Style and meaning

MANCHESTER
1824

Manchester University Press

Style and meaning

Studies in the detailed analysis of film

edited by

JOHN GIBBS and DOUGLAS PYE

Manchester University Press
Manchester and New York

distributed exclusively in the USA by Palgrave

Published by Manchester University Press
Oxford Road, Manchester M13 9NR, UK
and Room 400, 175 Fifth Avenue, New York, NY 10010, USA
www.manchesteruniversitypress.co.uk

Distributed exclusively in the USA by
Palgrave, 175 Fifth Avenue, New York,
NY 10010, USA

Distributed exclusively in Canada by
UBC Press, University of British Columbia, 2029 West Mall,
Vancouver, BC, Canada V6T 1Z2

British Library Cataloguing-in-Publication Data
A catalogue record for this book is available from the British Library

Library of Congress Cataloging-in-Publication Data applied for

ISBN   0 7190 6524 0 *hardback*
EAN   978 0 7190 6524 8
ISBN   0 7190 6525 9 *paperback*
EAN   978 0 7190 6525 5

First published 2005

14 13 12 11 10 09 08 07 06 05   10 9 8 7 6 5 4 3 2 1

Typeset in 10.5/12.5 pt Minion
by Graphicraft Limited, Hong Kong
Printed in Great Britain
by Biddles Ltd, King's Lynn

This book is dedicated to the late Andrew Britton

Contents

List of illustrations

List of contributors

Jonathan Bignell is Reader in Television and Film in the Department of Film, Theatre and Television at the University of Reading. He is Director of the Centre for Television Drama Studies, and General Editor of 'The Television Series' for Manchester University Press. He is the author of *Postmodern Media Culture* (Edinburgh University Press, 2000) and *Media Semiotics: An Introduction* (Manchester University Press, 1997, 2002), editor of *Writing and Cinema* (Addison-Wesley Longman, 1999), and joint editor of *British Television Drama: Past, Present and Future* (Palgrave, 2000).

Sarah Cardwell is Lecturer in Film and Television Studies at the University of Kent. She is the author of *Adaptation Revisited: Television and the Classic Novel* (Manchester University Press, 2002) and various articles that address television and film aesthetics, the philosophy of film, medium specificity and literary adaptation.

Edward Gallafent teaches Film Studies at the University of Warwick. His publications include *Clint Eastwood: Actor and Director* (Studio Vista, 1994) and *Astaire and Rogers* (Cameron and Hollis, 2000).

John Gibbs is Senior Lecturer in Film and Television at the University of the Arts London. He is the author of *Mise-en-scène: Film Style and Interpretation* (Wallflower Press, 2002).

Cathy Greenhalgh is Senior Lecturer in Cinematography at the University of the Arts London. She is the author of 'Shooting from the Heart: Cinematographers and their Medium' in *Making Pictures: A Century of European Cinematography* (Aurum, 2003). She studied at the National Film and Television School, UK, later working as a cinematographer in the film industry, and currently directs independent short films which combine dance, animation and documentary elements.

Jim Hillier is Senior Lecturer in Film Studies in the Department of Film, Theatre and Television at the University of Reading. He is the author of *The New Hollywood* (Studio Vista, 1992), co-author of *The Film Studies Dictionary* (Arnold, 2001) and editor of *Cahiers du cinéma Vols 1 and 2* (Routledge/ Harvard University Press, 1985, 1986), *Howard Hawks: American Artist* (with Peter Wollen, BFI, 1996) and *American Independent Cinema* (BFI, 2002).

Andrew Klevan is Lecturer in Film Studies at the University of Kent. He is the author of *Disclosure of the Everyday: Undramatic Achievement in Narrative Film* (Flicks Books, 2000). He has recently contributed a piece, entitled 'Guessing the Unseen from the Seen', to Russell Goodman (ed.), *Contending with Stanley Cavell* (Oxford University Press, 2004) and is currently completing his second book, entitled *Film Performance: From Achievement to Appreciation* (Wallflower Press, 2005).

Laura Mulvey has been writing about film and film theory since the mid-1970s and her essays have been published in *Visual and Other Pleasures* (Macmillan, 1989) and *Fetishism and Curiosity* (BFI, 1996). She is also the author of the BFI Film Classic *Citizen Kane*. Laura Mulvey co-directed six films with Peter Wollen, including *Riddles of the Sphinx* (BFI, 1978) and *Frida Kahlo and Tina Modotti* (Arts Council, 1980) as well as *Disgraced Monuments* with Mark Lewis (Channel Four, 1994). She is now Professor of Film and Media Studies at Birkbeck College, University of London.

Steve Neale is Professor of Film Studies at Exeter University. He is the author of *Genre and Hollywood* (Routledge, 2000), co-author of *Popular Film and Television Comedy* (Routledge, 1990), editor of *Genre and Contemporary Hollywood* (BFI, 2002) and co-editor of *Contemporary Hollywood Cinema* (Routledge, 1998).

Neill Potts is completing his PhD thesis on the television work of Alfred Hitchcock at the University of Warwick. His contribution to this volume grew out of his MA dissertation on characterisation in Hitchcock's films.

Douglas Pye teaches film at the University of Reading. He co-edited *The Movie Book of the Western* (Studio Vista, 1996) and is the editor of a forthcoming collection on Fritz Lang.

V. F. Perkins has lectured on film at Warwick University since 1978. He is the author of *Film as Film* (Penguin, 1972) and *The Magnificent Ambersons* (BFI, 1999).

Deborah Thomas is Reader in Film Studies at the University of Sunderland and a member of the editorial board of *Movie*. She is the author of *Beyond Genre: Melodrama, Comedy and Romance in Hollywood Films* (Cameron and

Hollis, 2000) and *Reading Hollywood: Spaces and Meanings in American Film* (Wallflower Press, 2001).

Michael Walker is a retired teacher who is on the editorial board of *Movie* magazine. As well as writing for *Movie* and for the *Movie* anthologies on *film noir* and the Western, he has contributed recently to *CineAction!* and to the BFI anthology *Alfred Hitchcock: Centenary Essays* (BFI, 1999).

Corin Willis is Lecturer in Screen Studies at Liverpool John Moores University. He wrote his PhD thesis at the University of Warwick on blackface in early sound film and is currently preparing a book based on this research.

George M. Wilson is Professor of Philosophy at the University of California at Davis. He is the author of *Narration in Light* (Johns Hopkins University Press, 1986) and *The Intentionality of Human Action* (Stanford University Press, 1989). He has written a range of articles in philosophy of language, philosophy of action and film aesthetics.

Acknowledgements

This book was inspired by a conference held in the Department of Film and Drama (now Film, Theatre and Television) at the University of Reading. We would like to thank all the contributors to the conference, and the department for playing host to the event. Colleagues in our two departments have been unfailingly generous in their support in all stages of the project. We are very grateful to MUP for their confidence in our proposal and their guidance and patience during the development of the book.

Chapter 14 includes extracts from students' essays. We are grateful to the students for permission to use these.

Introduction

John Gibbs and Douglas Pye

it is undeniable that in our reading of texts we inevitably run the danger of misunderstanding. Whoever is afraid of doing so can now comfortably withdraw into scepticism and dismiss striving for understanding as naive and obsolete. (E. H. Gombrich, 'Relativism in the Humanities', 1991a: 39)

I have expressed the belief elsewhere that the humanities ... would atrophy and die if they attempted to become 'value free'. Ideas originate with human beings and affect human beings and to discuss them with cold objectivity seems to me inhuman in the true sense of the word. (E. H. Gombrich, 'Relativism in the History of Ideas', 1991b: 55)

The study of film in the early years of the twenty-first century is characterised by a diversity of approaches. In an era dubbed 'Post-Theory' by David Bordwell and Noël Carroll – the title of their 1996 edited collection – the average university student will encounter a wide range of ways of engaging with the subject. This is what one might expect – indeed, a partial definition of a mature academic discipline in the arts and humanities might be its ability to sustain a number of approaches, underpinned by varied and even competing assumptions about the nature of the subject. What calling a volume of essays *Post-Theory* implicitly recognises is that this is a comparatively recent state of affairs in film studies, and one that merits a survey of the terrain now that the period in which the field was dominated by totalising theory is over.[1]

As a counter to what he identifies as the top-down approaches of subject-position theory and culturalism which proved so influential in the film studies of the last thirty years, Bordwell draws attention to another, more diverse trend in recent film scholarship. What he calls 'middle-level research' includes 'new film history', which has deepened our understanding of, among other topics, early cinema, non-Western national cinemas, industry practices, film reception and the history of film style; it also embraces work on film narrative, genre and point of view, as well as accounts of spectatorship which challenge the models presented by Theory. Crucially for Bordwell, much of this work has shown that 'an argument can be at once conceptually powerful and based in evidence', without a commitment to 'Grand Theory'. He concludes: 'In the Post-Theory era, sharply focused, in depth inquiry remains our best bet for producing the sort of scholarly debate that will advance our knowledge of cinema' (Bordwell and Carroll 1996: 29–30).

An important but, on the face of it, curious feature of Bordwell's account of middle-level research – given the significance of film style within the field he describes – is the exclusion of interpretation. 'These programs', he argues, 'have demonstrated that you can do a lot with films besides interpreting them' (Bordwell and Carroll 1996: 29). David Bordwell has developed at length in other publications the argument that led him to this dismissal of interpretation (see, particularly, *Making Meaning* (1989)). In a major dis- agreement with what is in many ways an admirable overview of the Post- Theory landscape, the position that underpins many of the contributions to this volume is that to be concerned with film style and its significance is inevitably to be involved in interpretation.

This view was one of a number of factors that led us to organise in 2000 the Style and Meaning Conference at the University of Reading as a way of re-examining the place of interpretive criticism, based on close reading, in contemporary film studies. It was clear from the widespread interest in the conference that many people welcomed the opportunity to engage with issues of detailed analysis, interpretation and mise-en-scène. At the same time, even in the context of greater plurality and openness in the field, for some a renewed focus on style and meaning seemed problematic and mis- guided. One feeling voiced was that to renew a focus on interpretation and style was to turn the clock back to the bad old days, before film studies was placed on a sounder, more rigorous, even a more *scientific* footing. Returning to these questions appeared to disregard more recent emphases in the field, and to be in some way reactionary.

Such objections are interesting in that they point to major fallacies that have haunted film studies since the 1970s – that new approaches invalidate old, that we progress by leaving behind the work we have defined ourselves by opposing. At times it seemed as though intellectual enquiry had become a branch of the fashion industry, dominated by the latest trend. One impulse in this book is to challenge some of these assumptions by reconnecting with strands of work in film criticism and theory that have been marginalised since the advent of Theory.

At the same time, work in film and cultural studies published during this period has changed the field definitively, in positive ways as well as negative. Issues of representation, of ideological orientation, deeply interwoven with investigation of modes of address and the development of forms and subjects in cinema, have significantly shifted practices of film analysis. As Bordwell writes of middle-level research: 'This tradition has been enriched by gay/ lesbian, feminist, minority, and post-colonialist perspectives' (1996: 27).

Among the consequences of this diversity of perspectives for the study of film was a challenge to the authority of the critic akin to post-structuralist assaults upon the author. The conception of the text as a site for the inter-section of cultural codes and forces that outran the ability of the author to control or channel meaning was paralleled by the shattering of the consensus which could be assumed by the critic. With audiences increasingly recog-nised as being divided by class, gender, race and sexuality, with critics and writers from previously marginalised groups making enthusiastic appropria-tions of films in relation to their distinctive experiences, the 'common pur-suit of true judgment' advocated by F. R. Leavis became a more difficult prospect than the shared endeavour he imagined.[2]

How can we establish a reasonable basis for interpretation in the face of these powerful objections? If the idea of a 'common pursuit' has been shown to rest on unacceptable assumptions about the homogeneity of the critical fraternity and reading public, how can any practice of interpretative criticism avoid falling into similar traps? One answer might be that it can't – that however hard one tries, these problems will continue to haunt us. Yet that is hardly the end of the matter. This is the case with almost any kind of discourse, not just the interpretation of films. Any act of conversation, any use of language, runs these risks, and the more significant in human and social terms the subject of the conversation, the more fraught with difficulty our interaction with others may become. Silence is a possible response to these problems; avoiding difficult topics is another. But these are hardly solutions, any more than shouting to impose your point of view might be. Talking with others inherently risks mutual incomprehension, unwarranted assumptions, failures of tone and address, conscious or unconscious playing of roles.

Recognising the significance of work developed from perspectives diver-gent from a white, male, middle-class hegemony is not the same as succumb-ing to a relativism where any interpretation of a film is of equal validity and relevance. In that view of making meaning, art disappears into its multiple social uses or into the inexhaustible play of signification. We want to propose an approach which allows for the inevitable variability of reading while not succumbing to the equal but opposed follies of believing that a text can have only one meaning or that meanings are infinite and indeterminate.

Interpretative criticism is, or has the possibility to be, a kind of conversa-tion about what we find in and what we make of films, and it should be governed by a process that can be evoked using the much disparaged words of F. R. Leavis: 'This is so, isn't it?' / 'Yes, but ...'. The 'Yes, but ...', often left out of critical accounts of Leavis's work, is crucial. In itself the question

('This is so, isn't it?') can seem too peremptory, demanding assent from a speaker/writer who assumes his own authority. Even 'Yes, but ...' may be too limiting: the implicit question, 'This is so, isn't it?' should also be able to elicit the response, 'No, because ...'.[3]

This is to suggest that processes of argument and of persuasion are involved, rather than merely the demonstration of a position: that what I have found in the film is not simply my view but represents an understanding capable of being shared or challenged and, in the process, enhanced, reworked or replaced. Interpretation developed through reasoned argument is therefore not simply 'subjective' or rooted in the tastes of an individual or group but, in establishing shared understanding, becomes a form of knowledge. It implies that a basis for dialogue and mutual understanding exists, that we are not locked either into our individual subjectivity or into our class, gender and ethnic identity to such an extent that dialogue and argument become hopeless or meaningless.

The knowledge produced in this view of interpretation can never be definitive and the processes involved are those of argument, not of deductive logic. As V. F. Perkins writes:

> No intra-textual interpretation ever is or could be a proof. Most often, it is a description of aspects of the film with suggested understandings of some of the ways they are patterned. Rhetoric is involved in developing the description so that it evokes a sense of how, seen in this way, the film may affect us, or so that it invites participation in the pleasure of discovering this way in which various of the film's features hang together. But the ultimate appeal for conviction is to the reader's memory and renewed experience of the film. (Perkins 1990: 4)

A central advantage of rooting interpretation in the detail of the film, the results of specific decisions taken by the filmmakers, is that it provides a material and verifiable basis for discussion. Appealing to what is observably present in the film provides a platform of shareable experience, with ready reference back to the film (once a far from simple matter) now facilitated by the availability of films on VHS and DVD. This does not mean that even description of what we see and hear in a film is likely to be uncontentious. While we can strive for objective recognition of, say, the action and the spatial and temporal dimensions of a shot, no description can be exhaustive and any description of the interaction of elements that make up even a simple shot will inevitably embody a viewpoint, a way of grading the elements we observe in their relationships with each other to register what we understand their priority to be. Description is inextricably bound up with interpretation. But being able to refer to the details of decision making in a film, and then to refer back as we engage in debate, is the crucial condition for meaningful critical dialogue.

Grounding writing about film in observable detail should be fundamental not to just one form of critical practice but to all, and not just to criticism but to theory. As Andrew Britton writes: 'No film theory is worth anything which does not stay close to the concrete and which does not strive continually to check its own assumptions and procedures in relation to producible texts' (1986: 3). Indeed, for Britton, 'the business of theory and the business of criticism cannot, in practice, be hived off from one another, and the cost of an attempt to do so is one of the fundamental lessons of the structuralist/ post-structuralist phase' (1986: 5). The linking of criticism and theory is fundamental, especially in the context of the split between them that characterised the period of Grand Theory and the widespread assumption in academic film studies that a criticism that focuses on style and meaning is inherently un- or anti-theoretical.

Like Britton, we take it that criticism has two basic functions: interpretation (or reading) and evaluation, the two dimensions of the process being inseparably linked. At the most basic level, films, whether apparently conventional or experimental, attempt to engage and/or challenge us and we are likely to respond to them in ways that untidily intermingle various levels of recognition and unfamiliarity, pleasurable and painful feeling, emotional engagement and distance, comprehension and puzzlement. In viewing most movies we will develop a quite complex grasp of characters and situations and possibly reach towards some sense of their wider resonance. Particular formal and stylistic features – the use of voice-over, extended camera movements, special effects – may strike us as significant. In our tentative, unfocused and often imprecise dialogue with friends after a movie we are all familiar with the mingling of these different responses and ideas as we struggle to articulate ways in which the film has affected us, what we take it to be trying to do, how it relates to other movies, to what we had expected, and so on. These are processes of interpretation, and the more systematic and analytical procedures that lead eventually to published interpretive criticism are tidier, more considered, selective and reflective versions of the same thing. This is a major part of what we take understanding a film to be.

Our sense of the fundamental link between movie-going and interpretive criticism is paralleled in Noël Carroll's article 'Introducing Film Evaluation' (in *Reinventing Film Studies*, Gledhill and Williams eds 2000), which is rooted in a similar appeal to the nature of film viewing. He argues that 'evaluating movies is something that we all do all the time'; debating whether a film is 'good' or not is central to our experience of film-going (Carroll 2000: 265). Film scholars should therefore 'talk to the film-goer where she or he lives' (Carroll 2000: 266). This is a welcome emphasis, and one manifestation of the revisionist impulses in contemporary film studies. Questions of value have been crucial to academic writing about film in the last thirty years while rarely being addressed head on. For instance, a good deal of symptomatic criticism, rooted in approaches to the ideological orientation of movies, erected 'subversiveness' and contradiction as criteria of value for popular cinema, within a politically informed critical practice. Value as part of an aesthetics of film has been a rather different matter. Not that the two things are necessarily incompatible. To quote Andrew Britton once more:

> Criticism is the systematic reading (that is, the evaluation) of texts. Like all other activities, it takes place in the present. Like all other critical activities it presupposes a principled attitude to the politics which constitute the present. The business of the film critic is to arrive at an understanding, on the basis of that attitude – which ought to be as alert and as conscious as possible – of what is of value in the past and present of the cinema and to ensure that this value is recognised for what it is, and has the influence it ought to have, now. (1986: 5)

'Politics' is used here in a very broad sense, but the intersection of broader and narrower meanings of the term suggests what is at stake for Britton in the work of criticism. He is arguing the key cultural importance of developing arguments about what is valuable in the arts and what is not.

Britton's view of criticism raises questions of the kinds touched on above. Critics and readers can embrace many political/social positions, or none. If interpretation and evaluation inevitably embody, consciously or not, such positions, is criticism inherently sectional and tainted? If I don't share a critic's politics should I reject her/his readings? The answer is again to insist on criticism as implicit dialogue, inherently requiring not just assent but question, and also to insist that it is dialogue about a text or texts that I also have access to and the meanings of which I can contest. Criticism ought to imply debate. Ideally, too, criticism should, just as Britton argues of theory, 'check its own assumptions and procedures', in this case making explicit the writer's sense of her or his 'position'. It will be part of the historical process of criticism to subject these and the unexamined assumptions made by even the most conscientious and self-reflexive critics to examination and to assess the extent to which (if at all) they invalidate the writer's insights. It is also fundamental to recognise that even criticism that is not insistently self-reflexive is not necessarily naive or blinkered about the subject position from which it is written.

Our emphasis on the examination of textual detail as the shareable basis for critical dialogue needs further elaboration. We cannot approach a film without expectations and without bringing to bear our more or less extensive experience of film viewing. Equally, creating a viable basis for critical dialogue depends on recognising that we are not simply trading opinions. It is the film itself, we have argued, that provides the basis for argument and understanding. If it is true (even a truism) that in film viewing we each construct our own film (of what experience wouldn't this be equally true?), it is also the case that individual ways of understanding a film often share more than sets them apart. We need to build on these shared understandings to create an adequate basis for extended argument and interpretation.

Works of art are not like shipwrecks on the sea bed which inertly form a home for different corals, but significantly organised artifacts which interact with and reflect upon the culture. They are more like a well-designed house: not every occupant will choose to use the rooms in the quite the same manner, but the building has been shaped to facilitate certain modes of living, certain ways of moving through it. Our readings can be similar because creating works of art involves skilful and complex attempts, through the detailed texture of the work, to channel our response to its areas of representation, dramatised subjects, themes, propositions, concerns. The objective features of a text are organised in such a way as to make some readings possible, and many others unsustainable.

The basis of a possible shared understanding is therefore the recognition that films exist in the world and in history, and that, like houses, they need to be understood in their own aesthetic and historical terms. As we begin to explore what we take to be interesting and valuable in a movie, we need to ask the extent to which we understand the kind of thing we are dealing with. One version of this question is posed by Gavin Lambert, in the final issue of the important British journal, *Sequence*, in 1952: 'Until we know how a film is speaking to us, we cannot be sure what it is saying' (1952: 7). This is an earlier passage from the same article:

> there are always cases of the work of art that one misunderstood or failed to grasp at the first encounter, came back to several years later and found wonderful, just as one can mistake something for a work of art at first and discover afterwards that it is nothing of the sort. In either case, the reason may not be emotional or intellectual immaturity; it is more probably a failure of communication, due to the fact that one has not really mastered the language in which the artist is speaking. (1952: 6)

As we seek to locate the film accurately and to grasp, in Lambert's words, the 'language in which the artist is speaking', we are also reaching for some sense of the film's purposes. This involves trying to grasp its identity as a work governed by sets of intentions. Writing in 1983, in the chapter on structuralism and semiotics within his brilliant explication and critique of literary theory, *Literary Theory: An Introduction*, Terry Eagleton developed one of the most lucid accounts of this idea:

> To understand a poem means grasping its language as being 'oriented' towards the reader from a certain range of positions: in reading, we build up a sense of what kinds of effect this language is trying to achieve ('intention'), what sorts

of rhetoric it considers appropriate to use, what assumptions govern the kinds
of poetic tactics it employs, what attitude to reality these imply ... Understanding these textual effects, assumptions, tactics and orientations is just to understand the 'intention' of the work. (1983: 120)

Intention has been a controversial issue in criticism but, as Eagleton makes
clear, this need not involve embracing naive notions of the work as
self-expression:

> None of this need be identical with the intentions, attitudes and assumptions
> of the actual historical author at the time of writing, as is obvious if one tries
> to read William Blake's *Songs of Innocence and Experience* as the 'expression' of
> William Blake himself. We may know nothing about the author, or the work
> may have had many authors (who was the author of the Book of Isaiah, or of
> *Casablanca*?). (1983: 120)

A key aspect of Eagleton's approach is that it involves recognising language as inherently social: 'When we understand the intentions of a piece of
language, we interpret it as being in some sense oriented, structured to achieve
certain effects ... It is to see language as a practice rather than as an object;
and there are of course no practices without human subjects' (1983: 114).
In normal conversation it is sometimes difficult enough to grasp what effects
a speaker is attempting to achieve, what the intentions of a particular use of
language might have been. Our experience is littered with misunderstandings
of tone, failures to grasp context appropriately, to adjust to audience, and so
on. It is correspondingly much more difficult to grasp the various orientations
implied by a poem, a novel or a narrative film. These problems can multiply
if the work was produced in a period removed from our own or in another
culture. It may be that historical and/or contextual knowledge can provide a
solid basis for initial placing of the work in relation to generic or other kinds
of categories and that further research can refine these broad recognitions.
But the kind of understanding implied by the quotations from Eagleton
cannot rest at these levels and can never be simply factual: grasping the
work ('What kinds of effect?', 'What sorts of rhetoric?', 'What assumptions?',
'What attitude to reality?') necessarily involves interpretation. Classification,
however subtle and historically well informed, can only take us so far. As
E. H. Gombrich writes: 'In the discussion of works of art description can
never be completely divorced from criticism' (1966: 81).

The kind of critical discussion we are envisaging may therefore begin by
asking what kind of thing we are dealing with, but when we proceed to try to
grasp the work in the specific ways Eagleton describes we inevitably engage
with the complex articulation of elements in the work and the relationships
to context, convention and reality which they imply – matters in which the
concept of style is inescapable.

The *Oxford English Dictionary* gives twenty-eight definitions for the noun 'style'. Like all complicated historical terms, it carries a great deal of baggage, and we can easily become weighed down by the range of usage and implication. For our purposes we will begin with a pragmatic view of the concept: style refers to 'those features of ... composition which belong to form and expression rather than to the substance of the ... matter expressed' (*OED*). Style, in other words, seems to refer to the 'how' rather than the 'what', although this formulation can seem to imply a separation that becomes unsustainable when we examine individual works. David Bordwell offers another definition: 'In the narrowest sense, I take style to be a film's systematic and significant use of techniques of the medium. ... Style is, minimally, the texture of the film's images and sounds, the result of choices made by the filmmaker(s) in particular historical circumstances' (1997: 4). At a basic level ('minimally'), style is the outcome of the filmmakers' material choices. Less basically, this is qualified by the words, 'systematic and significant', which imply the purposive and patterned nature of the decisions considered as 'style'.

The different essays that make up this collection will at times invoke further associations of the concept. There may be occasions when 'style' suggests 'the manner of expression characteristic' of an artist (*OED* again), a director's distinctive or habitual approach. The word 'style' can also be used to suggest the manner of expression characteristic of a period or an industry – what Bordwell has referred to as 'group styles' (Bordwell, Staiger and Thompson 1985: 3). But the book is less interested in the extent to which style is 'personal' (providing what Oscar Wilde calls a 'signature'), or characteristic of a 'group', than in the ways an approach becomes significant in particular instances. What is gained by the use of this technique here? How does the context in which it appears and the content to which it gives form, qualify or modify its impact? How does this choice relate to patterns developed across the length of the film? What are the consequences of articulating the action in those ways?

We can return here to our fundamental disagreement with David Bordwell about the role of interpretation, but now develop it in relation to our understanding of style. Outlining his position in the early stages of *On the History of Film Style*, Bordwell writes:

> Indeed, stylistic history is one of the strongest justifications for film studies as a distinct academic discipline. If studying film is centrally concerned with 'reading' movies in the manner of literary texts, any humanities scholar armed with a battery of familiar interpretive strategies could probably do as well as anyone trained in film analysis. ... But if we take film studies to be more like art history or musicology, interpretive reading need not take precedence over a scrutiny of change and stability within stylistic practices. (1997: 8)

The sense of 'interpretive reading' presented here is very odd. A process of ' "reading" movies in the manner of literary texts', which any humanities scholar can attempt, as though 'reading' had nothing to do with the specificities of expression, implies a view of reading literature that few literary scholars would recognise. That interpretation separated from consideration of medium-specific modes of expression is likely to be of limited interest is a view most people will readily share, but this is to erect a straw man that has little in common with the best practices of interpretive criticism in literature or film. At the same time, to pursue his vision of the study of stylistic history, Bordwell erects another version of the age old style/content dichotomy, where style can be studied free of the impurities of meaning.

Our understanding of interpretation and of style is very different. Interpretation has to be rooted in the concrete details of the text (its style) because it is only through these that we gain access to the film's subjects. Style constitutes the medium of expression, giving access to the story and simultaneously shaping in a variety of complex ways the film's relationship to its material, its audience and its traditions. In trying to develop an initial definition we suggested that style belongs to the 'how' of a film rather than the 'what', but for a more developed approach it is necessary to break down the implication of a clear separation between these basic analytical terms. Rather than seeing them as designating distinct realms we need to insist, to use a chapter heading from V. F. Perkins's book *Film as Film*, that ' "How" is "What" '.

Every decision taken in making a film – where to place the camera, which lens to use, when to cut, how to place actors in space, how to clothe them – is taken in a specific context, informed by powerful conventions but unique to this moment in this film. Each decision – made in relation to the multiple patterns being built up across the film – develops the narrative and thematic web. Every shot is a view of something, every cut is from one specific view to another, every costume decision bears on considerations of character, situation, fashion context, colour design, and more. Much filmmaking seems to encourage us to treat this complex tapestry of decision making as 'transparent', so that we are often unaware of the craft and artifice involved. But all this decision making is material and it has material effects on our experience of the film.

This emphasis provides common ground with a central aspect of David Bordwell's approach to the historical study of film style – the attempt to understand style in terms of specific problems encountered by filmmakers and the solutions they find. Drawing extensively on E. H. Gombrich's work Bordwell persuasively argues that this approach can enable us to focus on aspects of style while recognising that particular problems and solutions 'can intersect with one another or with other factors (technological, economic, or cultural)'; it grants a central role to practitioners' choices but recognises that they take place within specific social contexts and within the institutional frameworks of filmmaking (Bordwell 1997: 150–1). Our major difference with Bordwell is again over the relationship between style and meaning. In our view, style is constitutive – it is the heart of a material process of articulation – so that to understand style we must grasp how it works in its context to present and shape the film's dramatic world. To understand style is to interpret what it does.

Wide-ranging historical studies, such as those of Bordwell, Staiger and Thompson (1985) or Barry Salt (1983) are valuable and illuminating in outlining key tendencies in film production. But at the level of the individual film the mere presence of a formal element means very little. It is only when we can consider the specific decision within the context in which it appears, including the content to which it gives form, that we can grasp its significance. We need to understand the individual decision or formal pattern as part of the film's address to the spectator, and in relation to the norms and conventions upon which it draws. Historical studies can indicate a range of ways in which, say, a dialogue scene would have been likely to be filmed in a particular period. But, as in conversation we constantly have to judge a speaker's relationship to the registers of language she uses, so we have to assess the film's relationship to its stylistic registers, the status decisions take on by virtue of their specific use in context. The status of formal decisions, not simply the choice of a particular technique, is always crucial to their significance, and status can only be determined by interpretation.[4]

Metaphors seem almost inescapable in these discussions. Style is more than an accumulation of material decisions, it is a web, a network, a texture, a pattern, or, more mechanistically, a system.[5] These terms all insist that style involves relationships within and between the various areas of choice available to the novelist, painter or filmmaker. It is patterned, systematised decision making that achieves significance. This is not only important when considering the effects of style, but also for the ongoing discussion of critical method. Not all interpretations are equally successful and – as critical discussion will rapidly reveal – the extent to which a critical argument is able to take on elements of the film, and the degree to which it can identify significant patterns which give credence to the understanding of the part advanced, are major factors determining how persuasive it may be.

To think of style in these ways is to imply that films are significantly ordered, that they are shaped to some purpose or purposes, that, in ways that remain to be articulated, they are unified. To advance ideas of aesthetic unity is distinctly unfashionable, but to do so is not to reject the notion that a film has significance beyond the conscious intentions of its makers, nor the idea that a film is a kind of force field through which all sorts of strands within the culture find expression. Rather it is to suggest that the will to unity is a potent factor in movies – rarely simple, sometimes highly complex – and that unity and coherence remain crucial, though never straightforward reference points in any act of interpretation and most value judgements.

Even in order to identify the absences, gaps and fractures which have been such an important feature of much recent discussion of films, one needs to have a sense of a film's underlying levels of coherence. As Noël Carroll has argued, the absences commented on by symptomatic criticism are significant, structured absences.

> [H]ow does one go about identifying structuring absences? Obviously by determining the overall direction or tendency ... of a film in order to detect the countervailing tendencies which the film attempts to mask. But that, of course, involves holistic interpretation, and the assumption of some relative unity in the work. In order to interpret against the grain, one needs to find the grain in the first place. (Carroll 1998: 12)

'In point of logic,' Carroll concludes, 'to find that a film is disunified in certain respects already requires the presumption that it is somehow unified in others' (1998: 13).

Coherence and incoherence, unity and disunity, do not therefore present simple oppositions. Narrative film is so complex that the impulse towards unity encounters many obstacles (narrative, ideological, technical and so on). Equally, many forms of unity and coherence may be identified. We need an approach to coherence that recognises this complexity; which can aid our appreciation of a movie's attempt to wrestle with matters which prove intractable within its period, traditions and forms, or the film which refuses traditional modes of unity. Films can be profound despite (and perhaps partly because of) their failure to be entirely coherent. They may be valuable because of their intense embodiment of contradictions. More traditionally, we might point to those works which sustain different possibilities for interpretation simultaneously, or which balance different understandings of the events portrayed. As Terry Eagleton writes of the effects, tactics and assumptions of which a work's 'intention' is comprised: 'such tactics and assumptions may not be mutually coherent: a text may offer several mutually conflicting or contradictory "subject positions" from which to read' (Eagleton 1983: 120).

The writers who have contributed to the collection have varying ambitions for their work and represent a range of perspectives within the study of film. They also represent different generations within film scholarship. A lively conversation would result if all were to engage in a critical discussion. But there is also important common ground. Each of the essays is anchored in the specific material choices evident within the films (and in one case television drama) which they explore, but each writer also negotiates the relationship between detailed realisation and broader conceptual frameworks. The approaches employed are neither 'top-down' nor 'bottom-up', but focus on the exploratory process by which our experience of individual films and the tentative advance of concepts can inform each other. Moreover, most of the articles in the book are structured around a specific problem, or inspired by a particular experience, encountered in viewing films. The selection of texts has been made to reflect not only those areas of film history which have traditionally proved amenable to mise-en-scène criticism, but also areas such as the avant garde and television drama which have not tended to receive such detailed investigation. In these ways, the book conducts a series of dialogues with issues in film study which are specifically provoked by close analysis.

We hope the articles collected here extend the available critical responses to the specificity and complexity of cinema. Importantly, the complexity referred to here should not be mistaken for something which is only perceivable by the academic critic. We believe that interpretation is closely associated with normal viewing, but also that normal viewing is a highly sophisticated experience. As V. F. Perkins has written, 'Films are constructed so as to address our minds in the knowledge that mind is much faster and more comprehensively perceptive than intellect' (1990: 6). While in the cinema, we all have profound and intricate responses to film, but we tend to be less good at articulating these with a similar complexity when we leave the auditorium. One of criticism's major aims might be to capture something of the nuance and subtlety of our experience of, and involvement with, film.

This is why we are not simply arguing for interpretation to be added to the range of approaches available within the new film studies. Rather we have wanted to suggest that an awareness of the role, significance and consequences of film style is fundamental. An ability to understand filmic detail, to be open to the implications of tone and texture, and to be aware of the qualification and connotation given an element by its context, should provide a foundation for the full range of approaches to and interests in the products of cinema.

Notes

1 The full title is *Post-Theory: Reconstructing Film Studies*. Consider also C. Gledhill and L. Williams (eds) *Reinventing Film Studies* (2000), which similarly takes stock of the field.

2 Leavis takes the title of *The Common Pursuit* from an essay by T. S. Eliot: ' "The common pursuit of true judgment": that is how the critic should see his business, and what it should be for him [sic]' (Leavis 1952, 1958: v).

3   Indeed, Leavis writes in the preface to *The Common Pursuit*: '[The critic's] per-
    ceptions and judgments are his, or they are nothing; but, whether or not he
    has consciously addressed himself to cooperative labour, they are inevitably col-
    laborative. Collaboration may take the form of disagreement, and one is grateful
    to the critic whom one has found worth disagreeing with' (1952, 1958: v). See
    also Robin Wood (1989: 33, 374).
4   See Pye (1989) for a broader discussion.
5   Some of these metaphors echo the words of Robert Louis Stevenson's definition
    of style: 'The web, then, or the pattern: a web at once sensuous and logical, an
    elegant and pregnant texture: that is style, that is the foundation of the art of
    literature' (1885, 1905: 14).

References

Bordwell, D., J. Staiger and K. Thompson (1985) *The Classical Hollywood Cinema:
    Film Style and Mode of Production to 1960* (London: Methuen).
Bordwell, D. and N. Carroll (eds) *Post-Theory: Reconstructing Film Studies* (Madison:
    University of Wisconsin Press).
Bordwell, D. (1997) *On the History of Film Style* (Cambridge, MA, and London:
    Harvard University Press).
Britton, A. (1976) '*Mandingo*', *Movie*, 22, 1–22.
Britton, A. (1977) '*Meet Me in St. Louis*: Smith, or the Ambiguities', *Australian Jour-
    nal of Screen Theory*, 3, 7–25.
Britton, A. (1982) 'Metaphor and Mimesis: *Madame De ...*', *Movie*, 29/30, 91–107.
Britton, A. (1984, 1995) *Katharine Hepburn: Star as Feminist* (London: Studio
    Vista).
Britton, A. (1986) 'In Defense of Criticism', *CineAction!*, 3/4, 3–5.
Carroll, N. (1998) *Interpreting the Moving Image* (Cambridge: Cambridge University
    Press).
Carroll, N. (2000) 'Introducing Film Evaluation', in C. Gledhill and L. Williams (eds)
    Reinventing Film Studies (London: Arnold, 2000), pp. 265–78.
Dyer, R. (1977) 'Entertainment and Utopia', *Movie*, 24, 2–13.
Eagleton, T. (1983) *Literary Theory: An Introduction* (Oxford: Basil Blackwell).
Gledhill, C. and L. Williams (eds) (2000) *Reinventing Film Studies* (London: Arnold).
Gombrich, E. H. (1991a) 'Relativism in the Humanities: The Debate about Human
    Nature', in *Topics of Our Time* (London: Phaidon), pp. 36–46.
Gombrich, E. H. (1991b) 'Relativism in the History of Ideas', in *Topics of Our Time*
    (London: Phaidon), pp. 47–55.
Gombrich, E. H. (1991c) 'Relativism in the Appreciation of Art', in *Topics of Our
    Time* (London: Phaidon), pp. 56–61.
Lambert, G. (1952) 'A Last Look Round', *Sequence*, 14, 4–8.
Leavis, F. R. (1952, 1958) *The Common Pursuit* (London: Chatto & Windus).
Mulvey, L. (1977/8) 'Notes on Sirk and Melodrama', *Movie*, 25, 53–6.
Perkins, V. F. (1972) *Film as Film: Understanding and Judging Movies*
    (Harmondsworth: Penguin).

Perkins, V. F. (1990) 'Must We Say What They Mean? Film Criticism and Interpretation', *Movie*, 34/5, 1–6.

Pye, D. (1989) 'Bordwell and Hollywood', *Movie*, 33, 46–52.

Salt, B. (1983) *Film Style and Technology: History and Analysis* (London: Starword).

Stevenson, R. L. (1885) 'On some Technical Elements of Style in Literature', in *The Art of Writing* (London: Chatto & Windus, 1905), pp. 3–43. (First published in the *Contemporary Review*, April 1885.)

Wood, R. (1989) *Hitchcock's Films Revisited* (New York: Columbia University Press).

1

Where is the world? The horizon of events in movie fiction

V. F. Perkins

Some years ago a distinguished scholar in literature and film advised me that one should consider the idea of the fictional world as no more than a 'loose metaphor'. The phrase made an impression, and has stayed with me, for two reasons. I took it as the succinct statement of a belief that might well command acceptance within film studies, if the matter were attended to at all. And it seemed to be nearly the opposite of the truth. This essay sets out both to show that the fictional world of a movie is indeed a world and, by means of a few concrete examples, to sketch some of the ways in which it matters that a fictional world is a world.

I start with an ending, a familiar one. In the final sequence of *Citizen Kane* (Orson Welles, 1941) the journalists pack up and prepare to leave Xanadu, abandoning their quest for the meaning of Kane's last word. At this point two main issues are yet to be resolved: first, what was Rosebud; then, would the identity of Rosebud offer a key to the life and mind of the dead tycoon? When the 'The End' title appears the second question remains unanswered, left open to the speculations both of the on-screen investigators and of the movie's audiences. But before this, in the very last images, the spectator is privileged with a revelation of Rosebud as the name on the child Kane's sled. This knowledge is emphatically denied to the seekers within the fiction. The separation of viewpoint is developed with a grand rhetoric whose flourishes depend upon extremes of scale from the distended to the abrupt, from the weirdly distant to the impossibly close.

The setting is vast. The Xanadu hallway with its massive staircase is stacked farther than the eye can see with the trophies and detritus of Kane's wealth – everything from an old iron stove to classical statues and, we are told, a dismantled castle and a Burmese temple. In this huge vault voices in conversation are echoing as from distant domes and crevices. His departing colleagues start to quiz the chief reporter, Thompson, about his discoveries. To this point the image has tracked their course through the makeshift alleys of monument and keepsake. But now as they stand fixed to listen to Thompson's response the camera detaches itself, craning up and curling away to see them from on high. Thompson's admission of failure tails off with a doubt that one word can explain a man's life, and with his speaking of Rosebud as just a missing piece in a jigsaw puzzle. He leads his group towards the exit, urging haste to catch the evening train, but his sluggish movement suggests a reluctance to leave in defeat. Welles puts a period to this scene of departure by dissolving to a final, speechless, image of the newsmen as they move away through the labyrinth; here the high, static camera is so remote that individual identity is all but erased.

The sound in the scene has been strictly diegetic but now the entry of slow, doom-laden music dictates a mood which is the film's and not that of any of its characters. The declaration of an independent viewpoint is sustained through dissolves across an undefined stretch of time and space to yet another and another image of Kane's treasure-hoard. Now the camera glides high across a further – apparently boundless – expanse of boxed and unboxed stuff, taking a course unrelated to anything human. Its movement is not performable by any wingless being, and it surveys a vista of crates so jumbled and so close-packed as to deny access to man or woman.

The mood of detachment is assisted by contrast, through the disappearance of human comment. Moments ago a disparate chorus of reporters was yelling the inventory of Spanish ceilings and headless statuary; now there is only the whisper of music. In two large ways the image reverses the sense of the crane up from Thompson's group: a movement away has been replaced by a movement of advance; and this travelling camera is not approaching, as the other was drawing back from, a defined object. Nor is it showing interest in any of the articles that its view traverses; its eye is directed across the clutter below and is not seeking in it or sorting it through. The result is that Kane's treasure floats down through the frame in a stream of barely differentiated bits and pieces.

Yet the movement is deliberate. The camera advances in a straight line; portentous musical phrases underscore the fixity of its gaze and the evenness of its pace. Over a terrain without visible limits or shape, this camera knows where it is going. But it is not showing us its goal.

After nearly half a minute, and without having fixed on any singular feature, the camera begins to descend. It maintains its forward momentum as it drops closer and closer to the surface of the junk-ocean. Finally it shifts its angle of vision downwards and alters its forward course to veer round as it closes in on a child's sled, brought into view just as a labourer enters the frame to bear it away. A bass chime from the orchestra certifies that with the sled the camera has found its destination. In the memory game that the sequence has encouraged and frustrated we should recognise this object as a relic of Kane's childhood. We just about have time to take it in, lying at the edge of the store and close to a photograph of the boy Kane with his mother, before it is removed from the frame and the image changes.

With the removal of the sled comes a sudden change of pace as the film cuts and we are all at once given a great deal to absorb. For the first time the nature of the space is revealed, together with its difference from the hall where we observed the newsmen's exit. We must be in the cellars of Xanadu, as the new shot reveals the butler Raymond (Paul Stewart) directing the labours of overalled workmen who are feeding an enormous furnace with flammable scraps from the stockpile – a picture frame, a paddle, a cello case. The camera travels towards the inferno with the labourer who carries the toboggan. It continues its approach as the toy lands in the flames and the workman turns away out of shot, so that now we have a view of the sled that allows us to see, in the last moments of its existence, the inscription 'Rosebud'.

A new shot enlarges this detail to fill the screen, presenting the impossible image (Figure 1.1). The camera appears to have entered the furnace. Its view is held and tightened so that it sees only the flames that blast the Rosebud decal, and the paintwork tortured by the heat. A fade to black marks the end of the sled and its emblem. In an exterior shot the camera tilts up to follow the smoke that empties into the night sky from Xanadu's chimney. Repeating the imagery of consumption by fire, the black smoke functions as a sign of oblivion and declares the finality of Rosebud's loss.

Citizen Kane would need very little of this if the only, or overwhelmingly important, point of its finale were the answer to the Rosebud puzzle. For that

1.1 *Citizen Kane* (Orson Welles, 1941)

purpose, it would be necessary only to contrive the disclosure. The method would be optional, and the options would include a new flashback to Kane's childhood. Simplest of all would be to let the journalists make the discovery. Nothing in the enigma-resolution process demanded that the sled be destroyed, or required Welles to stress the completeness of its ruin. Nor was it necessary for the destruction to go, within the world of the film, unremarked. But these are the aspects emphasised in Welles's treatment: Rosebud is gone for ever and a significant moment has passed without notice.

The spectacle of Rosebud's immolation is presented in a context of defeat. Abundance has become clutter and 'America's Kubla Khan' has ended as the Ozymandias of his time. While the departure of the journalists could mean no more than that the truth of 'Rosebud' is as yet undiscovered, Welles's finale guarantees that nobody will ever find it. The location in the Xanadu vault gives the ironic sense of a near miss to the calling-off of the quest. Remember that the reporters are working for a movie newsreel, always taking pictures. Then the image we see of Rosebud's vanishing reverses the process of photographic development and undoes the snapshot that might have been. The presence of know-all Raymond gives the sled's end a further inflection as 'What the Butler Never Saw'. All these failures of vision are highlighted by contrast since they come at the climax of a movie whose process has been founded on a succession of assigned viewpoints, precisely on what various witnesses had seen and recalled.

Dissonance is crucial to the tone of *Citizen Kane*'s finish, most of all in the clash between the assertiveness of the camera's display and the insistence, within that, on the unseen and ignored. We are at once thrust into knowledge and informed that no one shall ever know. The music adds to this effect by filling our ears with the unheard screams of Rosebud's death-throes and by punching out chords certain of their finality over images that refuse to suggest how our knowledge of Rosebud has improved our understanding of Charles Kane, or whether the sled should stand as an instance of the triviality of trivia or of their momentousness. The effect is at its strongest in the shot of the burning decal, where the show of revelation collides most brutally with the erasure of all prospect of discovery.

That we can be present as an audience to witness the absence of witnesses is an index of the separation between our world and the world of the fiction. It climaxes the anomaly that places *Citizen Kane* both in and beyond our world, our 1941 world. Of course this is our world. It shares our economy, our technologies, our architecture, and the legal systems and social forms that yield complex phenomena like slum landlords, divorce scandals and fame. Its history is our history of wars and slumps and the rise of mass media. Its notorious people (e.g. Adolf Hitler) and its decisive events are the ones we know.

But of course its world is not ours. Kane is famous throughout that world, and we have never heard of him nor of Jim Geddes, his political rival. Susan Alexander's celebrated fiasco at the Chicago Municipal Opera House involves an occasion and a location without reality for us. Everyone there and nobody here knows about the construction of a new Xanadu (their Xanadu) in Florida (our Florida). These are some of the aspects that mark the world as fictional. They do not thereby negate its worldhood.[1]

The world of *Citizen Kane* is constituted as a world partly because, within it, there are facts known to all, to many, to few and to none. The phenomena of a world are independent of perception, though in principle and most of the time available to it. To be in a world is to know the partiality of knowledge and the boundedness of vision – to be aware that there is always a bigger picture. To observe a world humanly is to do so from a viewpoint, with angles of vision and points of focus whose selectivity is inflected by the seeing mind. The looking is governed by purposes and expectations, by interests, appetites, hopes and fears.

The camera's looking escapes some of the restrictions on our sight: those that follow from the fact that, for us, eye and ear always have to go with body. The movie can explore the opportunities of unembodied viewpoint but it can never escape the necessity of viewpoint itself. So one of the arts of the movie is to turn this condition to advantage – for instance, by articulating the condition as a topic within the film – by dramatising the distinction between the seen and unseen, or the relations between seeing and knowing.

I have begun with these moments from *Citizen Kane* on account of their peculiarly stark display of the connections between narrative, formal device, style, viewpoint, tone and meaning. My chief concern, however, is with the dependence of all these aspects on the worldhood of the fictional world.

Welles had freedom to choose how and when to reveal Rosebud because there is always more beyond the frame than any image can contain; more in space and more in time. In the first flashback to Kane's boyhood the name on the sled was only one of an infinite number of facets of that world – that world in those moments – that the camera did not display. The camera's selectivity means that the framed image and the (boundless) fictional world create and account for one another. As Bazin told us, on-screen presupposes off-screen.

Selection by the camera, however, asserts significance. The image is displayed not only to relay information but to claim that it matters and to guide us towards the ways in which it matters. Because this is information of and in a world it will be subject to many kinds of attention and assessment, with every shade available from obliviousness to obsession. Rosebud goes ignored. It must have been seen umpteen times. The sled is handled and moved by the labourers in the Xanadu vault but its name escapes notice.

It is not seen by those who have been searching for 'Rosebud' as the answer to a riddle, and to whom its sight would have significance, would be a discovery.

The music of the scene is interrupted only once, by Raymond's order to 'Throw that junk!' Finding junk and treasure in the same object, the film can put it in the context of revered and stock-piled antiquities. So it offers a token of boyhood memory for evaluation against the remnants of lost empires and against a host of objects that evoke ranges of purpose, history, cost and potentiality. Measured beside a Donatello Nativity or a headless Venus, a child's plaything can pose the issue of what any of these things may represent as achievements or attachments, just as the hungry furnace poses the issue of what is worth preserving. The question of value has been put explicitly into play in the journalists' remarks, among them:

'How much do you think this is all worth?'

'Millions ... if anybody wants it.'

As Rosebud burns, the strident music outlaws an 'Is that all?' response to the camera's disclosure. Welles demonstrates here that viewpoint is vastly more than an optical matter. *Citizen Kane* provides a stark instance of something that is always the case: that the material entities of a fictional world are also objects subjectively perceived – as talismanic, say, or intriguing or negligible.

The movie draws on our ingrained awareness that the things we treasure and the things that haunt us may be odd or unfathomable to our fellows. Reciprocally it invokes the knowledge, born of experience, that our access to the thoughts and feelings of others is uncertain and necessarily partial. None of us can legislate the distinction between the trivial and the momentous for the secret places of another's heart. Against this we know also that there are accepted scales of value, common senses of what matters and how much, in light of which any particular attachment may be seen as normal, individual, eccentric or outlandish. *Citizen Kane* places itself in a world of recognisable understandings: a *Venus* is valued at twenty-five thousand dollars, but 'that's a lot of money to pay for a dame without a head'.

The world as inhabited space and the world as communities of under-standing come together to underwrite the formal achievement of *Citizen Kane*'s finale. Welles is able to build a grand rhetoric of ruination by emphas-ising the distance you have to travel to encompass treasure-hoarding on the Xanadu scale, pitched at the outer limit of what is conceivable in relation to a wealth both real and – for most of us – unimaginable. Within this enormity he can then bring us to a littleness, a trinket not made to endure, remarkable for its survival rather than its fragility. So he can clash the huge against the tiny, the emphatic against the negligible, by sustaining the expansive rhetoric for the burning of a sled. A grand spectacle: flames in a furnace. A climax: smoke from a chimney.

In the moments I have discussed we see Welles making an appropriate style out of gross overemphasis. Still it should be clear that I have chosen to inspect this passage for its representative, not for its freakish, quality. It is representative inasmuch as the film's form and method are incomprehensible outside of a recognition that its story takes place, and its images are both made and found, in a world. I believe this to be true, obviously but importantly, of all movies.[2]

Yet film studies has in the main ignored the fictional world, at best taken it for granted. Lack of attention to the fictional world – what makes it a world rather than what makes it fictional – may be one product of the field's recoil from all that smells of realism. A new engagement with worldhood should be of value, not least in developing our grasp of styles and meanings. An immediate benefit could be to enrich our appreciation of film artistry both in the treatment of space and in the shaping of narrative. The on-screen/off-screen relationship should be opened to explorations that embrace issues far beyond those of spatial continuity. And we should see processes of narrative in more rewarding lights once we break from the narrowness of a concentration on the 'cause and effect chain'.

It seems to be a habit of narratologists, not only in Film Studies, to reduce a story to a succession of events – or rather to the synopsis of a succession of events. Since the synopsis is taken to be an adequate representation of the narrative, it becomes relatively easy to believe that the cause and effect account thereby produced is a revelation of the movie's narrative process. But film drama is more than a succession of events, and a cause-and-effect approach can confine us in a mechanistic view not only of human affairs but of narrative as well. It can also distort a movie's time-process since cause and effect are products of the retrospective view (whereby we see the two together) whereas motives and possibilities are among their dynamic counterparts. An event becomes a cause only in its relation to webs of circumstance, together with, say, desires and fears. Why a cause should be understood as a cause, and why an effect should count as an effect, are matters that can be assessed only within a world. It is, after all, a very particularly constituted world in which one man's death can be the occasion for squads of people to set off in an effort to identify the personal meaning of a familiar word.

The world is everything (in space and in time) surrounding and embedding our immediate perceptions. There is always an out-of-sight just as there is always an off-screen. Out of sight cannot be entirely out of mind: we may not know what lies beyond the horizon but we do know that there is a beyond. Fritz Lang can teach us about this. In *You Only Live Once* (1937) the thief Eddie (Henry Fonda) is paroled from jail through the good offices of the priest Dolan (William Gargan) and the lawyer Whitney (Barton MacLane). The day of his release is to be the day of his marriage to naively trusting, respectable Joan (Sylvia Sidney), who has been Whitney's secretary and who is the object of her boss's unspoken, unrequited desire. At just over ten minutes into the film, Eddie and Joan pass through the prison gates. They offer thanks to Whitney and Father Dolan, then leave. The camera returns to the two men, tracking them through an outer door where, framed together in mid-shot, they stand to talk. As they do so we hear the sounds of a car's departure – slamming doors, revving engine, and then fading, increasingly distant, motor noise. The combination of sound and image creates in our minds the event of Joan and Eddie's driving off. We have not seen it. The off-screen world is here constructed not only as space but also as action – and not just 'background action'. All things considered, the departure is more fateful than the Whitney/Dolan exchange.

This occurs in a film designed to provoke awareness of the dangerous power of images by making us repeatedly reassess the conclusions we have drawn from what we have seen and heard.[3] What do we imagine ourselves to have witnessed in these images? How may the camera's power of selection become an agent of misdirection? Here Lang offers an innocent example of our being led to understand more than we have seen. The construction of this one shot enables a variation on the film's themes of perception and prejudice. By watching Dolan and Whitney rather than the car, the camera guides us to observe the different attitudes in which the priest and the disappointed lawyer view this departure. Framed together, their faces and movements offer a study in contrast (Figure 1.2). Dolan's glance moves back

1.2 *You Only Live Once* (Fritz Lang, 1937)

and forth between Whitney and the leaving vehicle, sometimes fixing on Whitney to offer him support and understanding. The lawyer's gaze is entirely held by the car, so that his eyes and head perform one steady movement as he stares after it. Though he is in conversation with the priest, he looks at him not once. At the end, as Whitney remains staring into the distance, the fading car sound becomes emblematic of his vanished hope. Meanwhile priest and lawyer exchange thoughts about the prospects for Joan and Eddie, and their views are inflected by the optimism of the one and the dejection of the other. Issues of individual perception underlie everything that is said, most evidently in Dolan's response to Whitney's declared belief that Joan has made a mistake: 'It's only natural you'd think that, feeling the way you do about her.' The film has Dolan articulate the bias in Whitney's understanding. But nobody on-screen ever remarks how the priest's vision is skewed by professional cheeriness.

We are placed to observe, not share, the viewpoints of the two men. Lang discovered a vantage point from which to display the relationship between an event and the spirit in which it may be seen. He did this by concentrating on acts of watching, in a way that would not have been available if he had needed also to show us Joan and Eddie on the move. It seems to me important that we do not exactly picture the departing couple, and we do not precisely imagine the manner of their leaving. We assume it. It becomes part of our knowledge of the relevant data. Lang asserts the scale of relevance by a device that declares the unimportance of the particulars of the car journey while dwelling on the split between the two men's ways of observing it. This kind of device is available because there is always more to the world than we need to, or could possibly, see.

The extended world is continually manifest in the ways in which things enter and leave the space of the frame. The fictionality of the world is usually most marked in the characters' relationship to the off-screen zone which is the space forward of the frame – their unawareness of the apparatus through which their actions and images are relayed. Though the performers have to be aware of the camera's needs, their playing most often creates the camera's absence and thereby transforms the nature of the space in front of them.[4] It is not that these characters are oblivious to the camera. There is no camera in their world. Their situation is interestingly contrasted with ours as spectators. We are aware of the mechanisms of presentation and have to be so to make sense of the movie's devices; if we could mistake the screen for a window, the world would have gone mad. There is a projector in our world.[5] The projector is real and present; the absent camera confirms the fictional status of the movie image and the integrity of the movie world.[6]

On location and on the studio floor, the actors' work supports a similar labour by the technicians. A prime objective is to forestall intrusions upon the fictional world by the apparatus, whether in the form of camera shadows, microphone booms or studio noise. From time to time the image seems designed to demonstrate the camera's annihilation. A mirror shot in *The Lady in the Lake* (Robert Montgomery, 1946) shows off the ingenuity that puts the hero's image on screen while the camera is supposedly confined within his point of view. Through trickery, however, the shot is also making a display of the camera's absence. That could well be its most important function.

Performance and framing create a spatial world in our minds that may never – and in some aspects can never – have existed in the studio. In Lang's film it is virtually certain that there was no actual car driven or even present during the performance of the Whitney–Dolan dialogue. However, we should not fall into thinking that the off-screen space is in any special sense fictional or imaginary. That would oblige us to see the on-screen image as non-fictional or real. On-screen and off-screen are equally fictional and imagined; seen/unseen and heard/unheard draw many of the relevant distinctions.

The off-screen world is necessarily a world of time as well as one of space. Movies always take us into the middle of things because the film and its story begin, but the world does not. Joan, Eddie, Whitney and Dolan all have relevant histories. As the story of a couple, *You Only Live Once* faced its creators with familiar problems in screen dramaturgy: to start before or after the first meeting; if after, to introduce the couple together or separately; if separately, to start with the man or the woman and, in either case, how to fill in relevant backgrounds (Eddie's criminal past, Joan's having become involved) without loss of momentum.[7]

We are in the middle of things, too, because this is a world without end. It is, crucially, a world of possibilities where an event that comes to count as a cause may have ramifications that we cannot predict. Everything we see, or come to know, has some necessary and innumerable potential consequences. When we see a woman we know she had parents and a childhood some of whose circumstances may be disclosed to us. It is a safe assumption that Joan grew up in an American, English-speaking, household. She may have a sister (Joan has) who may enter into the action (Bonnie does). She may have cousins or an old boyfriend in Baltimore. (We shall never know.[8]) Her life thus far will have influenced the attitudes that bear on her situation and prospects.

As a zone of fact abutting on zones of possibility, the fictional world poses a relationship between all that we can assume and all that we cannot, or cannot yet know. Joan and Eddie have driven off. Is the car Joan's? Did she borrow it or rent it? And who is driving? We might take the film's not answering any of these questions as a consequence simply of its power to determine relevance via selection. Then we should look out. Lang has already warned us not to assume the completeness of our knowledge, or its reliability. The fact that Joan and Eddie are going off by car could become decisive for their fortunes – if, say, the vehicle turned out to have been stolen. We could imagine a Langian turn to the tale that would give crucial significance to the question of the driver's identity: Dolan and Whitney saw – as we did not – who was at the wheel. Five miles along the road a child is knocked down and left for dead. Dolan and Whitney come under pressure – since Joan is not a 'three-time loser' – to affirm that it was Joan who drove away from the prison. These are among the real, but not to be realised, possibilities ten minutes into the movie.[9]

Since the film's characters are in a world their knowledge of it must be partial, and their perception of it may be, in almost any respect, distorted or deluded. But that applies to us, too, as observers of their world and their understandings. In *You Only Live Once* Lang demonstrates how gullible we may become when we can be persuaded to limit the zone of possibility and so to carry our reading in a preferred direction. Given his skill and ingenuity, Lang can do this because he can rely on our willingness to ignore, by taking for granted, the profound mediation of our access to the fictional world and its events. We may take the mediation for granted; we may be overconfident that we understand its purposes.

We are offered an assembly of bits and pieces from which to compose a world. Fragmentary representation yields an imagined solidity and extensiveness. The malleability of the image is in a reciprocal relationship with the seamlessness and continuity that the image can evoke in our minds. Our imagination of the world is impressively independent of the means of representation;[10] this is most clearly so in flagrantly non-realistic media like cartoons, opera or puppet theatre. But in the movies too a journey may be conveyed by a car scene, a sound effect or even an animated diagram. We can take the meaning of an arrow travelling across a map between 'Abilene' and 'Dallas' as readily as we understand a departure–arrival dissolve. We do not have to see how the action occurs to understand it as taking place in its world, and thereby to know something of its character. There are as many ways of conveying any given thought, fact or event as creative imagination could devise. Even at our dullest we can see some of the options. That should not suggest that one way is as good as another. Any particular device has aspects and implications unique to itself.

Selective representation creates the stylistically relevant freedoms for the artist. I say this to distinguish expressive choice from the contingencies of production. It does not matter that most likely the set did not exist in which to film the counter-shot of, say, Joan getting into the car. Since that action did occur in the fictional world, it could have been shown. We might say that the availability of that shot is a dimension of the fiction. The camera's staying with Dolan–Whitney is a choice to which we respond in relation to our understanding of the pictured world, not in relation to the hypothetical economics of the shoot.[11]

A picture from a fictional world brings with it everything that goes without saying. *You Only Live Once* starts with an unpeopled image of the front entrance to a neo-classical building with electric lights and with 'Hall of Justice' engraved above its doors. It would be impossible to list all the things that we know from this four-second shot or all the frames of reference that it invokes. Among the most obvious are that we are in a modern town or city, probably in the USA, where recognisable systems are resourced for the proclamation and enforcement of law. We can reasonably suppose a society that erected this building to be in possession also of prisons, police, criminals, banks, armories, transport and communications systems. State murder of transgressors, if performed, may be by a number of methods, but boiling in oil will not be among them. There may, though, be some old citizens who claim to recall, with horror or nostalgia, the days when picking a pocket could get you tarred and feathered.

Surrounding all this will be attitudes to law and law-breaking some of which will be regarded as ordinary, some aberrant but comprehensible, and some outrageous. (There will be positions, too, on horticulture, music, navigation and palmistry but none of these becomes active in Lang's tale.) Concretely the film needs to tell us – because it does not go without saying – that in this jurisdiction a fourth criminal conviction entails life imprisonment and that murder is punished by a death sentence exacted in the electric chair.[12] (It does not need to tell us what is meant by 'electric chair'.)

The fictional world is a world not only when, and not because, it is *our* world but because it too has an infinity of goes-without-sayings. *The Wizard of Oz* (Victor Fleming, 1939) makes us witnesses to a world of the fantastic with many special rules and properties. Some of them are explained to Dorothy and to us.[13] We have to be told or shown the meaning of a pair of red shoes, instructed to see them as 'ruby slippers'. We are surprised to discover that a bucket of water can dissolve a witch. On the other hand the film can leave us to assume most of what matters. The physiologies of a man of tin and a man of straw – together with the threats from rust, fire or loss of stuffing – are easy to comprehend; and in Oz, as in Kansas or Coventry, the same things count as evidence of nerve, brain or heart.

If this were not so, fiction would be impossible. It could never get started if it needed to itemise all the factors of relevance to the actions of its creatures, particularly since these would have to include considerations of the possible as well as of the actual.[14] What the storymaker chooses to articulate is influenced by the needs of exposition to the extent that those needs are not covered by what can be assumed. Beyond that, as Welles and Lang

have shown us, articulation is less a route to clarity and more a device
of rhetoric.

We can take this further with the aid of Douglas Sirk and a moment from
his *All I Desire* (1953). Ten years ago, in 1900, Naomi Murdoch (Barbara
Stanwyck) left Riverdale, a small town in Wisconsin, deserting her husband
and three children in order to avoid a scandal and so as to pursue a career on
the stage. Now reduced to performing in low vaudeville, she has received a
message from daughter Lily entreating her to return to witness the girl's
graduation and her performance in a school play. She believes her husband
Henry, the school principal, to be a party to the invitation. In a tussle with
the ambivalence of her feelings she has allowed herself to be persuaded that it
would be fun to pay a visit. On the day of the performance, life in Riverdale
is sketched for us through its concerns with rectitude and gossip. While
Naomi completes the train journey and puts up at the town's one hotel, we
are introduced to the members of the Murdoch household. Now, thirteen
minutes into the film, it is evening and Naomi approaches the house walking
steadily, with controlled apprehension. On the porch she delays, holding
back tears. She stands in the shadows to look in on the domestic scene. The
film cuts to a head and shoulders shot as she glances about her, hesitating.
Her eyes move to a hanging flower basket in the foreground above her head.
She reaches up into the top of it to take down a door key that she holds for
a long moment in contemplation (Figure 1.3). She reacts in confusion to the
noise of an approach, hurriedly replaces the key and retreats further into
the shadows of the verandah.

Anyone who has experienced this scene through eyes not blinded by
snobbery about soap opera will recognise the brilliance with which Sirk

1.3 *All I Desire* (Douglas Sirk, 1953)

has defined a complex of thought and feeling in a great actress's gestures.[15] The richness of the moment depends on the clarity with which the filmmakers have sketched the world of the small town so that its spatial and its social dimensions provide some defining contexts. Design and lighting present an architecture of containment and exclusion that draws on the social, legal and familial aspects of space as property and privacy. To set foot on this threshold with whatever degree of boldness, anxiety or carelessness is to enact a sense of one's entitlement and an apprehension of the community's view of it. The meaning of a threshold as an area simultaneously within and beyond the embrace of privacy or intimacy makes Naomi's actions readable.

Again the film is drawing on information that it has not laid out for us, but that is accessible as required from our knowledge of this world. For a start it is drawing on layered notions of security where the house must be lockable and a key may be kept hidden for emergencies – hidden from the world at large but available for the family so that knowledge of the secret represents inclusion in its community. The hiding place is sufficiently removed and enclosed, on the porch, to be in space marked as private but it is easy of access to an adult and open enough to public sight to convey a confidence in the law-abiding tenor of the surrounding life. The key is special inasmuch as it has not been used in the family's ordinary coming and going.

Moreover it has been kept in the same place for a period of years. Naomi reaches up and finds, quite easily, what she thought she might find. The film has discovered the means to dramatise Naomi's familiarity with this environment, and to put it in tension with her knowledge of self-exclusion, her sense of coming back as a stranger. As she looks in upon the family scene it is as separate from her as a lit stage is from a darkened auditorium. There is no occasion for Naomi to use the key. That awareness shades our sense of her motives and feelings in reaching for it. There are degrees of definition, areas of possibility. There was nothing that Naomi was going to *do* with the key. Her motives in looking for it are associated with her emotions rather than her purposes. Given her apprehension in approaching the house, the nervousness in her delaying the moment of entry, she may be seeking reassurance through re-performing an old, old gesture. She seems to find it comforting that the key is still in place: some things don't change even while children are transformed in ways one cannot guess by time and growth. Some of her old knowledge remains reliable.

Note that there are real possibilities that do not seem to be in play. Though it is conceivable that Naomi's response might contain an element of irritation, say, or of contempt, nothing promotes such a notion. Such things remain conceivable rather than visible or to be assumed. But the key in its accustomed place is evidently being seen as an emblem of stability and continuity, the index of an unchanging way of life in a community once abandoned in the search for something more exciting, less predictable. Today's extraordinary return is experienced in its relation to memories of a once-familiar, even oppressive, routine of homecomings.

What is tentative in the gesture is felt in its pacing and through Naomi's dangling the key at a distance from herself (as shown up by her white, elbow-length gloves). Formality in dress and stealthiness in action conflict to present another register of uncertainty. Then her replacing the key, and doing so hurriedly, enacts her knowledge that she is now excluded from a routine that has been maintained without her participation.

We have not been told, and we could not have been told, all that we draw on to participate in these moments. That comes, we might say, with the territory. We did not need to be informed in advance that there is a key in the flower basket. We did not need this either for clarity or for emphasis.[16] We did not need to be told what it would mean for a key to be secured in this way. Instead, knowing what it would mean, we are able to understand more of the character of the community and to apprehend and enter into the development of Naomi's experience. It is important to the effect that Naomi's knowledge of the world was here larger than ours. Before it caught her eye the basket had featured in the shot only as foreground foliage absorbed by shadow into the surrounding darkness; it was brought to our notice by the movement of her glance. She knew about the key and we did not, so that what was revealed to us was what was confirmed to her.[17]

On the other hand, the film has already taken us inside the house, and has sketched the current situation of each of the members of the family, so that its figures are familiar to us but not to her. We have knowledge of what awaits Naomi whereas she can only speculate. We have been presented with possibilities of development that affect our response to Naomi's hopes and fears.[18] The special nature of our access to the fictional world has the important consequence that we can know things unknown to some, or any, of the characters.[19] It is equally important that each of them has a vast body of knowledge that is not detailed for us. They each have their own store of experiences and memories, just as we have in our world. (This is not a matter of our access to the events of the plot.)

The relation between what is articulated and what goes without saying is vital to the sources of emphasis that enable the assertion of significance, and the grading of significance. We can tell that Naomi knew that a key used to be concealed in the flower basket, so we can tell that she reached up to see if it was still there. The momentary oddity of the gesture gives way to an understanding grounded in our knowledge of what privacy, security and routine are, and what memories may be. The arc of our comprehension is different from the shape of Naomi's experience but it enables the moment's particular mix of observation and feeling.

The facts that ground our understanding here are sufficiently specific (a flower basket) and sufficiently ordinary (a reserve key[20]) to play tellingly within a modest rhetoric. There is music which because of our knowledge of the world we can understand as part of the film and not part of the fiction. It supports the understanding that Naomi's emotions are of an intensity that she must struggle to control and it affirms that we should be moved for her.

Alongside this the camera's gestures are delicately graded. The primary concern with interiority is developed through the pacing, since we are given an extended passage in which the action is stalled on Naomi's indecision. The film turns Naomi's approach to the house into an event, one that it studies when it could move more swiftly to resolve the immediate issues surrounding her arrival and reception. The image dwells on 'incidental' aspects of the scene: Naomi's shadow, the movement of her gaze across the exterior of the house. Then, in the mid-shot as she reaches up into the top of the basket, the camera lifts to keep her hand within the frame. It tilts down again, reframing as she lowers the key in contemplation.

A formalist of the more blinkered variety might despise this camera movement as a mere adjustment, a wasteful and unstructured manoeuvre that subordinates image to performance and demeans the camera to accommodate the actress. But Hypothetical Formalist would be ignoring the fact that a fractionally withdrawn camera, or a different lens, could have encompassed all the action without adjustment. The initial set-up was chosen so as either to allow the hand to go out of shot or to demand the reframing. Sirk made a rhetorical choice that gives a precisely graded emphasis to Naomi's reaching. The gentle, subtle quality of the emphasis is in tune with the reflective tone of this passage. The play with scale is available because the taking of the key is a large matter only in Naomi's consciousness. Within the world of Riverdale the gesture has a domestic character. Nothing great seems to turn on it – possibilities of embarrassment at most.[21]

Put this instance alongside *Citizen Kane* and I believe it becomes the clearer that the relationship between stylistic gesture and fictional world is crucial for the construction and understanding of tone, hence meaning. The extravagance of Welles's gesture and the modesty of Sirk's are palpable in the context of both the spatial measures and the terms of value obtaining in their worlds. In *Kane* the distance travelled across the Xanadu cellar is huge, and the height of it enormous, relative to what we expect of a cellar; it would be unremarkable in relation to a desert or an ocean, and absurd in relation to a corner grocery store. Sirk's small reframing on the Riverdale porch could be boldly declarative if it brought into view the hiding place of incriminating letters – or a deadly scorpion.

Sirk shifts to encompass Naomi's gesture, and the key, without moving away in the slightest from Barbara Stanwyck's face. A further index of the scale of stress awarded the gesture is found in the musical score. The composer gives the moment hardly any punctuation of its own within the flow of the scene's emotion; no little stinger solicits a special response.

This reticence is maintained as Naomi puts the key back. But here a repetition of the camera's tilt makes an acknowledgement in form that this act is an undoing of her first one. The repetition underscores the difference in mood between the tentative reaching and the hasty replacement. That the camera's moves could be regarded as primarily functional is an aspect of their discreet character (within the overall style of the sequence). Yet they are particularly implicated in the balance of distance and intimacy here, our sharing in and awareness of Naomi's confused, largely unacknowledged emotions in a journey she had portrayed to herself as an amusing adventure.[22] The adjustments of the camera give our eyes a degree of participation in the gestures of taking, inspecting and giving up the key. They make us sharers in the pacing of the actions as we take the force of the thought-feelings 'once mine', 'still here, not for me'.

Since the character is displaying the key to herself the actress is not required to make a further move to display it to the camera. No special illumination is employed; the key catches the light no more and no less than do Naomi's drop earrings. The moment is not punched up in the editing or by a change of focus. Within the rhythm of the scene the weight of emphasis is assigned simply through the reframings that serve to maintain the visibility of the gestures. The camera's procedures remain within the register of the ordinary. This is a choice of scale that acknowledges the unspectacular nature of a gesture uncomfortably caught between the routine and the transgressive, between what is likely to count, in Riverdale, as Naomi's entitlement and her presumption.

Every world has its own norms. Each world holds to beliefs and practices that place things on scales that stretch from the inevitable through the ordinary to the impermissible or the impossible. There is necessarily a relationship between the import and impact that a thing has in its world and the size of the gestures that display it on the screen. Since this relationship is not fixed, filmcraft can make it telling.

In Riverdale as we are shown it, work and gossip provide the two main points of contact and potential collision between home and the wider community. A place where Naomi's husband, an ambitious conformist, can abjure 'progressive nonsense' in his role as school principal, and a place where behind doors and in whispers a prurient fascination attends the new possibilities of scandal offered by Naomi's arrival – this is the same world in different but related guises. But of course it is not the whole world, and

definitely not the world in all its relevant aspects. By the time of Naomi's
arrival we have already been given glimpses of the city with its vaudeville so
low that it merges into burlesque, and of Riverdale's gunshop as a forum for
dirty talk between men, and we have heard of a zone 'out by the lake' that is
available, but not secure, for illicit meetings.

Within the larger world, the isolation of any one space or community and
its value-system (with its internal conflicts and sub-systems) is always far
from complete.[23] There are always Elsewheres that may be, for instance and
in various mixes, familiar, remote, rumoured, desired, feared, imagined,
sought, envied, shunned or demonised. A problem for Naomi, and potentially for her daughter, is whether a move from Riverdale should be welcomed
as a liberation or lamented as an exile. Riverdale is not the whole world but
it is the world that imposes the immediate context for the characters' actions
and prospects. At every moment the film faces stylistic choices over the
degree to which it will scale its gestures to the proportions and values of the
depicted world.

The movie works for an audience that knows the world always to be larger
and larger again than the sector currently in view. This knowledge entails
an awareness of selection, hence of the concentrations and emphases that
help to determine tone and viewpoint. *All I Desire* stays within the spectrum
of domestic emotional turmoil. Within that spectrum the worst that will
happen is heartbreak that may or may not be healed, and the best is some
occasionally pleasant, more or less tolerable negotiation of conflict.[24]

Of course the film could disrupt the tone it has established. It could have
Naomi's distress build to the point of madness or suicide. These are real
possibilities of the world, then and there or here and now. But they are not
within the movie's zone of choice. This suggests that a picture may define
itself generically and tonally – for instance as romantic melodrama rather
than tragedy – partly through the way that it incorporates and excludes
aspects necessarily entailed by its setting.[25] *All I Desire* chooses not to introduce material that would put domestic trauma into a withering perspective:
destitution, sadistic cruelty, warfare. On the other hand we see more striving
for fulfilment than we see instances of it. Real joy or satisfaction is as little
displayed as disease and death.

A contrasting example may be found in Lubitsch's *To Be or Not to Be*
(1942) with its extraordinary turns between political melodrama and farce.
The horrors of Nazi oppression in Poland are strongly depicted, with the
worst of them only just off-screen, though consistently so. A propagandist
distribution of good and evil sometimes occupies the foreground of the drama.
But the main action of the movie assumes all that as the backdrop to fantastic comedy where theatrical disguise can become effective as a weapon of
war and a bit-player can think it worthwhile to try to foil the Nazis with his

moustache-aided impersonation of the Führer. Meanwhile, with national and individual survival at stake, a troupe of actors finds that however desperate its fix it cannot escape its submission to theatrical values; the petty rivalries and vanities of the performing life repeatedly obtrude upon the immediate crises and threaten to wreck a breath-stoppingly precarious structure of pretences. The provision of a withering perspective is as crucial for the tone of Lubitsch's film as its absence is to the tone of Sirk's.

The collision of the darkest realities with comic absurdity was assisted by the casting, most obviously of the leading male role. Jack Benny, who was with reason one of the most celebrated of twentieth-century comics, brought his familiar radio persona (unmistakably American[26]) to the part of Josef Tura, an egocentric star of the Warsaw theatre longing to play his Hamlet on a larger stage. (A standing feature of Benny's clowning was his striving for cultural prestige through his efforts at the violin.) Seeing Tura as Tura, within the world of the action, alongside seeing Tura as Jack Benny, within our appreciation of the performance, is a main contributor to the success of this film's amazing experiment.

To Be or Not to Be shows us starkly that worldhood is not primarily an issue of realism, and is a concept that should work to illuminate artifice, not to deny it. Further useful provocations could be derived from the end of *The Road to Morocco* (David Butler, 1942) and from the brilliant essay in film aesthetics that Max Ophuls offers at the start of *La Ronde* (1950). However, my final example is from Charles Laughton's *The Night of the Hunter* (1955). Another ending, the coda to a tale in which John (Billy Chapin) and Pearl (Sally Jane Bruce), children of the Depression era, have been in flight from a nightmare of betrayal and persecution and, following the defeat of Robert Mitchum's evil preacher, have at last found safety with a fairy-godmother figure, a widow called Rachel played by Lillian Gish.

It is Christmas day and Rachel is in the kitchen cooking. She receives and praises the simple gifts brought by her orphan brood, then sends them off to find the presents she has left for them. Back at the stove tending to a steaming pan Rachel thinks aloud in the language of one who lives in daily communion with the King James Bible:

> 'Lord save little children. You'd think the world would be ashamed to name such a day as Christmas for one of them and then go on in the same old way. My soul is humble when I see the way little ones accept their lot. Lord save little children. The wind blows and the rain's cold, yet they abide ...
>
> 'They abide and they endure.'

At moments the sense of soliloquy is dominant. The camera approaches, not so as to exclude distractions (there are none), but so as to take us closer to the speaker. We are placed both to observe the inwardness of Rachel's

rumination and to take its meaning as a homily for us. On the final affirmation, Rachel looks out and faces us with her belief. She smiles, and it may be
that her faith gives her contentment; it feels, though, as if this is a smile of
reassurance for us. Yet how can it be Rachel smiling at us? Rachel is alone in
that 1930s kitchen; she has no audience. Lillian Gish was the one who knew
about the camera and who could assume the task of speaking to us through
it on the film's behalf.

If we insist too much on reason here we shall divorce criticism from experience. It is normal for a movie to stress and sustain the separation between
the fictional world and the world of the viewer. Imagination allows the movie
to work within that register. But imagination makes other registers available
as well. In one such, a world may be suggested whose beings can respond to
our watching. In another, the film may have its actors step aside from their
character roles and move apart from the fictional world so as to appear to
address or confront us in their own right.

A movie can change registers, or combine them in new ways. It has that
power because, in the cinema as in the world at large, there is a constant
interplay between background knowledge and immediate perception. Narratives work on the relationship between what we know – what we need to
have somewhere in mind in order to follow them – and what takes our
attention and engages our concern. The fluidity of that relationship allows
us, for instance, to delight in aspects of a movie's style and structure even as
we remain involved in the development of its action. It means that we never
cease to be aware of performance, however little attention we give it and
however much we become wrapped up in character and predicament.

One way that fictional worlds match the real world is in the meaningfulness of glance and gesture. It is hard to see how it could be otherwise in a
comprehensible movie. As projections or significant withholdings of what
the characters have in mind or at heart, perhaps nothing can attract our
interest with such ease and force as the actions of their eyes. Movies, as well
as our lives, have taught us to be alert to the implications of the glance,
boldly declarative, ambiguous or subtly nuanced as it may be. Our education
in this must be constant, and aided by the work we do to control the meanings that our own eyes convey. In film one may understand normal techniques, of cutting in particular, as serving to present clear eyelines that allow
interpretation and invite wonder.

Against this background, I am likely to have a strong response to moments
when a character's glance appears to be projected forward in my direction.
Whatever it seeks on the range between intimacy and confrontation, eye
contact ordinarily carries acknowledgement as its fundamental meaning.
Yet within the film frame acknowledgement can only be performed, played,
because it is without the essential condition for a real acknowledgement, the

recognition of my presence and selfhood. When I respond to the invitation of the outward glance I engage in the fiction in a new way, by imagining contact rather than separation between my world and the screen world. By no means all outward glances carry this invitation. Most of the time in Ozu's later films, for instance, such glances are not taken to enact any response either to the camera or to the anticipation of an audience. In *The Lady in the Lake* characters regularly project their words and looks in our direction; the effect is certainly odd but it is adequately covered, for the purposes of the fiction, by the claim that we are occupying the eyeline of the gumshoe hero.[27]

We are sufficiently attuned to the minutiae of eye use to make discriminations through such matters as focus and the set of the head, and degrees of tension or relaxation in the surrounding features. At the opening of *The Night of the Hunter* we first encountered the Rachel-to-be as a figure abstracted from time, and framed fantastically within an evocation of the night heavens. Here too as she delivered a Bible lesson about false prophets Lillian Gish faced out from the screen. Her words, her appearance and the tone of her delivery placed her in a dramatic situation that was given no concrete location; we understood her to be an old countrywoman speaking, with kindness and conviction, to a group of children. We also understood her to be delivering the film's epigraph, her words and image deployed to set up for us some of the terms in which we should view the drama to come.

Laughton's film is thus book-ended by moments of address from Rachel. The ones at the start prepare the ground for the final ones, to be sure, but in other ways the effects are quite different. At the opening there is an implied audience for Rachel's words within the world that she inhabits and though she is seen frontally there is very little sense, as she looks up, that her gaze is meeting or challenging ours. Her eyes and her speech project a gentle authority and her manner is fully that of one speaking impromptu to an audience of youngsters.

But at the end there is no audience for Rachel within her world. The setting, in the cottage kitchen, is realistic and familiar but it is shown now in a new way that suggests theatre: the 'fourth wall' has been removed to give us the view from behind the cooker. The last of the children, John, has left the kitchen before Rachel turns, seeming to shift her attention round to us, for 'They abide and they endure'. Her movement is matched by one of the camera's that, closing in, amplifies the effect of her turn. Her gaze is now clearly one that seeks to connect with ours (Figure 1.4). This special effect is placed as an *envoi* here, almost as clearly as the beginning was a beginning: by the music, by the completion of the main dramatic business, by the departure of the children from the stage of action, and by words that face into the future. The tale is over, the movie is all but over, and the world goes on. Rachel recalls the task in hand and resumes her cooking.

1.4 *Night of the Hunter* (Charles Laughton, 1955)

Three points seem equally important here: the special nature of this moment through its adoption of a changed register; its work as a formal device rhyming the picture's end with its start; and the embeddedness of most of its elements in the fictional world. The last of these is what we are most likely to miss. Yet the effect of the break must depend on the degree to which it is a break.

That the matter was of concern to the director is evident in his placing the moment as the climax of a sustained shot that pivots complex interaction and camera movement on the central figure. Most of Rachel's monologue has been spoken while the children are momentarily off-screen; they have run into the next room to open their presents. The reverie is interrupted when the four girls come back to thank her and scurry off upstairs with their gifts. A more weighty interruption, and a key context for the final affirmation, comes when the widow engages John in an exchange about his new watch. The boy's response offers the prospect that Rachel's care can heal the scars of his ordeal. Other elements of continuity are provided by the words themselves. Rachel has earlier spoken to John about his power of endurance, telling him that 'children are man at his strongest; they abide'. She remains in character in the final soliloquy since the children have remarked, and we have witnessed, that in her loneliness she talks to herself all the time.

By emphasis on the forward projection of the closing words as a claim on our consent – our willingness to grant that this figure can speak to us and for us – the film shifts the balance of prominence between the character and the player. What had been constants of our background awareness are now offered for more particular attention. Whether or not we could name the player we had always known that an actress was playing the role of Rachel.

Moreover, when delivered to the camera, the role of Lillian Gish is being performed no less than that of Rachel. In bringing the player forward the film moves to invoke Lillian Gish's particular screen history of abused innocence and to remind those who know it that guiltless victims are not always rescued. It presents us with the possibility that she too could have an unlikely, lovely faith in benign providence. The particular relevance of these moments to my theme is in the way that they explore some of the possibilities in movement between the fictional world and the means of representation.

Because the world is created in our imaginations it need not suffer damage from any foregrounding of the devices that assist its construction. We can, if we will, glide over inconsistencies and absorb ruptures, or delight in them. It is not difficult to see the image on the screen simultaneously as a world and as a performance. We do it all the time. The degree to which the filmmaker maintains the independence, solidity and coherence of the fictional world is a matter of choice and a variable. The decisions have great significance for style and meaning but no immediate bearing on achievement. The particular character of this ending depends on Laughton's having been able to hold the actress within her role even while bringing her forward as a spokeswoman. The movements towards and away from soliloquy are seamlessly performed, while the surrounding characters – the children – remain fully within the fiction and Rachel interrupts her musing to talk with them. Throughout, the central gesture of attending to the cooking is sustained. It contributes strongly to a mise-en-scène that keeps the figure of Rachel embedded in the cottage setting and does not seek to isolate her with effects of, for instance, lighting that would compromise the independence of the fictional world.

The result is that the central figure never ceases to be Rachel the cook and housemother (whose faith we may observe) when she presents herself also as Lillian Gish, an actress whose knowledge we must share. That sets up a conflict that I believe is vital for the significance and the emotional impact of this conclusion. 'They abide and they endure' might seem to be the film's final message of reassurance, allowing us to believe perhaps that the nightmare was just a bad dream. But that would be to ignore the precarious, all but magical, quality of the children's survival within the fiction. And from our spectating position, whether of 1955 or of the twenty-first century, it would be to disregard our knowledge of the fates of persecuted children in the world that the actress now seems to be addressing. Rachel always had the aspect of a fairytale being. When she recounted Herod's slaughter of the innocents her stress was on the survival of the baby Jesus. In her, generosity of feeling and hope for the future of mankind can outweigh knowledge, producing an assessment that we can only long to share. In our world, the world from which we weigh Rachel's words, the endurance of children is too often and too cruelly tested.

Conclusion

Has this chapter said anything more than that fictions are made for and by humans and that their strategies necessarily rely on the knowledge that we share? Perhaps not, but it has said nothing less. If, as it seems to me, this has been an exercise in exploring the obvious then it is an obvious that we have mainly chosen to ignore. My examples demonstrate, to my mind, that understanding the events of a movie as taking place in a world is a prerequisite of the intelligibility not only of plot but also of tone, viewpoint, rhetoric, style and meaning. If I am right it should be a priority in thinking about cinema – indeed in thinking about narrative more generally – to advance our grasp of what is involved in the worldhood of fictional worlds.

A priority but not an obsession. As a narrowly theoretical pursuit the fictional world is hardly preferable to any other. I would see no benefit in having worlds replace cause/effect, enigma resolution or order/disruption/resolution as a formalist distraction. It is an advantage of the fictional world that the concept is too broad to yield a methodology or an interpretive formula. It will not promise critical procedures that can replace attentiveness and dialogue. Not all our interests in film will be furthered by analysing worldhood. But as the point of convergence between space, community and the observing self, the fictional world surely earns a place among our central concerns.

Notes

1   I would be happy if anyone could suggest a better word than this but 'world-likeness' is not a candidate. To describe a fictional world as worldlike is to miss the point; a fictional world *is*, fictionally, a world.
2   By which I mean all motion-picture fictions. In fact I think it must be true of all narrative, whatever the medium, but my concern is with the movies.
3   See the brilliant essay in George M. Wilson's *Narration in Light* (1986).
4   Cf. portraiture, where the subject's complicity is often displayed through pose and vital to the picture's meaning. In line with regular usage I shall often use 'camera' to stand in for the entire apparatus of filmmaking – lights, microphones, crew, wind machines and so forth. Writing this chapter I have been more conscious than ever of some problems attached to our use of the word 'camera' to deal with the mobility of frame and viewpoint in movies. There is a gap in our vocabulary here, apparently irreparable since the alternatives to 'camera' are all more misleading or more cumbersome. We seem to be stuck with expressions like 'looking into the camera' to describe some images where that is not what either the character or the actor can be supposed to be doing.
5   For me, there is a lost magic of cinema-going, though my lungs are grateful for it, through the removal of the tobacco fog that once gave the projector's beam so strong a presence in the auditorium.

6   Note that the converse does not hold. The actors' occasional acknowledgement of the camera cannot be without effect. But the effect is not necessarily to break the fiction or to detract from the worldhood of the world. In their appeals to our complicity or compassion Oliver Hardy's camera-looks seem often to increase the sense of intimacy rather than to produce a new detachment. I shall say more on this point in discussing *The Night of the Hunter*.

7   *It Happened One Night* (Frank Capra, 1934) provides an interesting set of contrasts in its address to these issues.

8   The film can construct zones of relevance beyond which an issue like this one has no reason to arise.

9   A relevant further instance could be *Strangers on a Train* (Alfred Hitchcock, 1951) and the matter of Miriam's shattered glasses. When last seen they are in her husband's keeping and, potentially, damning evidence of Guy's complicity in her murder.

10 For more on this see Perkins (1999: 40–1).

11 For some critical and scholarly purposes the economics are, of course, vital.

12 The make-up of this 'us' is a matter of the constituency addressed by the filmmaker's assumptions. This huge topic might, for a Western readership, be forwarded by considering the opening shot of *Sansho Dayu* (Kenji Mizoguchi, 1954) or the matter of Noriko's handbag at the tea ceremony in *Late Spring* (Yasujiro Ozu, 1949).

13 And some of them are not. While the Munchkins can direct Dorothy to the Emerald City, we should wonder why none of them may escort her there.

14 See Sterne, *Tristram Shandy*, passim.

15 This is a scene of homecoming to compare with the equally fine one at the start of Nicholas Ray's *The Lusty Men* (1952).

16 Cf. *Notorious* (Alfred Hitchcock, 1946).

17 Take it another way round. If she were going to reach into the basket to react to the *absence* of the key then the film (if it wanted immediate understanding rather than to set a puzzle) would have to have found a way to let us know that a key is or was normally stowed there. This illustrates the difference between a created expectation and a possibility inherent in the presented world.

18 For instance, it could become a major issue that Naomi's husband might not be the father of her son, or that she has misrepresented the nature of her work in the theatre.

19 For instance that the sled called Rosebud has been destroyed.

20 In this world: a key left available to passers-by in Scorsese's New York would have different meanings; one left at the entrance to an igloo would present an enigma and we should have to speculate on its function until we were informed.

21 Cf. *Notorious* again; or replace Naomi with a crook hired to abduct her daughter.

22 Soon she will claim, in the family kitchen, 'Now I know I'm really home', where she might say only that she knows herself to be back again.

23 Overtherainbow offers Munchkinland, Oz and the fortress of the Wicked Witch as distinct but adjacent environments, with Kansas as a world away.

24 Cf. the movement towards catastrophe in *Rebel Without a Cause* (Nicholas Ray, 1955) or *Written on the Wind* (Douglas Sirk, 1956). Sirk reflects interestingly on the matter of scale in *All I Desire*, with reference to the choice of school play, in Jon Halliday, *Sirk on Sirk* (London: Secker & Warburg, 1971), pp. 89–90.

25 Here I want to draw attention to the interest and importance of Deborah Thomas's discussion in her book *Beyond Genre* (Moffat: Cameron & Hollis, 2000) where – with reference to films that include *All I Desire* and *To Be or Not to Be* – relationships between genre, tone and world are differently explored.

26 And, as William Rothman reminds me, identifiably Jewish.

27 In its relentlessness the effect soon becomes tedious. *The Lady in the Lake* is a useful marker for the contribution that variety of posture and eyeline make elsewhere to the liveliness of film drama.

References

Perkins, V. F. (1999) *The Magnificent Ambersons* (London: BFI).

Wilson, G. M. (1986) *Narration in Light* (Baltimore: Johns Hopkins University Press).

2

From detail to meaning: *Badlands* (Terence Malick, 1973) and cinematic articulation

Jonathan Bignell

This chapter focuses on an overlapping series of journeys. It offers several interpretive journeys from moments in *Badlands* to critical frameworks for discussing the meanings of the film as whole. These movements from detail to meaning also entail the linkage of aspects of the film to broader film-theoretical problematics such as genre, narration, gender and familial roles, and the placing of the film in a historical context within the American film culture of the 1970s. While the interpretive discussion of *Badlands* demonstrates the power of detailed film analysis to open up a vista of theoretical and cultural study, the purpose of the analysis is not only to explore the meanings of this film in particular (an enterprise necessarily restricted by constraints of space), but also to reflect on the discursive process of film criticism. I shall begin at the beginning, by discussing three brief moments from the opening of the film, then consider the film more broadly, in less detail. The chapter ends with a series of theoretical reflections on the methods of film analysis and criticism in general. Starting with a detail from *Badlands* is not a theory-free approach, since after all the decision to start with the text, to subordinate my discourse to that of the film, is already laden with assumptions about the relationship of the critic to his or her object of study. Indeed this chapter focuses on what is at stake in the relationship of critic to film, and the relationship of theory to its object.

The motif of the journey is used here to suggest that there is a plausible critical movement from detail to theory, and also to question the notions of progress entailed in journeys, whether literal or discursive. *Badlands* is itself a film about journeys, notably the journey undertaken by the two main characters as they escape from a small town and travel cross-country towards Montana. I shall argue later that the journey in *Badlands* undercuts assumptions about self-discovery in the road movie, and about the frontier (the badlands of Montana) as the locus for a discovery of identity. The motif of the journey as a progression towards an origin, a truth or a self will also be used as a means to reflect on the procedures of film analysis. *Badlands* is a suitable site for exploring these issues because the film uses distancing techniques which can be noted at the level of the shot, the sequence and the structure of narration, as well as in tropes or themes, and these distancing techniques focus attention on details at the same time as calling for an interpretation which reflects on and surpasses what the spectator is given to see and hear. However, I am going to argue not that *Badlands* is a 'radical film' either in its cinematic construction or in its 'message', but that it functions as a metacommentary on the film's relationship to American cinema's histories, genres and tropes. From this perspective, *Badlands* becomes a film about film, in the sense that it foregrounds the different interpretive schemas which might be used in moving from immanent analysis of detail to film-theoretical discourse in general.

I shall begin this journey from a specific sequence, in fact the first shot of the film, before even its title has appeared on the screen. What we see is Holly (Sissy Spacek) sitting on a double bed, playing with a large dog, while the camera moves in a slow tracking shot from the side of the bed to a slightly elevated position at its foot (Figure 2.1). Holly's voice, relatively unemotional and flat in tone, describes how after the death of her mother, she and her father moved house to the town of Fort Dupree, South Dakota. A similarly slow, somewhat mournful or nostalgic musical accompaniment begins during the shot. The scene seems to be set in the house which the family left when the mother died. This opening moment is then a kind of

2.1 *Badlands* (Terence Malick, 1973)

memory-image, a flashback to a lost time in which the family was complete. Holly is probably sitting on her parents' bed, and her caresses and games with the dog signify both a childlike playfulness and affection, yet her actions might also represent a certain sensuality at the same time as a disavowal or repudiation of the adult sexuality which the bed and the animal make available for this interpretive pathway. Holly's voice-over comments that her father must have been dismayed by the presence of his daughter, as a reminder of her mother and a mark of the mother's loss.

One of the stories which film studies might tell about the film is to cast it as a family romance, and the journey here is from detail to psychoanalytic criticism. Holly, from this point of view, stands in the place of the mother but cannot fulfil that place. The attempts of Kit (Martin Sheen) to leave with Holly, taking her from her father, lead to Kit's shooting of the father in a contest over the role which Holly occupies. For Kit, she is at once a child whom he meets after school or under the bleachers at the school sports field, and also a lover with whom he wants to run away. For the father (Warren Oates), Holly is a child who needs protection, but also a beloved whose role as substitute for and sign of his own wife renders her a love object for him too. Later in the film, when Holly and Kit are living in a stockaded treehouse reminiscent of Tarzan and Jane's dwelling in the Johnny Weismuller films, and also redolent of the defensive tunnels and camps of the fighters in the Korean War against whom Kit had fought, Holly takes on a maternal and wifely role in her relationship with Kit. She wears make-up, puts her hair in curlers, decorates their treehouse, and reads to Kit from Tor Hayerdal's *Kon-Tiki Expedition*. The adventure of their escape into a pastoral dreamworld involves adult roles (Kit practises the guerrilla warfare techniques which enable him to defeat the law officers who attempt to capture them), but also perpetuates their childlikeness. Holly still has her schoolbooks with her, because Kit doesn't want being on the run to make her fall behind in her education, and the couple dance to pop music on their radio. As the song they are dancing to claims, 'Love is strange / A lot of people / Take it for a game'. Presenting love as a game of roles and positions both questions ideologies of husband and wife, masculine and feminine, parent and child, and also questions the violence which erupts when those roles are shifted. For the beginning of Holly's journey away from the family involves the killing of her father, and along the way as the journey unfolds, further characters threatening an enforced return to that starting-point are gunned down by Kit.

The film could be read, then, as being about the loss of an originary maternal security, and the forces which are consequently released as sexual desire, violence and struggles to either repudiate or repeat the nuclear family. This is a variant on the Oedipal logic discerned by psychoanalytic film criticism (see for example Raymond Bellour in Bergstrom 1979). My first journey, then, has been from the opening shot of Holly and the dog on her parents' bed, with its accompanying voice-over, on a track through the film that frames it as the collision of several 'family romances': the family that existed before the film's present tense, the family without a mother at the film's opening, and the fantasised family constructed by Kit and Holly. Masculine, feminine, maternal, paternal, filial and sexualised adolescent roles are rendered volatile and placed in conflict with each other in this interpretive journey.

My second journey is from the opening shots of the film to questions of genre prompted by Holly's framing comment in her voice-over that the film is a story of a journey from 'the alleys and back ways of this quiet town' to 'the badlands of Montana'. This voice-over draws attention to a number of ways in which the film is articulated with and against certain binaries in cinema and in cinema studies. The quiet little town of Fort Dupree, South Dakota, is at once the heart of America, but also one of those places at the edge which embodies a mythic America outside of the cosmopolitan urbanism of the contemporary. The value of this mythic America can be both positive and negative, both innocent and banal, both communitarian and oppressive, and the still shots of the town, showing picturesque but static unpeopled views, provide evidence to support the voice-over's implication that the town is a boring place. The badlands of Montana, to which Holly and Kit escape after Kit shoots Holly's father, are similarly multiple in their possible significance. The badlands are the empty space in which an authentic identity might be carved out, as in the Western (see Pye 1999), but they are also a null space, in which the activities of the characters leave no mark on the blank page of the prairie, and in which the story of Holly and Kit is finally insignificant and delusory. The beautiful close-ups of prairie animals later in the film, accompanied by haunting marimba music, show a world going on beyond Kit and Holly's story, a world which is oblivious to them (similar shots in Malick's *The Thin Red Line* (1998) have a similar function). If the film alerts us to genre, by signalling the small-town film and the Western, it also asks us to consider the ambivalent significance of mise-en-scène and setting as parallels with, and contrasts to, the human drama of the film.

In these respects, the film is also about storytelling, since the kinds of stories we might expect in the small-town film and the Western are significantly different, and the film counterposes these kinds of story without privileging either of them. So another journey which begins from the issue of genre raised by Holly's voice-over is about how different kinds of narrative invest details with meaning. *Badlands* can be interpreted as a film about how significance is achieved: how stories, narration, fantasies of escape and memory are attempts to give meaning to a depthless surface. Neither Holly nor Kit seems to feel or desire anything, a mood which is conveyed by the deadpan

2.2 *Badlands* (Terence Malick, 1973)

tone of Spacek's voice-over, and by the inadequacy of the attempts by Holly and Kit to mark out significant moments in their journey and their relationship. The first time that Kit and Holly have sex, for example, by the bank of a river, Holly asks whether that's all there is to it, and wonders what everybody had been so excited about. Kit picks up a rock to take away as a souvenir of their encounter, but casts it away because it is heavy, and simply chooses a smaller stone. There is nothing necessary about the sign which marks the moment, and nothing intrinsically interesting about it. The couple bury some of their possessions in a bucket on the prairie, as a memorial for future people to find, and when captured finally by the police, Kit carefully allows time to build a cairn of stones to memorialise the place where his journey stopped (Figure 2.2). These little monuments are attempts to mark space and to fix meaning, but they remain heaps of rocks and a bucket of dusty bric-à-brac.

The film shows attempts by the couple to fit their behaviour into story structures, like the teen romance or the outlaw pursuit, but the characters and their actions cannot carry the mythological weight of grandeur and notoriety that they aim for. When Kit is shown recording a message to posterity explaining the motives for killing Holly's father, he runs out of things to say before the recording time has finished, and the record player on which the record plays outside Holly's house is seen being consumed by fire in a long sequence showing the burning of the house. Kit's attempt to memorialise his actions does not survive. In the only visual sequences which are beyond the consciousness of the main characters, Holly's voice-over describes the

excessive precautions taken by people across the Midwest to protect themselves from Holly and Kit, who have become notorious outlaws. The monochrome newsreel-style shots accompanying this voice-over reveal the distance
between the banal but violent actions of Holly and Kit themselves, and the
hysterical but patently unnecessary precautions of townspeople. When Kit
and Holly are captured, they are guarded at a military base by an excessive
number of soldiers and police. Kit is admired and liked by these officers not
because he is notorious, but because he is ordinary, friendly and talkative.
Following an American tradition which goes back at least as far as *The
Adventures of Huckleberry Finn*, storytelling is a vital component of identity
and self-definition in American culture, but also a diversion from the actual
banality of crime, violence and heroism. The making of meaning, the telling
of stories, and the distance between the banal and the mythic, are part of
what *Badlands* articulates. One of the key points that a study of detail in
Badlands makes clear is that the film thematises the construction of significance in the lives of the characters. In marking this issue as significant, the
film also poses a question to its interpreters (to its spectators and also to film
theorists) about how they make the journey from detail to meaning. The
attribution of meaning and value, and the discursive terms in which significance is framed, are already questioned in the film before debates about
interpretive legitimacy are raised in critical discourse about the film.

In *Badlands* identity is a matter of performing the conventions of an identity, and shifting from one position to another in structures which provide
a contingent and partial significance to the characters' lives. At the moment
of Holly and Kit's first meeting, Holly is performing with her cheerleader's
baton, while Kit presents himself as a teen idol, a James Dean-style rebel.
When they meet, cuts back and forth between them suggest a mutual recognition that they are both playing out roles, and this is the common factor
which enables their relationship to begin. Andrew Britton (1981: 4) argued
that American films of the 1970s 'are primarily of interest for the various
ways in which they seek to negotiate a historical moment which includes not
only Vietnam and Watergate, but also the critique of the family, and the
questioning of gender roles developed by the women's and gay movements'.
For *Badlands* to open with Kit masquerading as James Dean, and Holly
listlessly practising her moves with a marching band baton, is to signal at
once the gendered roles that the characters initially play out, and which they
will renegotiate together. Their journey is not simply away from these roles
to more authentic ones, however, since for example when Kit is finally captured by two police patrolmen, he is delighted when one of them describes
him as looking just like James Dean.

In his discussion of the war film, and especially films around the subject
of Vietnam, Britton argues that a problem arises when a film retains a

hero-function, but places him/it in a situation which is both inexplicable by the film and also calls into question the values like masculinity or morality which underlie the hero's agency. The contradiction between the hero-function and the situation produces 'a hero whose activity (still deemed of value) remains "tragically" unrealised; a hero who is passive – not acting, but acted on; or a hero whose assertion of agency appears as compulsive and psychotic' (1981: 5). Britton later quotes Norman Mailer as a voice support-ing a view of the hero as the American existentialist, where in response to a deadening social order 'the only life-giving answer is to accept the terms of death, to live with death as immediate danger, to divorce oneself from society, to exist without roots, to set out on that uncharted journey into the rebellious imperatives of the self' (1981: 13). This form of agency is complicit with the forces of the social order, in willingly falling into its Romantic valuation of the individualist frontier hero, its metaphorical substitution of a physical journey for a moral one, and its inverted, negative version of the theory that heroism consists in realising in behaviour a supposedly 'true' selfhood which has been hitherto obscured by the quotidian demands of getting on with other people.

Badlands offers a contradictory and unresolved attitude to the hero, who is both effective, active, attractive and nice, but also irrational, unpredictable, excessively violent and criminal. The fact that Kit both resembles and imit-ates James Dean makes him doubly out of place: he is a throwback to the iconography of the rebellious teen, complete with car, chewing gum, and white T-shirt, but he is also distinctly working class (a garbage man and a cattle-pen worker, as opposed to Dean's suburban middle-class milieu) and too old to be a rebel without a cause (ten years older than Holly, and not at college). In contrast to the teenage rebel's actions, Kit's behaviour seems excessive, useless, childlike and inconsistent. On one hand, it keys into the Romantic myth of childhood as an originary, true selfhood uncontaminated by society and its demands, a utopian childhood which meshes with the myth of the frontier and the open plains as a Garden of Eden, a playground in which one finds oneself. On the other hand, this regressive, defensive and immature behaviour is part of an unwinnable Oedipal struggle where parental figures, and maturity itself, are aggressively and pointlessly resisted. The film's allusions to myths of masculine self-realisation do not therefore produce a narrative progression in which a heroic identity is achieved. It is symptomatic that Holly gradually becomes bored and frustrated with the couple's journey, and begins to engage in minor defiances of Kit's grand narrative about their outlaw grandeur. The film offers the spectator a sequence of scenes in their car as they rush headlong across the prairies. Holly almost ceases to communicate with Kit, and her voice-over informs us that instead she spells out whole sentences on the roof of her mouth with the tip of her tongue. By doing this, she articulates an unseen, unspoken alternative writing in her mouth that, together with the voice-over retrospectively accompanying the sequence, denies Kit mastery over the terms in which their journey's meaning can be framed.

Badlands can be regarded as constituted by a movement from one space to another (from town to prairie to airport, or from home to nature to sky) where the narrative journey of the road movie as a journey to the inside of the self contrasts with the journey from contained spaces to open spaces of transcendence. In this reading, there is progression though space and progression towards an achieved personal identity, each of which is a metaphor for the other. But this progression is problematised by the film's final aeroplane journey, an image both of transcendence and of entrapment simultaneously since the visual beauty and freedom of the airborne shots of clouds touched by evening sunlight is counterpointed by the knowledge that the aeroplane is taking Kit and Holly towards their punishment by the institutions of the law. Furthermore, there is an ironic counterpoint between Holly's voice-over at the end of the film where she tells of her eventual marriage to another man and settling down into conventional domesticity, and the images in the film's final minutes. The final sequence is only the last in a series of disjunctures between the image-track and the retrospective voice-over narration. The whole film raises questions about the primacy of either the voice-over or the image as a fixing element, for what is articulated by the image-track or articulated in voice counterpoint each other – sometimes to confirm meaning, but sometimes to question it. The fact that Holly's voice-over is retrospective tends to privilege her version of events since it is reflective and interpretive, offering a means of articulating the film's scenes together into a story. Yet the nature of the voice-over, delivered in a deadpan tone and reducing the complexities of the actors' performances and the visceral violence of some of the characters' actions to simple statements (like 'Kit was the most trigger-happy guy I ever met' as a coda to the gunning-down of his friend in a field) is distant from the visually represented action and often inadequate to channel its impact on the spectator. The disjuncture between image and voice produces a necessity for the spectator to make a journey from detail to meaning that is not mapped out definitively by the visual and aural articulations of the film itself, but requires instead a spectator enagaged in trying out a number of possible routes through the film.

Badlands can also offer, therefore, a site for the exploration of the multiple meanings of the term 'articulation' which I have used so often in this chapter. Articulation refers to the vocal articulation in voice-over as supplement to the image-track, and to the articulation of images and sounds together in this or another film, and also to the enunciation of theory as an interpretive discourse. Having made some remarks about the first two kinds of articulation so far, the remainder of this essay considers the third sense of articulation; the discourse in which my remarks have been made. What film studies does is to supplement one kind of articulation with another. The film, which is itself an intervention in culture, could be described therefore as an articulation, a contribution to the dialogues of the public sphere. In accounting for the specific nature and effects of a film, accounting for its meaning, it becomes necessary to give an account of it in a language other than its own. The film is articulated by film criticism. Furthermore, for readers to judge the correctness or perspicacity of a critical articulation about a film is to consider it in two other related ways. First, does the critical discourse give the sense of how the film works – its meaning, but also its tone, its mood, its affective relationship with its spectator? Second, does the critical analysis itself intervene in a cultural debate, and by doing so bring to notice the fact that the film has something to say? This second question draws attention to the fact that film criticism is not a pure articulation, if such a thing could exist, but necessarily one which is engaged in the movement of public discourse more generally. To put this another way, film criticism is inherently political because it is articulated in relation to culture. Articulated, in this sense, means both that film criticism is a discourse which voices itself among the other competing discourses of culture, and also that it exists as a discourse by working on and with a cultural object, a film, to which it is linked or hinged.

Since film criticism in the sense that it is practised in this book is part of the academic and pedagogical world, another question arises in considering the ways in which film criticism responds to a film's articulacy, and tries to articulate this again in other terms which further the movement of debate and enquiry in culture. That question is how the study of a film can enable further articulations by students, among fellow researchers and in the arena of publication (this is the project of, for example, Elsaesser and Buckland 2002). By offering to write about *Badlands*, I am implicitly suggesting that the film has something to say to me, to you, to the film studies community more widely, and to all those who have an interest in film, in culture and in criticism. In this respect, there is a journey from detail to meaning in my analysis of the film itself, but also a journey from a particular object (*Badlands*) to a set of ideas which claim a greater purchase. *Badlands* becomes the locus of an articulation which begins from what I say that the film has to say, and therefore the film becomes not simply the contingent, happenstance object that I chose to write about, but also a privileged place from where my wider observations can make sense.

My choice to write about *Badlands* is motivated then not only by my view that the film has something to say (about the hero, about gender, about narrative structure, about genre), but also by the specific ways in which the film articulates these things. My journey of interpretation through the film can become a metaphor for the processes involved in film study itself. For the interpretive journey through *Badlands* travels in parallel with the trajectory of film analysis from detail to meaning, from the particular to the general, from the object to its theorisation. *Badlands* becomes privileged by this selection and analysis, but at a certain point the film is also neglected in favour of the place where it allows me to go. *Badlands* is the starting-point of this journey, a commentary on this journey, but not the journey's destination, since the theoretical points about film studies which I am making here exceed the film as a particular object, and reflect back on the very activity of selecting the film as my object of study in the first place. So the study of detail necessarily produces a relation to theory. The example is always placed in relation to a metalanguage of criticism which it supports, affects or challenges, and the further theoretical issue raised by this becomes a question about the authority of film-theoretical metalanguages.

In the context of an analysis of *Last Chants for a Slow Dance* (Jon Jost, 1977), Jim Hillier (1981: 109) argued that 'even the supposedly "progressive" American cinema of the seventies (Altman, Hellman, Malick, Rudolph, Rafelson and others) belongs, fundamentally, to "Hollywood", to the dominant system, both economically-industrially and formally'. For Hillier, the potential progressiveness of Altman's films is circumscribed by their belonging to 'Hollywood art movies'. It is the issue of belonging that I would like to focus on, as a way of considering how film-theoretical categories articulate the political meanings of films. Robin Wood (1981: 42) proposed that in the 1970s social structure was questioned, to the extent that the decade was one in which 'the dominant ideology *almost* disintegrated'. The importance of this '*almost*' for my reading of *Badlands* is that the film is articulated in and against a wide range of categories and genres of film, and offers itself for readings which articulate the cultural and historical debates about American cinema of the 1970s in terms of gender, the family, violence, freedom, individualism and mythmaking. *Badlands* is more available for readings of this kind, because of its reflexivity, than American films outside the sub-category of 'Hollywood art movies'. It is perhaps too easy an example to choose in order to articulate these ideological and representational issues. But historically, film studies has perpetually increased the number of films regarded, after a detailed analysis has been carried out, as examples of critical commentary despite being apparently mainstream. Jean-Louis Comolli and Jean Narboni's (1969) 'Category E' is a class of films which are neither complicit with dominant ideology nor radical critiques of ideology, but from within a mainstream cinema tradition raise questions about ideology without being able to resolve them or offer alternatives. However, once any film is analysed in detail, it tends to drift into Category E. Once a film is taken out of a general category, like the categories of complicit or radical, and analysed in detail, it reveals itself as an articulation rather than an object, and it becomes a site of conflict, ambiguity and interest. At the extreme of this view, no film can be dismissed as a straightforward example in a category, and this problem therefore collapses the divisions between categories like radical or complicit, and requires the elaboration of new categories which further sub-divide films.

My interest in this issue is less in the specific form of these categories, and which films can be definitively established as members of them. Instead, I want to draw attention to the fact that the process of analysing detail in films throws the activity of categorisation into doubt (see Brunette and Wills 1989). This is most obviously the case with generic categories, but occurs whenever a trait of belonging is identified. Every film, once it is considered in detail as an articulation, and is supplemented by another articulation, namely the discourse of film-critical theorisation, has a crucial and problematic status. Such a film becomes the interface between considering a film as a represent-ative object for theoretical discourse on the one hand, and on the other hand considering it as a unique articulation which exceeds the ability of a metalan-guage to master it (see Bignell 2000). Indeed, this problem affects every use of an instance or example as a location for remarks of a general and theoretical nature. The journey from detail to meaning is both essential to film studies as a discipline, and also enables the discussion of questions of origin and destination, trajectory and aim, on which that journey is necessar-ily based. Finally, then, what I am arguing for in this essay is not only the value of *Badlands*, nor yet the value of any particular theoretical discourse as most pertinent for its interpretation, but for the reflexivity of any critical discourse that cites films as examples and moves from detail to meaning.

References

Bergstrom, J. (1979) 'Alternation, Segmentation, Hypnosis: Interview with Raymond Bellour', trans. S. Suleiman, *camera obscura*, 3–4, 87–103.
Bignell, J. (2000) *Postmodern Media Culture* (Edinburgh: Edinburgh University Press).
Britton, A. (1981) 'Sideshows: Hollywood in Vietnam', *Movie*, 27/8, 2–23.
Brunette, P. and D. Wills (1989) *Screen/Play: Derrida and Film Theory* (Princeton: Princeton University Press).
Comolli, J.-L. and J. Narboni (1969) 'Cinema/Ideology/Criticism (1)', trans. S. Bennett, *Cahiers du cinéma*, 216, 11–15.
Elsaesser, T. and W. Buckland (2002) *Studying Contemporary American Film: A Guide to Movie Analysis* (London: Arnold).
Hillier, J. (1981) '*Last Chants for a Slow Dance*', *Movie*, 27/8, 108–16.
Pye, D. (1999) 'Writing and Reputation: *The Searchers* 1956–76', in J. Bignell (ed.), *Writing and Cinema* (Harlow: Longman), pp. 195–209.
Wood, R. (1981) 'The Incoherent Text: Narrative in the '70s', *Movie*, 27/8, 24–42.

3

Narrative and visual pleasures in *The Scarlet Empress* (Josef von Sternberg, 1934)

George M. Wilson

In her widely influential essay, 'Visual Pleasure and Narrative Cinema', Laura Mulvey includes a brief discussion of the films that Josef von Sternberg made with Marlene Dietrich, citing them as prime exemplars of one of two regimes of cinematic scopophilia that she distinguishes as informing the foundations of classical narrative films. According to Mulvey, Hitchcock's work represents a brand of 'voyeuristic' scopophilia, while the von Sternberg/ Dietrich movies instatiate a 'fetishistic' mode. Her remarks on Hitchcock and von Sternberg are brief and rather abstract, and it is not altogether easy to follow the critical characterisation she means to offer. On several important matters, her claims strike me as suggestive and on the right track. But, in two key respects, to be discussed in this chapter, I believe that her succinct analysis is, at a minimum, misleading. First, Mulvey apparently assigns very little aesthetic or thematic importance to the narrative construction of these movies. Here, she is in agreement with the majority of commentators on von Sternberg's work. Nevertheless, I think that this partial consensus is quite mistaken. The design and narrative mechanics of the stories in these movies are unquestionably non-standard, but that is not to say that the non-standard design is not worthy of close attention nor that the non-standard machinery does not produce rich and interesting results. Second, Mulvey does not give any notice to the fact that the films in question are focused systematically upon some of the chief themes to which her own theoretical arguments are addressed. That is, the movies investigate questions of dominance and submission in gender interactions. More specifically, they depict the various ways in which the sexually charged gaze – not just the male gaze but the female gaze as well – give force and expression to these potential relationships of power. Given the importance of these matters to her analysis, the omission is surprising, and it deserves to be addressed.

In my opinion, the two claims sketched above apply to all of the von
Sternberg/Dietrich films, but I do not have the space to support this conten-
tion in the present setting. Therefore, I will examine, in considerable detail,
the narrative structure of *The Scarlet Empress*, the penultimate film that von
Sternberg and Dietrich made together.[1] In fairness, I should note that Mulvey
does not herself discuss this film. The movies she explicitly cites are two
earlier works: *Morocco* (1930) and *Dishonored* (1931). However, it is reasonably clear that her major theses are supposed to apply across the full range of
the Dietrich/von Sternberg collaborations. My objective here is not to attack
the theoretical framework of her essay. I am not sure that I understand some
of its components well enough to do so, and, in any case, the framework
has been extensively discussed by a host of other commentators over the
course of many years. I am much more interested in elucidating the subtle,
self-conscious complexity of the von Sternberg films themselves. That they
exemplify a complex visual style is almost universally acknowledged. However, the notion that they also exhibit a self-conscious complexity of narrative meaning is much more controversial. My aim is to correct what I take to
be a wrong impression of the von Sternberg films that Mulvey's terse analysis
is likely to convey. If I am right, then her use of von Sternberg as a primary
example of 'fetishistic scopophilia' needs to be modified and qualified in
a number of ways. And yet, this is a result that would not, I suspect, disturb
Laura Mulvey at all. Her essay, as I read it, is a challenge to say more on each
of the different topics she introduces. However, if my observations about *The
Scarlet Empress* are right, they raise some nice problems about the possible
relations between the type of symptomatic interpretation that Mulvey practises in her article and the sort of practical, internal criticism that I deploy in
mine. I will not pursue those questions here.

Let us begin with the question of narrative structure. Mulvey states:

> Sternberg once said he would welcome his films being projected upside-down
> so that story and character development would not interfere with the spec-
> tator's undiluted appreciation of the screen image. This statement is revealing
> but ingenuous: ingenuous in that his films demand that the figure of the woman
> (Dietrich, in the cycle of films with her, as the ultimate example) should be
> identifiable; but revealing in that it emphasises the fact that for him the pictorial
> space enclosed by the frame is paramount, rather than narrative or identification
> processes. (1989: 22)

This passage seems to conceive of von Sternberg's films as painterly in character, revelling chiefly in the exquisite perversity of their formal visual design,
a design constructed around the 'fetishised' figure of Marlene Dietrich. In the
dynamics of the narration, the stories such as they are, are punctuated by
crucial episodes in which, 'The beauty of the woman as object and the screen

space coalesce; she is no longer the bearer of guilt but a perfect product, whose body, stylized and fragmented by close-ups, is the content of the film and the direct recipient of the spectator's look' (1989: 22).

Now, as we will see, there are important episodes in *The Scarlet Empress* that satisfy Mulvey's description, and these are often episodes in which narrative development can seem to be more or less on hold – the action virtually frozen. Nevertheless, it is essential that even these episodes be scrutinised within their larger narrative context, because, as I will argue, these segments do play a significant, if unusual, role in advancing and defining the nature of the story being told. In fact, I want to begin by considering a central segment of *The Scarlet Empress* that contains such a moment of 'frozen' contemplation of Dietrich's loveliness. It will take us some space to unravel the significance that this segment ultimately suggests.

The plot environment of the targeted segment can be minimally summarised in the following way. Princess Sophia, played by Dietrich, has been brought to Russia to be married to the future czar – 'the royal half-wit' Peter. By marrying Peter, the erstwhile Sophia becomes Catherine of Russia. In the first part of the movie, Dietrich renders Sophia as an innocent virgin, shy and kittenish in demeanour. The performance in this stretch of the movie is fun and utterly preposterous. Dietrich seems to be more playing with her role than playing it. She is conveyed to Russia by the incredibly handsome and utterly self-absorbed Russian ambassador, Count Alexey. Thus, Alexey, as he is portrayed by John Lodge, comes across as a kind of male counterpart to Dietrich, fully as gorgeous and narcissistic as she. It is wholly natural, therefore, that the Dietrich character falls for him like a ton of bricks. However, just prior to the action in the relevant narrative segment, Catherine has discovered that Alexey, apparently like everyone else at the Russian court, has been sleeping with her mother-in-law. She regards this as very bad news and reacts crossly. In anger and distress, she throws a locket containing Alexey's portrait out of her bedroom window and then runs down to the palace garden to retrieve it. It is nighttime as she searches, and as she finds the locket, she encounters a handsome young lieutenant of the guard in the dark. He, with no difficulty whatsoever, seduces her on the spot.

This encounter opens an extraordinary sequence. As it proceeds, it is not always easy to say with real confidence just what is going on. The lieutenant announces at the very outset, 'On a night like this, *anything* could happen.' Given the various things that subsequently do happen or seem to happen, his remark comes across as flagrant understatement. Catherine submits to the guard, and we see the token of her submission, the relaxation of her hands upon his back. That image then is dissolved into images, themselves intercut in dissolves, of huge bells ringing and mighty guns firing. At first sight, this appears to be a rather vulgar cinematic metaphor – an instance of the kind of ersatz Freudian symbolism that stands in for the act that can't be shown in classical film.

And yet, this inference is immediately complicated by what follows. These shots of bells and cannons are gradually edited into shots of happy crowds out celebrating some momentous event, and it is briefly unclear what these celebrations are about.[2] One has the brief impression that most of St Petersburg is in a state of exultation because Catherine has lost her virginity in the palace gardens. And yet, of course, that isn't right. As the sequence continues, it emerges at the conclusion of some exuberant montage that a considerable period of time has passed, and, in fact, the cheering crowds are celebrating the birth of a royal heir. But even this realisation is conveyed to the movie audience in a confusing fashion. In the ensuing scene, it is the dowager empress, Elizabeth, who is shown in bed with a new baby, and she is the one who is receiving congratulations from a band of courtiers for *her* splendid achievement. It is, at this moment, as if Catherine's midnight indiscretion in the garden had caused her mother-in-law to conceive a child. (This is not the kind of causal connection one would like to see raised to the status of universal law.)

Eventually this confusion gets straightened around as well. We realise that nine months have passed. Catherine is the person who has mothered the infant, engendered presumably by the 'lucky' lieutenant in the garden. The dowager empress is triumphant because, thanks to Catherine, the royal line has been continued. Nevertheless, just this far into the sequence, the filmmaker has already established what seems to be an attitude of calculated playfulness concerning familiar standards of temporal and causal exposition. What is more, the last part of the segment is, if anything, more disorienting. First, we have the oddly moving and oddly uncommunicative scene in which Catherine lies in bed thinking her private thoughts, a rather characteristic moment in a von Sternberg film. That Catherine's thoughts and feelings are veiled from view is visually signified by the veil-like bed hangings that blur and soften her unreadable expression (Figure 3.1). This is a moment at which, in Mulvey's words, 'Sternberg plays down the illusion of screen depth: his screen tends to be one-dimensional, as light and shade, lace, steam, foliage, net, streamers and so on reduce the visual field' (1989: 22). (Here it is lace and net that chiefly effect the reduction.) Although the overwhelming impression from these shots derives from the carefully contrived visual aesthetics, it is not as if the story had simply halted. Catherine is plainly thinking something through, and it appears that the reflections Catherine is entertaining here are of some importance, since the camera lingers on her pensive face for an extended time, scrutinising her impassive gaze. It is as if she is reaching some fundamental decision or conclusion, but we don't know what it might be. We do know from the action a moment before that her lover's locket has now been

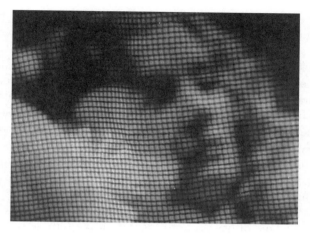

3.1 *The Scarlet Empress* (Josef von Sternberg, 1934)

3.2 *The Scarlet Empress* (Josef von Sternberg, 1934)

replaced by a jewelled political medallion, awarded to her for her splendid service to the state. Presumably she partly contemplates the ironic lessons that are implicated in that exchange, but the contemplation is unfathomable (Figure 3.2).[3]

Soon afterwards, we see Catherine emerging again upon the public stage, but the Catherine who emerges in this scene is by now dramatically transformed. Gone is the wide-eyed virgin princess of the first half of the movie, and in her place we discover an altogether different being – a startling metamorphosis of Dietrich's character. To put it bluntly, we discover the powerful, well-established star persona of Marlene Dietrich, the persona we know and love so well from her earlier movies with von Sternberg. Suddenly, up on the screen, we have Catherine the Great rendered in the familiar Dietrich style. One has had the feeling all along that the 'real' Dietrich has been withheld from us, hidden from us behind the implausible Princess Sophia facade. But, here at last, the real Dietrich, with very minimal narrative motivation indeed, has been released into the story world. Sophia/Catherine has become the knowing, audacious, sexually exploitative figure who ambiguously seems to promise uncharted possibilities and who is coldly and exquisitely in complete control. One of the movie's odd, old-fashioned intertitles explains that Catherine is presently consolidating her position in court and that she has 'discarded all of her youthful ideals'. This strikes me as another case of loopy understatement. Actually, it is more as if she had discarded the whole of her previous identity in the film. It is as if she had stepped, in the space of an intertitle, into an entirely new and yet oddly familiar role.

The transfigured Catherine is introduced to us conversing with a gray-bearded old man, and in this conversation she practises her new sexual and political sophistication upon him (Figure 3.3). In a particularly sardonic stroke, the old fellow is the head of the Holy Russian Church, although he really doesn't seem, in any way, to be out of his league in negotiating cynically with her. Like a second-rate mobster, he assures her that he has considerable control of 'the political machine' at court, and, as he confides that assurance to her, he ostentatiously fingers the emblem of his grasp on power – the crucifix of the church. And Catherine, when she responds,

3.3 *The Scarlet Empress* (Josef von Sternberg, 1934)

likewise plays with the token of her newly realised power – the frothy, flirty handkerchief that she holds.

The obvious question that all this raises is the following: how is it that the Catherine-character is so strikingly and abruptly transformed in this manner, suddenly stepping forth in this novel instantiation of the Dietrich persona? Why does this enormous change take place without any serious attempt at psychological elucidation or development? The dramatic transition here, taken as a subject for psychological explanation, is enigmatic. Still, I think that it is worth pressing the question, 'What sort of interpretative rationale, if any, can be offered for this delirious stretch of film?'

In point of fact, the story of *The Scarlet Empress* is structured around a whole series of transformations, each having stylistic similarities to the key example I have just described, and this should cue us to the fact that the question deserves to be pursued. For instance, all of these scenes of transformation are punctuated by a more or less elaborate montage sequence in which shots of the great tolling Russian bells recur and mark the passage of time. In this respect, *The Scarlet Empress* does fit the one additional general remark that Mulvey makes about von Sternberg's storytelling. She says, 'Despite Sternberg's insistence that his stories are irrelevant, it is significant that they are concerned with situation, not suspense, and cyclical rather than linear time, while plot complications revolve around misunderstanding rather than conflict' (1989: 22). Certainly, the film's narrative is divided by the following transformations. First, there is

1   the transformation of Catherine (Sophia) as a young girl into Catherine as a sexually mature woman.

Next, there is

2   the transformation of the young Catherine, at her wedding, into the wife of the czar-to-be.

Third, there is

3   the central transformation of Catherine's passage from sexual and political naivety into worldly sophistication.

Fourth,

4   the death of her mother-in-law raises her to a position of genuine political power and rivalry for political ascendancy with her husband.

And, at the end of the movie, we have

5   Catherine's final and complete triumph – her apotheosis as the all-dominating Catherine the Great.

In agreement with Mulvey's observation, each of these stages or stations in her development involves little in the way of serious dramatic conflict. What conflict exists is chiefly played out in terms of broad melodrama or farce. However, each stage (or, using Mulvey's term, each 'cycle') is a step in the rise to power of Catherine the Great, and each stage or cycle marks a type of worldly knowledge and experience she has to acquire in order for her dominance at the drama's end to be possible at all. It is precisely the application, in this instance, of her shrewd but vague observation concerning the 'cyclic' character of von Sternberg's stories that should have encouraged further enquiry into the unusual strategy and interesting nature of the narrative in *The Scarlet Empress*. It is a narrative that may not be primarily driven by dramatic conflicts, but it is carefully constructed nonetheless.

From the very beginning, *The Scarlet Empress* makes it clear that it means to invoke for its audience 'the Legend of Catherine the Great' and the associated myth of her political and sexual omnipotence. In the dialogue and in the absurd intertitles, the idea is repeatedly expressed that she is a character who has a fated, legendary destiny to fulfil. She is, the very first intertitle tells us, 'the Messalina of the North'. In the opening scene, following this title, the young Sophia falls asleep listening to fantastic tales and legends of past Russian rulers, tales whose violent content the movie encapsulates in a burst of Vorkapich-style montage. Catherine, we are later informed, is 'chosen by destiny', but she, the intertitles assert further, 'is unaware of the fate that awaits her'. When she leaves for Russia, she is instructed by her father 'to be worthy of her glorious destiny', and so on, from various sources, in the same vein. The narrative, defined in stages, charts out the fulfilment of that pre-ordained destiny.

In this connection, I believe, we need to distinguish between the flesh-and-blood person from history, Catherine the Great, and the fictional character of the same name, created by myth and popular lore. Naturally, the fictional Catherine of legend is, in some sense, 'based upon' or 'derived from' the historical figure, but they are separate entities nonetheless. (They are related to one another very much in the way that St Nicholas, the storied Christmas character, is linked to the historical St Nicholas.) I suggest that we are meant to see and comprehend Marlene Dietrich, in this movie, as playing the *already* fictionalised Catherine and not as attempting to re-enact the 'real' Catherine at all.

In other words, *The Scarlet Empress* drops the standard pretence of biographical fiction film that the filmmaking is to take us back in time and show us a selection of the historical events in question. That dramatic ambition is altogether foresworn in the present case. Actually, in the movie biographies of the classic period this imaginative pretence was almost always pretty shallow.[4] When George Arliss played Disraeli in *Disraeli* (Alfred E. Green,

1929), or Delores del Rio played Madame DuBarry in *Madame DuBarry* (William Dieterle, 1934), they were cast for their roles in important part because it was supposed that they carried with them, from other films, the kind of screen persona that would plausibly sustain the intended, usually stereotyped, conception of the historical individual in question. Of course, this is just a special instance of the still more ubiquitous practice, already mentioned, of conjuring up a major dramatic character on the basis of the star's already acquired motion-picture image. As usual, von Sternberg pushes this common moviemaking practice to its limits. While Catherine is seen reflected in the 'Dietrich' figure, Dietrich is revealed to be a 'Catherine' counterpart, and each of the two 'roles' is played off against the other during the remainder of the film. This is an especially nice example of the way in which familiar, problematic dramatic devices are used by von Sternberg but are exaggerated, made especially salient, and exploited as a content-bearing stylistic motif.

Moreover, in this movie, it is very much the von Sternberg/Dietrich *version* of the legend of Catherine the Great that we are offered. And this version is idiosyncratic and highly stylised, constructing the figure of myth in its own terms of delirious parody and satirical fantasy. The character of Catherine is marked specifically as a creation of the filmmaking, erected from the bare framework of the fable of Catherine the Great, and elaborated, in the movie's second half, in terms of the daunting screen persona of Miss Marlene Dietrich. If this interpretative proposal is right, then we already have some reason why we might expect *The Scarlet Empress* to deviate from our ordinary conceptions of the continuity of the self and of plausible dramatic evolution. The movie aspires to be, it seems to me, a kind of exemplary tale concerning the will to sexual and political power and, as such, its narration is fully prepared to abstract from ordinary ideas of psychological reality.

In fact, a moment early in the movie raises a brief uncertainty about the ontological status of its narrative, albeit playfully and in passing. That is, it is unclear at an early juncture whether the film is supposed to be recounting a piece of history, a legend or Catherine's private fantasy. In the very first scene, Princess Sophia is ill, and, as the scene closes, Sophia is being prepared for sleep, and a servant (her tutor perhaps) is going to read her tales of past Russian rulers. Sophia's image is then dissolved into the beginnings of an incredible montage of pillage, torture and oppression, and these horrendous incidents are depicted as illustrations in a book whose pages appear to be turning on the screen. The last of the 'illustrations' shows a half-naked man being swung as the clapper in a huge, tolling bell, and this shot dissolves into a visually rhyming image of a teenaged Sophia being pushed by her companions in a garden swing. This image of Sophia (Dietrich's first appearance in the movie) surely represents a return from the montage to the main story, but, in visual terms, it is continuous with whatever it was the preceding montage had presented, i.e., a young girl's dream? Anecdotes of violent Russian history? Or cautionary fairytales of cruelty? That is, nothing formally marks a definite point where the action re-emerges from the hallucinatory segment of the montage, and the formal indeterminacy this suggests is wholly appropriate to the preoccupations and strategies of the larger film. It is equally unclear what kind of 'reality' the movie as a whole presents.

The Scarlet Empress takes almost no interest in the 'realistic' depiction of any of its characters. Louise Dresser plays the empress like an egregiously belligerent fishwife from 1930s Brooklyn. And, as Andrew Sarris once pointed out, Sam Jaffe's portrayal of Peter renders him as a kind of malignant Harpo Marx. All of these characters are presented, so to speak, as if they were automatons made of flesh, all of them driven, in the most crudely determined ways, by lust or greed or the will to power. The movie draws a broad contrast between the human characters, who seem devoid of significant emotional and spiritual life, and the huge statues with which they are constantly surrounded. The statues appear in poses of religious ecstasy and world-weary despair. They assume the postures of agony, shame and grief. And these are states of mind and soul that the human characters seem largely incapable of experiencing.

If this film, whose scenes are obsessively filled with statues, dolls and carved figurines, has an emblematic equivalent for the characters it portrays, these would probably be the grotesque, mechanical figures that intermittently appear. One of them strips off its garments at midnight, a second pounds another with a club, and the members of a third group creep around in sinister circles, each tracking down the one ahead. The metaphorical linkage of human behaviour with the idea of the mechanical is extended in various other directions. For example, as I mentioned earlier, the old priest speaks anachronistically of 'the political machine' in court that he controls. And, at the conclusion of the famous marriage scene, an intertitle reports that 'the machinery of the wedding ceremony' grinds on to its conclusion.

It is not simply that the characters surround themselves with artifactual representations of human beings – the statues, the dolls, the paintings of human forms and faces, the mechanical figures. There is at least an equal emphasis on the theatricality of self-presentation and the continuous 'audience' scrutiny to which these dubious histrionic outbursts are subjected. When Count Alexey comes to fetch her from Germany, Sophia is subjected to a cold, critical inspection by the members of her own family. Or, arriving in St Petersburg, she is poked and peered at from all quarters in the court. A kind of culmination of this motif occurs at the spectacular marriage of Peter and Catherine. Here Catherine is offered up as a subject of a vast ceremonial spectacle and as the object of Alexey's private and penetrating stare. Moreover, at the same time, she is marrying a goggling idiot who surveys the scene blindly and simply stares through her as they wed.

These considerations introduce the second objection to Mulvey's discussion of von Sternberg that I mentioned at the outset, i.e. the curious absence of any consideration of his own treatment of questions of the potency and implications of 'the gaze'. She claims, 'The powerful look of the male protagonist (characteristic of traditional narrative film) is broken in favour of the image in direct erotic rapport with the spectator' (1989: 22). However, in *The Scarlet Empress*, the chief male protagonist, Count Alexey, is the bearer of the powerful, sexual gaze, although its intensity and narcissism are presented as absurd. When Alexey arrives in Germany to fetch Sophia to Russia, he surveys her appraisingly with a fatuously forceful look that parodies the gaze of the supposedly dominating male, and, in the early parts of the film, he repeats this ridiculous self-absorbed scrutiny of her many times. Moreover, by the end of the film, whatever power his look may have had for her before is broken. As she progressively rules the line of action, she dismisses him and humiliates him, replacing him with a legion of other lovers, other looks. By the time she ascends to the throne, he is merely a minor aide to her final seizure of total power, and he figures as just one admiring member of the audience that contemplates her culminating, triumphant transformation. In fact, after her crucial transformation to sexual maturity, it is Catherine who comes to be the one who surveys the male world with her own appraising, dominating gaze. For example, in the wonderful scene in which she inspects her troops, dressed herself in military garb, she looks over the more attractive specimens among them, awarding honours and accepting offerings from those who seem that they might be most promising 'in action'. One soldier presents her with a bag of spectacular diamonds, and she gives him a spectacular gaze of approving assessment in return. 'Rich too!' she comments smilingly. So, it is not exactly as if 'the controlling gaze' is simply absent from the 'screen scene'. Rather, it is very much embodied in her parting look.

The potential implications of casting or averting one's gaze in one or another way are developed in a most elaborate fashion. When Alexey, Sophia and her mother stop at an inn en route to Russia, there is a bizarre scene between the lovers, where he warns her not to look him in eyes, the power of the attraction in her mere glance being more than he can bear. And, when she does look at him again, he demonstrates his complaint by being, as it appears, so overmastered by passion that he grabs her and kisses her intensely on the lips. (All of this is accompanied by some fetching by-play with a whip.) Later, having arrived and settled in Russia, Alexey and Sophia have a rendezvous in the royal stables. She is holding on to a rope that hangs above her head and swaying her body in an odd, mechanical manner. She stares at Alexey as he approaches, looking as if either she is hypnotised

3.4 *The Scarlet Empress* (Josef von Sternberg, 1934)

herself or has the aim of hypnotising him. In this scene also, the impossibility of resisting the power of her gaze is conveyed once again, although in both of these scenes the power of her look is to fire the passion of the man but not to dominate or control the interaction with him. But this will change. Even in the scene with the head of the church, just after her central transformation to maturity, we first begin to see her gaze as one that takes in the scene with shrewd appraisal, one that expresses her intention to act on her own and for herself.

These issues of seeing and being seen reach a zenith of complexity in the famous wedding ceremony, and I will not attempt to analyse the many nuances that are involved in this elaborate context. The spectacle of the marriage is virtually triangulated by three powerful lines of gaze. Catherine, moved by mixed but powerful emotions, stares straight ahead, the impact of her laboured breathing almost causing the candle she is holding to be extinguished (Figure 3.4). Count Alexey stares balefully at the proceedings from a position in the crowd that is never specified, but, by means of the editing, one is given the impression that (metaphorically) he is staring into her eyes – his look being one key cause of Catherine's emotional response. In one way, he still can control her feelings to a significant degree, but in the sphere of action he is helpless. And, presiding over the affair, dominating the spectacle as a whole, is Elizabeth, watching triumphantly as the union she alone desires is brought to culmination. Ironically, the idiot groom, Peter, stares around the church, grinning vacuously, but his overwhelmed vision has no power of effect and takes in nothing but an overwhelming chaos of sight and sound. Here and elsewhere in the movie, Peter is a male, but one whose spying gaze is impotent.

In Mulvey's short analysis, the Dietrich/von Sternberg films are simply treated as 'symptomatic' manifestations of a recurring proclivity for a purportedly basic mode of scopophilia. But, really, there is every reason to suppose that von Sternberg was very much alive to many of the issues that Mulvey seeks, in her much later article, to raise. No doubt his conception of the issues and their broader import was very different from hers, and no doubt various aspects of his views on such matters were, at a minimum, perverse and problematic. Nevertheless, these themes and variations are present in *The Scarlet Empress*, and von Sternberg's treatment of them in that film achieves a certain level of complexity.

Related to the motifs concerning the dynamics of visual scrutiny, much attention is also devoted to the various roles that the main characters perform within the political drama or, alternatively, to the roles that others expect or require them to undertake. The central conflict between the dowager empress and Catherine lies in this range. On the one hand, the Empress Elizabeth repeatedly demands that Catherine learn her proper role as a royal Russian wife. That role demands the observance of established forms of duty, submission and female enticement. Above all, it demands an outcome – the breeding of male heirs. On the other hand, Catherine's successful acquisition of supreme power depends, as she herself remarks, upon mastering a very different role. Catherine must learn the highest arts of sexual politics, at least as von Sternberg conceives of these. She learns the manoeuvres of ambiguous sexual promise and the payoffs of strategic sexual manipulation. She acquires freedom from romantic illusion, and she learns to wear the countenance of self-control and to wield the power of the dominating gaze. At the end of our highlighted segment, she tells the priest, 'You need have no fears for me. Now that I know how Russia expects me to behave – I like it here.' Somewhat later on, she adds, 'And I am taking lessons [in the expected behaviour, she means] as quickly as I can'. [5]

One lesson that Catherine apparently has to learn is given by her formidable mother-in-law. Elizabeth humiliates Catherine by having her prepare the way for the entrance of Count Alexey into her (the empress's) boudoir. Now, this piece of cruel instruction is quite effective. The humiliation leads to Catherine's seduction, and her seduction leads, as we have seen, to the crucial transformation of the Dietrich character. What is more, the transfigured Catherine actually replays this same scenario later, recasting Alexey in the role that she originally had played. In fact, it is my proposal that her subsequent transformation is itself to be conceived as her self-conscious adoption of a radically new role. Seen in this fashion, the fact that the movie offers only a minimal psychological explanation of the enormous change in her personality comes to make an obvious sort of sense. Normally, we do not expect that a person's character, outlook and sensibility can alter so swiftly and extensively. But if we assume that the fictional characters in *The Scarlet Empress* are largely empty of any significant core from the very outset, then it is not implausible that the canniest among them should drop one role that isn't playing very well and take up another better suited to her needs and circumstances. This is what I make of the musing Catherine, veiled by the delicate curtains around her bed. I see her as making just this sort of calculation about the content of her future performances.

At one juncture, the empress says to Catherine, 'We women are too much creatures of the heart', and Catherine has to comprehend the hypocritical posturing expressed in such a speech. This is just one facet of the expertise in histrionic self-presentation she acquires. In the course of the whole movie, Catherine's progressive acquisition of her fated role as 'Catherine the Great' demands the blurring, or perhaps even the obliteration, of many standard roles, and gender roles are definitely among those left in the rubble. Czar Peter rages and dithers more and more hysterically as Catherine grows correspondingly more assured and self-controlled. This double transformation culminates at the instant when Peter, in his billowing white robe and flowing white hair, is struck down helplessly before the crucifix in his bedroom. And, at this moment, Catherine, mounted on her white stallion and wearing her white soldier's gear, takes her place upon the throne. Even Count Alexey characterises these changes in theatrical terms. 'Exit Peter. Enter Catherine,' he announces, and the revolution (of several kinds) is now complete. In the world of *The Scarlet Empress*, Catherine enjoys an almost alchemical mutability, a power available to 'those extraordinary people' (this is Alexey's phrase) who have the intelligence to discern their theatrical options and go on, as Alexey says, 'to create their own laws and logic'. He means, of course, the laws of conduct and the logic of high style.[6]

Notes

1 I have given an extended interpretation of the final von Sternberg/Dietrich film, *The Devil is a Woman* (1935), in my book *Narration in Light* (1986: 145–65).

2 Douglas Pye has pointed out to me that one faintly hears among the hubbub of the cannons firing and the bells ringing, the words 'It's a boy.' The cry is so faint that I had missed it in seeing the movie several times. But it is present, and since it does offer some clue as to the nature of the celebrations, it complicates the argument in the text concerning the segment under discussion. Still, there surely is an issue as to why this 'clue' is presented so recessively, when it would have been easy, in various ways, to make the relevant temporal and causal connections quite obvious. It would be nice to know how and when these words were introduced into the soundtrack.

3 At the Style and Meaning Conference, V. F. Perkins suggested that Sophia/Catherine, lying behind the veils of web and lace, gives the appearance of a being

in a chrysalis – a suggestion that fits well, of course, with the character's imminent transfiguration.

4   For a helpful discussion of this and related issues concerning film biographies made by the Hollywood studios, see Custen (1992).

5   For a short discussion of *The Scarlet Empress* that approaches the movie in a similar way and with several points of significant agreement, see Robin Wood's liner notes for the Criterion Collection DVD version (2001).

6   This chapter derives from the lecture I gave at the Style and Meaning Conference. The present analysis of *The Scarlet Empress* constituted the heart of that presentation. However, the lecture eventually evolved into a longer essay on questions of narrative structure in the last three von Sternberg/Dietrich films. That essay appears as 'The Transfiguration of Classical Hollywood Norms: On von Sternberg's Last Films with Dietrich' in *The Creation of Art*, edited by Berys Gaut and Paisley Livingstone (2003). The framework of the present chapter, i.e., the discussion of Laura Mulvey's views on von Sternberg, was not a part of the original lecture and does not appear in the longer paper just mentioned. Also, the material on *The Scarlet Empress* has been reworked for this chapter. For comments, advice and encouragement, I would like to thank David Bordwell, Marshall Cohen, Greg Currie, Karen Hanson, V. F. Perkins, Douglas Pye, Murray Smith and William Taschek. I have been especially helped by Karen Wilson.

References

Custen, G. (1992) *Bio/Pics: How Hollywood Constructed Public History* (New Brunswick: Rutgers University Press).

Gaut, B. and P. Livingstone (2003) *The Creation of Art: New Essays in Philosophical Aesthetics* (Cambridge: Cambridge University Press).

Mulvey, L. (1989) 'Visual Pleasure and Narrative Cinema', in L. Mulvey, *Visual and Other Pleasures* (Bloomington: University of Indiana Press), pp. 14–26.

Wilson, G. (1986) *Narration in Light* (Baltimore: Johns Hopkins University Press).

4

The Dandy and the Magdalen: interpreting the long take in Hitchcock's *Under Capricorn* (1949)

Ed Gallafent

> There were walls flying up into the rafters as we walked by, all the lights were movable. ... The whole floor was filled with numbers and everybody had to be on the cued number at the right moment or the shot was ruined. It's the only time I ever cried on set. (Ingrid Bergman, quoted in Spoto (1983: 310))

In addressing the long take, I am conscious of looking at an element of film style that cannot be subject to a simple, fixed definition. The practice of filming using long takes is described by David Bordwell and Kristin Thompson in *Film Art: An Introduction*, with the deceptively plain phrase 'unusually lengthy shots', acknowledging that what is at stake here can only be understood as a matter of difference (1993: 235). The perceived length of a shot depends on many considerations, such as the length of shots in the rest of the film, the average shot length in the specific area of cinema and historical period of the film's production, and not least the content of the shot, how it draws our attention to its length or chooses not to do so. Obviously camera movement is important here – a long take in which there is little or no camera movement is very differently perceived from one in which the camera movement is unmistakable.[1] The latter is the case in *Under Capricorn*, as Ingrid Bergman's words above make clear, and what is not disputable is that the film is marked by a number of sequences in which single shots are experienced as unusually long, and in which the mobile camera follows the actors as they move around the sets. It has been remembered, commonly as a footnote to *Rope*, for this, but not all of the commentary on the film has tried to address the function of the style.

As a way of introducing the film and proposing an argument as to why it has proved problematic for Hitchcock's viewers, I wish to begin by looking at a single image, that of the feet of Lady Hattie Considine/Ingrid Bergman, and how it has been understood (Figure 4.1). The image is privileged in two ways. It announces the appearance of the film's major star. It is also positioned at the moment of cutting between two long takes, a bravura

4.1 *Under Capricorn* (Alfred Hitchcock, 1949)

five-minute take in which the camera tracks Charles Adare/Michael Wilding as he meets the guests at the dinner party held by Sam Flusky/Joseph Cotten, and the first part of the conversation between Charles and Hattie at the dinner table, a take of approximately one and a half minutes.

The dinner is about to begin, over the saying of grace. Faces turn to the entrance of the dining room, and Hitchcock cuts to the bare feet of Lady Hattie. Robin Wood writes of Hattie's 'incongruously bare feet' and Lesley Brill comments that 'pathetically trying to play her proper part as hostess, she arrives drunk and shoeless' (Wood 1989: 329, Brill 1988: 276).

I suggest that the bare feet are more than incongruous. They are part of the imagery, which is sufficiently extensive in the film as to be unavoidable once we are conscious of it, of religious penitence. The subject is presented to us in two ways. One is through the imagery traditionally associated with St Mary Magdalen (the patron saint of penitent sinners) in religious iconography: the bare feet, the skull, the flail, the looking glass in which the beholder's image is not always reflected, the jewels cast down to the floor. Sources for such imagery that Hitchcock might perfectly well have had in mind are the paintings *Saint Mary Magdalen With a Candle* [*c.*1630–35] and *Saint Mary Magdalen With a Mirror* [*c.*1635–45] by Georges De La Tour. It is striking that every one of the elements of their imagery occurs in *Under Capricorn* in various places and guises. By this point in the film we will have already have seen feet, flail and – a neat adjustment appropriate to the Australian setting of the film – skull, here in the form of the shrunken head.

If this were not enough, Hitchcock gives the sequence a kind of title, or statement of its subject, if we can but read it. As Charles's buggy draws up in front of the Flusky house, he reads its name – Minyago Yugilla – and the driver supplies a translation: 'Why weepest thou'. Charles does not respond here to the words, or appear to recall their source. But the origin of the phrase is not all that obscure. It is used twice in chapter twenty of St John's gospel, both times spoken to St Mary Magdalen, once by the angels and once by the risen Christ (whom Mary does not recognise), the occasion being Mary's response to the absence of Christ's body from the sepulchre.[2] So the figure invoked is that of the saint, and the moment is something about the failure properly to mourn, the sense of a horror that cannot be worked through to its conclusion.

We should see Hattie as someone whose appearance at the dinner-table can be read not as a random act brought about by inebriation, but as a moment of deliberate self-abasement. It is theatrical, a performance which is both a penance in itself and an embodiment of the figure of the penitent sinner. (It is one which is arguably slightly derailed by the discovery that one of the guests is a visitor from her childhood.)

In the light of this some of Hattie's behaviour in the film becomes more comprehensible. Rather than reading her simply as a passive addict, we can say that she allows the housekeeper Milly/Margaret Leighton to feed her alcohol, using it to assist in her own humiliation, just as she allows Charles to kiss her – without responding to him – in the sequence in her locked bedroom. Both things can be read as self-abasing acts of penitence; while she is no more a committed drunk than a real adulteress, she will tell us that she does experience the urge to go 'down, down, down, to where I can go no further down'. Thus we may say that we learn that Hattie is a penitent, while it is not clear exactly what is the subject of her penance. This will emerge only in the latter half of the film, in the sequence (usually referred to as the 'confession sequence') in which she tells Charles the story of her elopement to Gretna Green with Sam, her marriage and her shooting of Dermot, her brother, which was the crime for which Sam was tried and sentenced to transportation to Australia.

Why is this image, of Hattie as a penitent, not more commonly noted in accounts of the film? I want to suggest a reason, and offer a set of terms for an interpretation which I hope will make more substantial the connection between Hitchcock's style and his meaning.

I suggest that the reason why the behaviour of the Bergman character has been puzzling to Hitchcock's interpreters is that it has been read in the shadow of *Gaslight*. George Cukor's 1944 version of the Patrick Hamilton play, starring Bergman, Charles Boyer and Joseph Cotten, must have provided a major context for responses to *Under Capricorn*. In *Gaslight*, the Bergman character is famously persecuted by one man (her husband) and rescued finally by an unattached male. *Under Capricorn* has been read as a variant of this plot in which we reassign the role of the persecutor of the wife from husband to servant (with a nod acknowledging *Rebecca*), thus exculpating the husband and allowing him to retain the attachment to his wife.

But what the satisfying map of plot variation leaves out is the matter of the nature of motivation, which marks the two films as crucially different from each other. *Gaslight* is built around a conscious campaign of persecution of the wife by the husband – he knows pretty well what he is doing and why. Equally it turns on the quality in the Bergman character that Florence Jacobowitz (2000) has called 'her refusal to be guilty', even when driven and tortured. As for the third party in the triangle, again his clear motivation – to solve a crime, to rescue a woman in distress – could be summed up by his being cast in this plot as a detective. If we think in terms of guilt and innocence, then one of these characters is guilty (of the brutal murder of an innocent woman) and knows it perfectly well. The other is innocent, and equally knows that, and the function of the detective is to help her to express it, 'reintroducing her to language' in Stanley Cavell's words (1996: 58).

Consider the parallel issues in the three central figures in *Under Capricorn*, where matters of guilt and innocence and their relation to punishment are set out quite differently.[3] The Bergman character is aware that she once killed (in self-defence, a brutal man), a crime for which a punishment has been exacted, but not on her. The Cotten character is aware that his behaviour was a part of the circumstances which led to this killing, and that although he was not the perpetrator, he was punished for it. The Wilding character carries with him a past of which we learn little, except that it consists of a number of escapades and nothing in it is much to his credit.

The difference between the two outlines I have sketched, and thus between the basis for behaviour in the two films, is expressible as the distinction between guilt and shame. Eve Kosofsky Sedgwick puts it as follows: 'What most readily distinguishes shame from guilt is that shame attaches to and sharpens the sense of what one *is*, while guilt attaches to what one *does*' (1995: 212).[4] Thus I suggest that *Gaslight* can be associated with guilt (and actions and objects) and *Under Capricorn* with shame (and the assertion of what the self is). The success of *Gaslight* may have had an unfortunate influence, both on the audience's expectations of Hitchcock's film in 1949, and on subsequent critical thinking about it, in that it has blurred this difference, which now needs to be elicited by close reading of some long takes in *Under Capricorn*.

Shame and the long take

The use of the long take in *Under Capricorn* relates to three elements of the film's meaning. These are:

1   Ideas of accessible and inaccessible space as expressed in the gothic
    house.
2   The form in which the characters inhabit their past.
3   The divergence or convergence of eyelines – the gaze that cannot, or
    must, meet another's.

All three of these elements can be linked to concepts of guilt and shame. In
1 and 2 the question is how something is felt to be present. In 3 it is the
difference between a locked or concealed physical space and a mental secret,
with no physical presence. In 2 it is the difference between the representation, or sharing, of the past as flashback, and of the past as spoken narrative,
where part of what is being articulated is precisely the inaccessibility of the
past, its experience being locked inside the speaker. Both cases here follow
the distinction that I quoted earlier, between guilt (as something done, marked
by a relation to objects and actions) and shame (as the sense of what one is,
marked by no other reality). As for 3, the avoided gaze is the determining
physical sign of shame. Writers on the subject continually insist that the
'proto-form' from early infancy is the avoidance of the look: 'eyes down,
head averted' (Sedgwick 1995: 211).

    I will consider some sequences in order to explore how these issues are
expressed in practice, beginning by returning to the passage which opens
with Charles's arrival for dinner at the Flusky house. At this point Hitchcock
uses a series of long takes which dominate the style of the film as it records
this evening, from the moment of Charles's decision not to ring the doorbell
of the house, through his encounter with Sam's household and then his
dinner guests, Hattie's initial appearance, and the conversation between Sam
and Charles after the guests have departed.

    The point made by the first of these, the take in which Charles walks down
the side of the Flusky mansion, eventually entering through the kitchen door,
is one addressing expectations of the gothic, which other elements of the
scene (the previous conversation with the coach driver, the accompanying
music) have set up. The unbroken motion of the take relates to what the
mise-en-scène indicates, that this is no conventional gothic house, in which
a secret is locked in an attic or a cellar (as in, say, the attic in *Gaslight*). The
front door stands open, but Charles ignores it and proceeds past a series of
open French windows. As he arrives at the kitchen he does seem to encounter something that might look like a scene from the attic at Thornfield Hall,
two women restraining another, but this turns out to be a kind of plant, or
lesson. The woman is not Hattie, nor some other concealed madwoman,
some confirmation of expectations of gothic excess. All this is just a few convict servants fighting. It seems to make a point to Charles (and to us): make
no assumption that you will find a horror, for there are no such apparent

secrets to be spied on here, simply by opening the right door or looking in the wrong window.

In both the mise-en-scène and the long takes of the sequences that follow, the treatment of the physical spaces emphasises their openness and interconnectedness, a series of arches and open doors, underlined by what Hitchcock referred to as the 'easy flow' of the long take (Truffaut 1978: 230). I have already argued that the roles of both Hattie and Sam in the dinner-party sequence are performances, and the style is expressive in that it seems to emphasise this openness, underscoring the claim to be making a display of what one is. The sequence is a ritual, not a revelation; Hattie's penitential drunkenness and Sam's inverted snobbery are not shown as causing surprise to anyone present. There is almost a quality of aggressive triumph in showing something shameful so overtly.

Yet shame is marked by both performance and aversion. The same sequence insists continually on the difficulty of meeting the gaze: the effect of the long takes is to present the Flusky mansion as a house where no door is closed, but where nobody can look anyone else in the eye. It is as if the knowledge of shame, and its flamboyant exposure here, creates a shame in the witnesses to it which is marked by the averted face, the desire, while being completely aware of the presence of the other, to look away.

Of course the dominance of this mode of aversion throws into sharp contrast the moments opposite to it, the meeting of the gaze. There are two in the sequence, both involving Sam and Hattie. They occur on her lines 'I married Sam Flusky, but that must have been a long time afterwards' and 'The man and the woman: nobody knows about Sam and me'. (Sam and Hattie are looking directly along the length of the table at each other, and the effect of the matching sets of candelabra on the dining table is important to emphasising the meeting of the gaze here, by giving a clear geometry to these shots.) Thus the one aspect of the world which is free of the averted gaze of the shamed is the marriage. The lines anticipate and prepare for the moment in the confession sequence when Hattie looks Charles directly in the eyes (one of the few moments in the scene in which she does so) to deliver the line 'Sam is part of me and I am part of Sam for ever and ever'.

After the end of the dinner party, Sam and Charles walk outside the house and the first version of the story of the elopement is told, in two long takes separated by a crane shot of Hattie on the balcony of her bedroom.[5] Robin Wood has discussed this sequence at length in terms of identification; another perspective on it is given if we think of it as a conversation which might conventionally be shot by cutting on eyeline matches, where the force of the long take and thus the absence of such editing is to emphasise that the characters are talking but not looking at each other, unable to do so more than momentarily. A way of underlining the effect is by demonstrating that the usual signs of attention in conversation will not work here. The averted gaze means that the speaker cannot tell if his auditor is looking at him, which becomes a piece of business; Sam, turning towards Charles to find that he is looking away, says 'I'm wearying you' and Charles has to insist that he is listening.

It is also at exactly this point that for (I think) the first time, we see a character's eyes not just averted but clearly fixed on something that we cannot see, a vision of the past. As he describes the young Hattie riding, Sam is staring into space off-camera. There is a small movement of the hands as if he is gesturing towards something that he can see, something projected in front of him. But not in front of us – the sustaining of the long take, rather than the move into flashback, is an assertion of Sam's privacy, that what he sees is incommunicable, part of his being rather than just another story that can be told after dinner.[6]

My last comment on this sequence will be on a single crucial image (about twelve seconds of film), when Hitchcock breaks the men's conversation into two halves by having his camera find Hattie on the balcony of her bedroom (Figure 4.2). I do not think that this has any narrative function, such as Hattie overhearing the men. It can be observed that Hitchcock places her at the end of the balcony that is facing way from them. As she appears in the frame, she turns away from the balcony and leans on the window glass, facing into a breeze. Her eyes flutter open, then close as she leans back, exposing herself to the camera as the wind plays across her face and hair. I suggest that the shot offers the paradox of self-exposure (as an image,

4.2 *Under Capricorn* (Alfred Hitchcock, 1949)

a woman, a penitent) and privacy, or self-containment; it invokes what Stanley Cavell has called the woman's unknownness (1996: 106). It relates, of course, to the most famous case of it, the shot of Greta Garbo at the end of *Queen Christina* (Rouben Mamoulian, 1933). I take it that Hitchcock's intention in using the device of the wind on the woman's face is to prompt this connection. The image tells us that it does not matter whether Hattie's eyes are open or closed: whatever she sees is in her mind's eye, and she will allow us no access to it. It is related to the quality of Sam's isolation that is displayed through the style, that in part he is talking not to Charles but to himself.

The same terms are in play in the final spectacular use of the long take, Hattie's confession sequence after she has fled the ball and returned home with Charles. The effects we have seen are repeated in a single take of over eight minutes, in which Hattie prowls and circles Charles as she experiences her past. We see the movement between meeting the gaze of the auditor and the inability to look at him for the most part, and the invocation of the past without flashback. Hattie partly tells her story, and partly sees it, as if what can be dramatised is less the series of events and actions and more the expression of what inhabits the being of the speaker. We might say that Hattie's subject in the scene is what has defined her self – she begins it with the line that I quoted earlier about Sam being part of her. Close to its end, her whole body thrown back in a gesture of deliberate self-exposure, she speaks of waiting for him: 'all that hot misery: it became me'.

Thus the effect of the long take here, and of the concentration of the camera on Hattie, is to expose her to us, to our interpreting eye, but what is exposed is not knowledge but unknownness: we understand that we will not be able to see and that we cannot know. Rather than an offer of privileged access, we might think of the long take here as expressing refusal, a kind of default position that applies when there is an inability to move into the other ways of knowing, or offering or experiencing the world. It speaks of Hattie's self, and what we cannot know of it.

Shame and meaning

If I have successfully argued that the use of the long take expresses the intensity of the shame felt by the principal characters, how does this form part of a larger interpretation of the film? I have already suggested that the death of her brother is experienced by Hattie as a matter for penance, as a crime for which she feels she has never been sufficiently punished, although it would be easy to point out that her life during Sam's sentence was a self-imposed punishment. More substantial, perhaps, is the realisation that the death in part defined what her elopement meant, or has involved. In her account of the past, Hattie recalls this exchange as in effect the proposal of marriage and her acceptance:

SAM: This is killing me.

HATTIE: Dear Sam, then I'll save you.

At that moment the words 'killing' and 'save' functioned at a metaphorical level. Eloping could be seen as, in Hattie's mind, doing no violence to anyone else, only rescuing Sam. What Hattie does not realise – what she will not confront until forced to do so – is that her action was to involve a severance from her family so violent that it would result in the deaths of one or other of the Considine children. (Hattie states that Dermot was trying to shoot her, not Sam.) And so the loss of her family and her past, her childhood, which would have been the inevitable result anyway of such a marriage but for which she had not prepared herself, is given emphatic embodiment in the death of her sibling.

How can this situation be retrieved? One thing which needs to happen, and which is a clear element of plot-structure, is that the characters need to have what Chris Marker in his essay on *Vertigo* calls a 'second chance', to re-enact the past (1995: 130). What she can do is to recreate her family and make her peace with it.

From their first meeting Hattie begins to invoke Charles's role as a brother through the mention of his sister Diana, and uses him as a route back to her memory of her childhood as an Irish aristocrat. In due course Sam's behaviour causes her to flee another Irish aristocratic world (the Irish Society ball at Government House), and the tussle for the possession of Hattie between Sam and an aristocrat (now Charles rather than Dermot) is re-enacted, with Charles sounding like a threatening sibling: 'I'll be back tomorrow and if you ...'. Sam's line 'you bloody murdering gentleman' clearly invokes the past: it is the line that he never spoke to Dermot, spoken here as he fires the bullet that he was unable to fire then. So the bullet is relocated in two ways – fired by Sam rather than Hattie, and this time not proving fatal. Rather its effect is benign in the sense that the brother figure will recover and will treat the moment not as attempted murder but catharsis, and will act in a way that confers his blessing on the revived marriage of aristocrat and groom.

The effect of Sam's shame on his actions is pervasive. Hitchcock introduces him in sequences that contradict the idea that Australia is a place where pasts are forgotten, where criminal acts are put aside once the sentence is served and where social class can be reinvented. That Sam is obsessively concerned with social class is demonstrated continually – we could observe it, say, in his hiring a 'gentleman' (the transported convict Winter/Jack

Watling) while simultaneously asserting his contempt for Winter's class background. It also appears in his employment of a markedly working-class figure
in Milly, who he can assert to the world is one of his own kind.

We might argue that Sam, far from making a new life in Australia with
Hattie, is locked into a view that his marriage to her is still the violent
violation of class barriers which it was at the point of their elopement, a
matter which he has no more resolved than she has. The dinner party at
Minyago Yugilla expresses this. Does Sam truly think that the presence of
Charles at his home will overturn the status of himself and Hattie as social
pariahs? Even Milly knows this won't happen; unconsciously (or even perhaps consciously) Sam knows it too. The sequence can be read as a piece of
rhetorical performance, in which Sam invites the colony's society wives to his
home exactly in order to demonstrate that they will not come. Rather than
a confrontation between sober, controlled husband and pathetic, inebriated
wife – the interpretation courtesy of *Gaslight* – it is an occasion of two
theatrical performances, of penitent sinner and self-made master. Both of
them want to use this public occasion to insist on what they are.

The opening scenes at the house demonstrate that Sam has in a way
arrested time at the point of his unwitting courtship of Hattie, that he desires
her but has no idea how to address the aristocratic world that still intimidates
him. At the heart of this is the contradiction that his deep distrust of aristocrats of course involves being distrustful of this quality in Hattie.

Thus when Charles turns up in Australia, Sam finds the opportunity to
play again the drama of his life, his second chance. He does this by allowing
Hattie to be reinserted into the aristocratic Irish world of the ball, and then
as I have said, he asserts his right to take her away from the world of gentle-
men and offers defiance to a father figure. I take it that a crucial part of this
psychic process for Sam is his row with the governor/Cecil Parker at the ball,
which clearly stands in for the missing part of his behaviour of long ago, his
claiming of Hattie from her father.

One moment of the action illuminates some of these attitudes. I am thinking of the sequence in which Hattie, dressed in the new gown in which she
will accompany Charles to the ball, descends the staircase at Minyago Yugilla.
We may take this as a climactic moment in the recovery of Hattie as an Irish
aristocrat engineered by Charles with Sam's consent. Visually, when Hattie
appears at on the staircase, it is in a gown that denies her sexual experience,
makes her again the virginal daughter of the house of Considine. Sam, after
having allowed Charles to produce this effect, also seems to wish to intervene, to add a little red to this whiteness, in offering her a necklace of rubies.
The symbolism is not obscure; it is, I think, a first move towards claiming her
as his wife, to mark her not so much with his wealth (the gown already does
that) as with sexual experience.

4.3 *Under Capricorn* (Alfred Hitchcock, 1949)

But what is marked here is his manner of offering the gift. Hitchcock shoots Sam from behind so that we see the gems concealed behind his back; he is concealing them from both Charles and Hattie (Figure 4.3). At first Hattie accepts the suggestion of the jewels ('Do you think so, Sam?') But when Charles objects to the idea of rubies and Hattie agrees (observing that she has no rubies), we see the jewels concealed – not simply folded into the hand of the giver, but dropped swiftly into the convenient pocket of the tailcoat.[7] The point is again that Sam seems to be constructing a moment of rejection, performing a failure, which is perhaps a response to a psychic drive or expectation. It is exactly appropriate that the moment is followed by the sequence in which Milly returns and fills Sam's ear with insinuation about Charles and Hattie, which is presented at its opening and closing moments with the voice of Milly unlocated, almost as if it is inside Sam's head.

We can now turn to the figure of Charles, where the keynote is the presentation of the young aristocrat as a dandy.[8] This is partly a visual point – it is made by Charles's impeccable appearance throughout the film, and his interest in, or say fascination with, the possibility of social rebirth being expressed through clothing (male and female) and appearance, and the linking of these matters to the creative, to works of art. The link is clear in the moment in which the appearance of Hattie restored to her youthful beauty and ladylike dress takes the form of a mirror shot, but the image appears in the form of unwrapping a mirror that has been covered with paper. The effect is to pun on portraiture, as if this were a framed portrait of Hattie being unpacked. Charles also has a line of dialogue: 'The first work of art I've ever done.'

There are other qualities that define Charles as a dandy. He is intensely conscious of his aristocratic blood, and of the class positions of others (see not only his attitudes to Sam and Hattie, but his response to the various guests at the Flusky dinner, and to Milly.) He appears content to be without occupation, and his one family relation, to the governor, is one in which he is viewed as a species of 'black sheep'. Apparently he has a history which, while its exact content is never specified, implies insufficient diligence or application. (He tells Hattie, 'I've spent most of my life warding off boredom', and the governor pleads: 'Now look here Charles, I hope you're going to try hard this time'.) Of the three principals he is perhaps the most purely associated with shame in that his past is viewed as a series of actions that are completely unknown and remain so throughout the film – except in so far as they constitute his sense of what he is, and what he cannot be.

Significantly it is not suggested that his past has to do with any sexual misdemeanour. (There is a space made for such a suggestion at the point of introducing Winter, who has 'got a girl into trouble', but there is no response to this story from Charles.) My suggestion here is that paradoxically, rather than a passionate sexual attraction to Hattie, the emphasis of Charles's interest in her is that of a dandy, which is to say he wishes to flirt, even to make a conquest, but his ultimate aim is not so much to claim Hattie for himself – after all, he knows he has no means of supporting her – as to take her away from Sam and return her to Ireland.[9] At first he wishes to make her over, dress her, to reinstall her as both the mistress of a well-appointed mansion and as the reborn young Hattie Considine, the belle of the Irish Society ball. In all this his feelings are most profoundly engaged at the level not of sexual desire but of class superiority. Only when Sam has intruded into the ball does he move on to trying to take her away, and even here the emphasis is on separating her from a 'lout' rather than demanding a response to a sexual advance.

There are two sequences in the film in which this interpretation can be tested, the two obvious moments of Charles's physical advances to Hattie: the encounter between the two in her locked bedroom, and the confession sequence. In the bedroom sequence, Charles certainly acts the role of the lover, kissing Hattie with evident force in response to her sense of dispossession, but his reaction to her explicit lack of sexual response to his kiss is not to speak of love but to take them both, in imagination, back to the Ireland of their shared past, of gorse and sea and power/control, 'the turf pounding under your horse's hooves'. As they ponder this vision, Hitchcock poses them. They are not facing each other; Hattie leans on Charles and both of them look in the same direction, as if they could see the past he is evoking. The significant pose will be repeated at the end of the confession sequence, where what we see are not lovers looking into each other's eyes, but a pair of dispossessed Irish aristocrats, looking towards the world that they can reconstruct only in imagination. Of course Charles wants to be thought of as a lover, even perhaps wants to think of himself that way, but perhaps what he most strongly suggests is a life without direction. In his wanting to recreate Hattie as if she were still young Hattie Considine, he desires his own form of the second chance, to return to the point in the past where he might start afresh, without the shameful emptiness of his adventures so far.

Resolution and film style

We can measure the deliberateness with which Hitchcock has constructed the style of *Under Capricorn* by looking briefly at the film's resolution. We have seen Sam re-enact the drama of the elopement, defying a 'father' and wounding, but not killing, a 'brother'. At first it seems that this is disastrous. Coupled with Hattie's decision to turn a matter of shame back into one of guilt by confessing her murder of Dermot to the governor, the effect of the events is to make Sam, fixed on the memory of the stable boy surrounded by aristocrats, experience what has happened not as a second chance but as a more malign version of the past. It is as if we are back in Greta Green: Dermot/Charles lies wounded and the father/governor proposes to take the wounded son and the errant daughter away, back to Ireland. Sam's rage and jealousy in the scene after Hattie comes back from visiting Government House is that of a disappointed lover, as if the stable-boy had been given the treatment he always expected.

Something has to happen which will release the couple, and finally inter-rogate Sam's conviction that what is opposed to them has always been entrenched class interest. This is the lesson of Milly's attempt to poison Hattie. Literally it offers a different figure of the murderer, relocated from aristocrat and family member to working-class figure and servant, and thus a chance to rethink what prompts such violence. It also speaks to the fantasy of adultery. Hattie's instant dismissal of the thought that Sam and Milly are lovers ('Hattie, you don't think that ...' 'No no of course not, no ... but ask her why she did it') enables Sam to lay to rest his fantasy that Hattie is romantically interested in Charles.

The style of the sequence, reversing the terms of the earlier moments I have discussed, is central to its meaning. The gothic note is now present but conventional, as a storm rages outside the closed window. Now that the subject is not shame but guilt and crime, the shooting emphasises actions and their objects, the poison bottle, the shrunken head, the balloon wine-glass.[10] The length of take is conventional; the averted gaze is replaced by an insistence on watching and looking, the power of the gazing eye. So Milly's preparations for Hattie's murder are the subject not of a long take but a series of actions interrupted by no less than seven shots of Hattie's face as she watches and pretends drowsiness, ending in her scream, her eyes locked on Milly's: 'Sam!!' He rescues her from Milly – she will in turn rescue him from the chain gang, and from the aristocrats of Government House as the film concludes.

Interpreting Hitchcock's commentary

In his interview with François Truffaut, Hitchcock offered a limited defence of the use of the long take in *Rope*, arguing that 'the mobility of the camera and the movement of the players closely followed my usual cutting practice'. He described its use in *Under Capricorn* in harsher terms: 'As an experiment, *Rope* may be forgiven, but it was definitely a mistake when I insisted on applying the same techniques to *Under Capricorn*' (Truffaut 1978: 224–30). The interview continues in largely negative terms, Hitchcock talking about his own 'infantile' behaviour in wanting to bring Ingrid Bergman to England, calling it in retrospect 'stupid and juvenile'. He seems to accuse himself of poor judgement as to what would make an effective Bergman vehicle and queries the rest of the casting, particularly that of Joseph Cotten. Further, he sheds doubt on the quality of the adaptation (by Hume Cronyn, of a novel by Helen Simpson for which Hitchcock had 'no special admiration'). This series of comments is perhaps the more surprising in that the production background appears to have been paradoxically benign, a deal with Sidney Bernstein which offered Hitchcock considerable freedom.[11] Hitchcock could further rely on knowledge of two of his leading actors from his own previous films (as well as their success in *Gaslight*), and a substantial rewrite of the Helen Simpson novel was undertaken.

What is only briefly mentioned in the interview is the disastrous performance of the film at the box office, but it can be read as Hitchcock (director-producer) reflecting long after the event on his poor judgement, in this instance, of what was commercial. It seems clear enough that he wished to locate issues such as the use of the expensive star and the audience's expectations of this genre as reasons for its failure. But the interview seems interestingly unable to elicit exactly where or how, or even if, Hitchcock felt that the film was an artistic failure. His comments are all in some way related to the materials or externals of the film. He does not tell us what he was trying to do, and we are given no terms here for illuminating whether he was able to do all or some part of it.

The conversation is sprinkled with hints of another evaluation, or rather a sense of the occasion of making the film which implies another attitude: 'I would have liked it to have been a success', 'all the enthusiasm we invested in that picture', 'it's true that I liked the story, but not as much as *Vertigo*'. (High praise indeed.) The most striking of these hints may be Hitchcock's parting shot, his last word on the film. He is talking about Bergman, and her desire to play in 'masterpieces': 'How on earth can anyone know whether a picture is going to turn out to be a masterpiece or not? ... I might say to myself, '*Psycho* will be a nice little picture to do.' I never think 'I'm going to shoot a picture that will bring in fifteen million dollars; that idea never enters my mind' (Truffaut 1978: 224–30). So talking about *Under Capricorn* leads to a description of Hitchcock's philosophy: ignoring the commercial payoff in favour of working on a film in an experimental spirit – one might, or might not, be making a masterpiece.

I am conscious that these observations only touch the surface of the complexity of Hitchcock's art in this project. I hope that I have demonstrated some ways in which the long takes in film can be read, and that any account of the meaning must address the specificities of the style. Full analysis of the use of eyelines as an expressive device in the whole film would I think be valuable. But there is also another direction to consider, which is the relatively unexplored relation of Hitchcock's film to some of the major films of the period. I am thinking that, say, looking at the commitment to flashback in Ophuls's *Letter from an Unknown Woman* (1948) might help to read the refusal of it here. A further connection is with a closely contemporary film in which there is a triangle and in which the dandy does not win the aristocratic woman: set the plot in an American context and you have Wyler's *The Heiress* (1949). In all these cases it may help to bear in mind the issues of display and aversion involved in shame, and those of concealment and challenge involved in guilt.

Notes

1   I am indebted in my thinking about the long take to my reading of a recent thesis by Donato Totaro: 'Time and the Long Take in *The Magnificent Ambersons*, *Ugestu* and *Stalker*' (University of Warwick, 2002).

2   'And they say unto her, Woman, why weepest thou? She saith unto them, Because they have taken away my Lord, and I know not where they have laid him' (John 20: 13). 'Jesus saith unto her Woman, why weepest thou? Whom seekest thou? She, supposing him to be the gardener, saith unto him, Sir, if thou have borne him hence, tell me where thou hast laid him, and I will take him away' (John 20: 15).

3   The opening situation of the plot is briefly as follows. A young couple fall in love; she is an earl's daughter, he a groom in the household. They elope and marry, but are pursued by the girl's brother. The girl shoots her brother; the new husband takes the blame, and is sentenced to transportation to Australia. The wife follows him to the colony. After his release he becomes rich, but the household is not happy. There are no children, and the wife drinks to excess. At this point they encounter a young Irish aristocrat who has known the wife as

a child; this is the figure played by Michael Wilding, with whose arrival in Australia the film begins.

4   Thinking about one great artist can throw light on another: my understanding of *Under Capricorn* has been greatly aided by Eve Kosofsky Sedgwick's writing on shame, albeit in the context of a different medium and another figure earlier in the century.

5   The crane up to the balcony is the final camera movement of the first long take.

6   Relevant here is Stanley Cavell's discussion of flash insets in his *The World Viewed*, enlarged edn (1979: 135–7).

7   The resonances of this moment, which can be taken as a kind of blocked primal scene, are outside the scope of this study. I have written elsewhere about use of lost or concealed jewels in *Gaslight*, but the key film here may be John Brahm's *The Locket*. See John Fletcher's helpful account of *The Locket* in his 'Versions of Masquerade' (1988); see also E. Gallafent, 'Black Satin: Fantasy, Murder and the Couple in *Gaslight* and *Rebecca*', both in *Screen*, 29, 3 (Summer 1988).

8   I make no claim for the originality of this perception, although its implications do not seem to have been explored. It is noted in passing by Thomas Elsaesser in his 'The Dandy in Hitchcock', a 1981 essay recently reprinted in Allen and Ishii-Gonzalès (1999: 13, n. 21).

9   The definition of the dandy often seems to involve an attitude to women which is limited by coolness and lack of direction, and certainly does not involve the consummation of any sexual relation. See Moers (1960: 36–8 et passim).

10 Was Hitchcock recalling the business of reading labels and drinking potions, and of remembering simple rules, as laid out in *Alice in Wonderland*? His poison-bottle, with the label attached to its neck, seems to recollect visually John Tenniel's illustration for Lewis Carroll's book.

11 'Bernstein offered him a production set-up of his own, something to be called Transatlantic Pictures which would enable him to make films in Britain or America, co-produce them with Bernstein, and have complete control of subjects, casting and budgets. Hitchcock was delighted' (Taylor 1978: 206).

References

Allen, R. and S. Ishii-Gonzalès (eds) (1999) *Alfred Hitchcock: Centenary Essays* (London: BFI).

Bordwell, D. and K. Thompson (1993) *Film Art: An Introduction*, 4th edn (New York: McGraw-Hill).

Cavell, S. (1979) *The World Viewed: Reflections on the Ontology of Film*, enlarged edn (London: Harvard University Press).

Cavell, S. (1996) *Contesting Tears: The Hollywood Melodrama of the Unknown Woman* (Chicago: University of Chicago Press).

Brill, L. (1988) *The Hitchcock Romance: Love and Irony in Hitchcock's Films* (Princeton: Princeton University Press).

Fletcher, J. (1988) 'Versions of Masquerade', *Screen*, 29, 3, 43–7.

Gallafent, E. (1988) 'Black Satin: Fantasy, Murder and the Couple in *Gaslight* and *Rebecca*', *Screen*, 29, 3, 82–105.

Jacobowitz, F. (2000) '*Under Capricorn*: Hitchcock in Transition', *CineAction!*, 52, 18–27.

Marker, C. (1995) 'A Free Replay (notes on *Vertigo*)', in John Boorman and Walter Donohue (eds) *Projections 4.5* (London: Faber), pp. 123–30.

Moers, E. (1960) *The Dandy* (London: Secker & Warburg).

Sedgwick, E. K. (1995) 'Shame and Performativity: Henry James's New York Edition Prefaces', in David McWhirter (ed.) *Henry James's New York Edition: The Construction of Authorship* (Stanford: Stanford University Press).

Spoto, D. (1983) *The Life of Alfred Hitchcock* (London: Collins).

Taylor, J. R. (1978) *Hitch* (London: Faber).

Totaro, D. (2002) 'Time and the Long Take in *The Magnificent Ambersons*, *Ugestu* and *Stalker*' (PhD thesis, University of Warwick).

Truffaut, F. (1978) *Hitchcock* (London: Paladin Books).

Wood, R. (1989) *Hitchcock's Films Revisited* (New York: Columbia University Press).

5

Character interiority: space, point of view and performance in Hitchcock's *Vertigo* (1958)

Neill Potts

There has been a dearth of work on character in film studies. General distrust surrounds the idea of considering characters as analogues of humans, since they are obviously not real. Murray Smith has ascribed this to the theoretical mauling character received in the twentieth century by literary and structuralist narrative theorists (1995: 17). However, characters are filmic references to real human beings and, as such, it is possible and fruitful to study them as if they are real, in a manner not resulting in the 'impressionistic quality and "imbecilities of rhapsodic gush" associated with most writing on the subject' (Smith 1995: 228).

To study film characters is to contemplate a fundamental concern of film itself: humanity. Stanley Cavell, in his essay 'What Becomes of Things on Film?', identifies 'the meaning, or limits, or conditions ... of human identity' as a central subject taken up by film (1984: 179). In her writings, frequently indebted to Cavell, Marian Keane states: 'In my experience of viewing films, the medium of film – and specifically the camera – takes the nature of human interiority as its fundamental subject' (1993: 38). Film concerns itself with the nature of its own creators. As analogous humans, characters are a major locus of meaning and provide rich material for filmic analysis.

Cavell concludes his article on filmic human presence by stating: 'The question what becomes of things when they are filmed ... has only one source of data for its answer, namely the appearance and significance of just those objects and people that are in fact to be found in the succession of films, or passages of films, that matter to us' (1984: 182–3). Cavell's philosophical question finds the focus of its possible answer to be film itself: 'To express their appearances, and define those significances, and articulate the nature of this mattering, are acts that help to constitute what we might call film criticism' (1984: 183). Cavell's philosophical question becomes a problem for film studies.

Cavell's approach provides the context for the discussion that follows. Each section acts as both argument for the article's main premise of the importance of character in the comprehension of film, and also as a small passage of interpretation of a film which 'matters' to me. The study of character does not militate against analysis of film form; textual analysis is a key tool in the elucidation of film character. Character-centred analysis shifts critical emphasis to elements which enhance the understanding of movies through a comprehension of the characters who inhabit them.

The scepticism Murray Smith noted in relation to literary analysis of character stems from 'real-world' philosophical cynicism related to the self and others as discrete minds. Cavell notes: 'virtually every philosopher who has been gripped by the skeptical question whether and how we can know of the existence of so-called other minds has found himself or herself saying something of this sort' (1988: 162) and as an example, he quotes Wittgenstein: 'Other people cannot be said to learn of my sensations *only* from my behaviour – for I cannot be said to *learn* of them. I *have* them' (Wittgenstein in Cavell 1988: 162; emphasis in the original). The scepticism of this statement is a problem for real-world analysis of human interiority, and correspondingly for analysis of character in film. However, such an argument is tempered by writers such as George M. Wilson. In his discussion of Hitchcock's *North by Northwest* (1959), Wilson writes of the '"directness" of ordinary perception', that we believe, in reality and in the cinema, 'that outer appearance is not a veil of deception' (1986: 78–9). Furthermore, we extrapolate belief in the existence of 'other minds' through our own self-knowledge. We can know other people have an interior life because we know we ourselves possess one. We equate ourselves with other human selves and assume they also have and maintain an internal, non-language-dependent mind. The reactions of our own interior minds to external events help us analyse and deduce the likely reactions of other human minds. To a large extent, the inner life of all humans becomes known (and real) to us through everyday experience of our personal internal processes.[1]

Moreover, most films aim to make readable the gestures, movements and expressions of their characters. Film characters are given traits intended to be communicative, expressive, evocative and comprehensible. Their external behaviour is largely designed to convey interior states. When one recognises this rather straightforward concept, it becomes even more surprising that film studies has taken such issue with the concept of characters as analogous humans.

Through detailed analysis of the first scene at Ernie's restaurant from *Vertigo* this chapter argues for the importance of characters for an increased comprehension of narrative film. The analysis is organised around the presentation of three filmic elements through which character interiority is conveyed: spatial relationships, point of view (POV) and performance.

Seasoned viewers of *Vertigo* may map out each main character's multiple roles in terms of who they are performing to in the Ernie's scene.[2] There are numerous layers to each performance which only become apparent with hindsight. It seems useful to briefly discuss these roles before moving into the analysis:

Gavin Elster   Primarily Gavin Elster (Tom Helmore) is performing to deceive Scottie (James Stewart). Scottie believes Elster is showing his wife to him to recruit him to follow Madeleine (Kim Novak) and understand her strange behaviour. In fact, Elster is plotting to embroil Scottie in an elaborate murder plot, to place Scottie as a witness to the staged 'suicide' of his real wife, and the woman played by Kim Novak is not his wife but his mistress, Judy, impersonating Mrs Elster. Elster is performing to Scottie as an attentive husband, talking intimately with Madeleine at their table, pulling out her chair as she stands to leave. However, he is also sufficiently lax in his husbandly attentiveness (an apparently intentional lapse) to talk to the maitre-d', allowing Scottie to see Madeleine's insecure, distracted and nervous behaviour when she is left alone. Elster has already indicated these traits to Scottie in the preceding scene.

Scottie Ferguson   Scottie is at the restaurant at the request of Elster, to view Madeleine from afar. He has expressed his reluctance to become involved and his scepticism about her 'possession' by a dead relative. Scottie believes he is deceiving Madeleine by watching her without her knowledge and he is anxious not to be seen to be looking. Actually, she knows she is being observed. The scene marks the beginning of Scottie's obsession with Madeleine.

Madeleine/Judy   *Vertigo* is a film of deceptions, many perpetrated against its audience. Charles Barr's (2002) BFI monograph on *Vertigo* summarises the levels of performance for Kim Novak in the first Ernie's scene: 'Kim Novak is not simply, as a first viewing suggests, playing for Hitchcock the role of a woman being voyeuristically observed; she is playing, for Hitchcock, the part of a woman who is playing, for [Gavin] Elster, the part of a woman being voyeuristically observed' (2002: 11). This formulation is correct, but elides the problem of where the performance of Madeleine stops and where the performance of Judy begins, and vice versa. There is no answer to the conundrum of Novak's characters, no definite place to draw the line.

This is Scottie's first sighting of Madeleine. We are told later, before Scottie discovers it, that this Madeleine is not Elster's wife; it is Judy Barton performing as Madeleine Elster for Gavin Elster as part of his plan to use

Scottie. On first viewing, Madeleine's behaviour at Ernie's is readable as evidence of Elster's claim that she is nervous and distracted. It may break down some of Scottie's scepticism surrounding Madeleine's strange reputation as previously reported by Elster. Once it is known that Madeleine is being performed by Judy, a further possibility arises. Maybe the nervousness is a result of her fear that her performance of Madeleine might disintegrate under Scottie's scrutiny.

Space

For the beginning of the scene inside Ernie's restaurant, Hitchcock creates a complex moving camera shot which, although not from any character's point of view, is highly evocative of Scottie's (James Stewart) sense of the situation. The spatial relationships between the camera, Scottie and the Elsters are crucial to the shot's meaning. There are also other elements such as the music, costume and Scottie's movement which enhance the overall emotional effect.

When we first see Scottie in the restaurant, he has already arrived.[3] He sits at a bar and once this image has taken full precedence over the dissolve from the previous exterior shot, Scottie begins to lean back. As Scottie moves, the camera begins to track back, quite swiftly at first, simultaneously panning left. The movement immediately picks up on Scottie's own casual lean backwards, echoing its measured surreptitiousness and steadiness. The camera then gradually slows throughout the rest of its magnificent movement.

The camera takes in an opulent restaurant interior, separated from the bar area by an archway and plush partition. Scottie disappears from view, still leaning back on his stool, but the camera continues its movement, surveying the assembled diners. Clanking cutlery, glasses and crockery mix with the largely indistinct conversations of the customers. The camera slows down, then stops its tracking movement backwards for a brief moment but continues to pan left, its overall motion thus made continuous. It then begins to track forward, with slight pans and a small downwards crane. As this forward track commences, the music, 'Madeleine's First Appearance', the film's recurring romantic theme, is heard for the first time.

Within the crowd of diners sits a figure with her bare back to camera. She is dressed in an emerald satin dress. The camera moves towards her. It is only as the camera gets closer, craning down slightly to the eye level of the diners as it does so, that we recognise Gavin Elster across the table from this figure, whom we take to be his wife Madeleine. Yet this passage of camera movement is tentative and not as fluid as it might be. The slight pans left and right and the downwards crane give a sense of awkwardness not present in the earlier moments of the shot. The end of the shot also maintains a distance from the target of the camera's gaze. This denial of intimacy with the subjects

is compounded by Madeleine having her back to camera. The shot's perceptible 'jostling', its slow pacing and its resting at some distance from Madeleine
all express the nervously attentive, surreptitious vigil maintained by Scottie.
The shot also expresses what Scottie sees as his discreet observation of the
couple.

The camera's proximity to the subjects of its view strikes a fine balance
between declaring fascination and practising caution. Despite the distance
maintained, it is evident that the focus of attention is the couple at the table
in the middle distance, mainly because they inhabit centre-frame. However,
costume colour also emphasises these diners over others. Madeleine's green
gown visually separates her from the other clientele and the vivid red restaurant decor.[4]

Previous academic discussion of this shot has declared it a moment when
the camera asserts its authority over events. Following Raymond Bellour's
(1977) article on *Marnie* (1964), Tania Modleski (1988: 91) says the 'camera
itself takes over the enunciation' of the scene. Both Bellour's and Modleski's
arguments posit the final focus of the camera's searching movements (for
Bellour, Marnie, for Modleski, Madeleine) as the 'object of desire' (Bellour
1977: 86) or the 'object of man's romantic quest: the eternal feminine'
(Modleski 1988: 92). Such emphasis on the 'scopic drive' (Bellour 1977: 86)
as the force behind this shot fails to fully consider its function.

Robin Wood argues more persuasively that:

> The fascination [with Madeleine] is conveyed in the sequence's first shot
> starting from Scottie at the bar, and as if taking its impetus from his look,
> the camera draws back over the restaurant ... It is not (cannot possibly be) a
> point-of-view shot yet it has the effect of linking us intimately to the movement
> of Scottie's consciousness. (1989: 383–4)

In other words, the camera may detach itself from Scottie's 'searching gaze'
(Modleski 1988: 91), but movement and the spatial relationships this creates
between him and the Elsters, although not presenting his physical POV,
nonetheless articulate his view or opinion of the scene. It is not a shot which
imparts vital information contained in the mise-en-scène. Little information
as such about the restaurant would be lost by using a shot from Scottie's
POV in its place but the cinematic style of the shot is designed to evoke
Scottie's emotions without representing what he sees.

The use of Bernard Herrmann's music is also vital to the scene since it is
another key method through which film evokes emotion. The theme begins
as the camera starts its track towards the figures of Madeleine and Gavin
Elster. 'Madeleine's First Appearance' is dominated by stringed instruments.
The melody line, played on violin, is unpredictable and slips into minor
keys at musically surprising moments. These elements of construction and

orchestration create a piece which strongly evokes romance. Yet it is romance inflected by sadness and yearning. Like the music's insertions of minor keys, the romance it conveys will be unpredictable and melancholy.

If the connotations of the music seem to define aspects of Scottie's developing feelings, its emergence over the image of Madeleine also acts to strongly associate its melancholy mood with Madeleine's story of possession. In Elster's story, her happily married life is blighted by her obsession with her dead relative.[5] However, one might also consider the music as additionally aligned with Scottie in that the music and the emotions it evokes are crucial in articulating the softening of the 'hard-headed Scot'. The music implies Scottie's acceptance, following his first view of Madeleine, of Elster's story, that she is the tragic, romantic figure whose life is blighted by mental problems or supernatural intervention.

The combination of elaborate shot and evocative music enables Hitchcock to create complex effects in which music and mise-en-scène can be associated with more than one character. The spectator strongly experiences Scottie's response to Madeleine, but is also encouraged to contemplate and interpret Madeleine herself.

Point-of-view and viewpoint

In his discussion of POV, Murray Smith argues that the POV shot's 'privileged place in discussions of "identification" in film' is not truly justified: 'POV shots are thought to represent, synecdochically, the entire mind of the character – an assumption I am tempted to call the "fallacy of POV"' (1995: 156). A consideration of the Ernie's scene bears out Smith's observation.

Hitchcock's use of POV structures begins with what I will call Scottie's 'optical POV', where the image presents Scottie's physically possible field of vision. During the rest of the scene, however, the images we see of Madeleine become divorced from Scottie's optical POV, and through Hitchcock's construction of the scene, become linked with Scottie's thoughts and feelings.

Within Scottie's optical POV, the Elsters are shown preparing to leave. Their activity is the reason for Scottie's nervousness, conveyed through his readying movement in the previous shot. Madeleine wraps her emerald-coloured shawl around her shoulders. We cut to see Scottie again, motionless at the bar, in a similar shot to the previous image of him, and then cut back to the Elsters, again from Scottie's optical POV. Gavin Elster walks around the table and pulls his wife's chair back as she stands up, a gesture of attentiveness which chimes with the brief view we had of them at their table: a contented couple, engrossed in one another's company. She turns clockwise, a little towards the camera, but looks down at the floor as she does so. Her face is still being denied to us and Scottie. The information he needs to do his job (if he accepts the role of Elster's detective) is being withheld. His determination to see her face is expressed through this set of repeated shots of him looking fixedly in the Elsters' direction, a sense further reinforced by the next shot of Scottie still looking into the restaurant. It is a closer shot than the preceding two, a medium close-up rather than a medium shot. He moves his head towards the bar but his eyes demonstrate some reluctance to look away completely. The end of this shot shows Scottie looking towards the bar, relinquishing his optical POV through the restaurant archway which has been articulated twice by the camera.

However, at this point, despite Scottie's facing the bar, the camera returns to the same image through the archway in the next shot. It has taken up the exact position which Scottie's look at the bar has just shown him to have relinquished. Madeleine and Gavin Elster walk towards Scottie through the restaurant. Her walk is serene and graceful; he walks behind her, visible over her left shoulder.

Now the camera takes in far more visual information than would be available to Scottie. His orientation towards the bar means his current optical POV is not what the camera shows. Scottie, acutely aware that he must not be seen by Madeleine to be interested in her, must look away. The vision of Madeleine becoming larger in this wide frame of the restaurant is now an evocation of his sense of her moving closer rather than a representation of his optical POV.

Bernard Herrmann's music, which started as the roving camera moved towards Madeleine, begins to climb the musical scale and gain in volume. Conversely, the diegetic sounds of the restaurant are faded down, overtaken by the dominant strains of violins. This creates a build-up to the crescendo of aural and visual effects which mark the affective climax of the scene.

As the Elsters pass through the doorway to the bar, Gavin stops to talk to the maitre-d'. Madeleine glances back at him and walks on to a space just behind and to the left of Scottie (as one looks at the scene from behind the bar). The camera pans with her to the right and she stops in profile, facing frame-right. This is the key image of the scene, one which will return later in the film, projected from Scottie's consciousness over the picture of Carlotta Valdes in the gallery catalogue (Figure 5.1). The camera's panning right to follow Madeleine further distances the camera image from the physically possible optical POV of Scottie, yet the fact that he recalls this striking image later shows he has internalised it – on a psychological level, he possesses it. In the same way that the first camera movement through the restaurant is evocative of Scottie's feelings and situation, again the camera creates images evoking Scottie's sense of the scene without depicting his optical POV.

The climax of the Ernie's scene is rendered in a number of briefly held images which indicate 'Hitchcock's concern for the precise management of

5.1 *Vertigo* (Alfred Hitchcock, 1958)

the "look" in this scene' (Barr 2002: 11). From this point on, the pattern of shots runs as shown in the table.

Shot	Description	Time
1	End of pan-right, holding Madeleine in profile. As she stops walking, she swallows once. The lighting on the restaurant wall in the background becomes brighter.	–
2	Scottie in profile, shot over his right shoulder. He looks out of the corner of his eyes, but his head points towards the bar.	1.5s
3	Madeleine in profile. Different framing than shot 1. She blinks and swallows again, then turns her head slightly to her right, towards the camera.	1.5s
4	Scottie, framing as shot 2. He looks even more directly at the bar, turning his head to the left.	1.5s
5	Madeleine looking over her right shoulder, her eyes facing off-screen left. She twists her body so her face is briefly in profile facing left. As she executes this twist, the lighting is dimmed on the restaurant walls behind her head. Gavin Elster goes by left to right, between the wall and Madeleine. As he passes, Madeleine turns her body back towards frame-right. Her face remains visible as she turns. She walks off frame-right after Elster.	4.5s
6	Scottie shot over his left shoulder. He turns into profile and looks past the camera frame-left to watch the Elsters.	2.3s
7	Scottie's optical POV. The Elsters leave the restaurant.	3.5s

5.2 *Vertigo* (Alfred Hitchcock, 1958)

At the end of shot 1, a lighting effect is used to underscore the moment. With Madeleine in profile, the general lighting of the blurred red restaurant walls behind her head (especially that portion to the right of the frame) becomes brighter. It serves to give a visual uplift, a small background effect which subtly enhances the emotional high-point to which this scene was leading.

There is then a cut to Scottie, from over his right shoulder (shot 2). The side of his face is visible and his eyes move away from the camera and down to the bar (Figure 5.2). The highest note of the music's melody is reached at the very end of this shot and bridges the cut to the next image of Madeleine in profile (shot 3). This is the moment when it still seems possible their eyes might meet. It is as if they already know one another, but this must not be publicly acknowledged. It is a painful, heart-breaking moment which pre-figures both their future love and its tragic demise.

A few frames into shot 3 and the moment swiftly dissipates. Madeleine's forward-facing gaze is broken by her distracted look down and to her right, towards (but not at) the camera. Immediately, the strong lighting on the red wall begins to fade. The highest note of the music's melody ends and the notes tumble down the musical scale. The heightened tension, created by the possibility their eyes might meet, blowing Scottie's cover (and maybe Judy's), dissipates as the next images depict their lack of eye contact.

In shot 4, Scottie looks away until only the side of his nose is visible. He looks down at the bar once again. At this moment the camera's view of Madeleine is most at odds with Scottie's own physically possible optical POV.

Despite having presented his optical POV, the camera has gone on to break from a realistic depiction of it. Instead, it supplies idealistic images of Madeleine as a vision of nervous beauty, unapproachable yet vulnerable. These images are created by a camera fulfilling Scottie's inner desires rather than his vision. The camera is working on behalf of Scottie, seeing Madeleine as he wants to see her. This is why the profile image of Madeleine, which Scottie could not physically see, is available for him to recollect as he looks at the 'Portrait of Carlotta' in the gallery catalogue: the scene implicates him as the co-creator of its images of Madeleine.

In addition, the alterations in sound echo the images. The soundtrack moves from a believable representation of the restaurant environment to the mysterious-romantic music which peaks at the moment when Scottie's half-imagined view of Madeleine is most vivid. The soundtrack draws attention from the scene's restaurant setting when the images are closely aligned to Scottie's inner desires, across shots 3 and 4. Taken with the visual rhetoric of the bright red walls and their increased illumination, it is clear we are being encouraged to view this moment as within the realm of imagination, rather than a faithful depiction of a narrative event.

In this scene, an 'imaginative' POV is used at its emotional high-point, the moment when Scottie's and Madeleine/Judy's gazes almost meet. The images are more felt by Scottie than viewed by him; the shots are more a reflection of his character, his thoughts and emotions. The camera takes over his optical POV, then stretches the physical possibility of this view. Despite the supposed break from depicting his optical POV, the camera captures a key image in that part of the scene which Scottie later recalls from his mind.

Performance

Performance has always been concerned with 'the revelation of the interior states of characters', but this area of film analysis 'has had the least attention paid to it' (Smith 1995: 151). Whatever the reasons for this omission on the part of film studies, there exists a body of film analysis that recognises the importance of performance in film. One example is V. F. Perkins's article 'Must We Say What They Mean? Film Criticism and Interpretation' (1990). Perkins considers a moment from *Caught* (Ophuls, 1948) to highlight the importance of film performance in film criticism: 'It is necessary to reflect on what the gestures mean and where they come from. The camera cannot directly show what is on Leonora's [Barbara Bel Geddes] mind, but her aims and feelings are as much a part of the narrative of *Caught* as the fact that she is sitting in a millionaire's car' (1990: 1). Perkins is arguing for critical sensitivity to human content in narrative film, rather than concentration on bald taken-for-granted facts of the film world evident in plot synopses and much film criticism. The inner life of characters is an integral factor in the movement of narrative. In terms of motivation, desire and aspiration, key elements of any analogous human, would Leonora be in the millionaire's car if it were not for that part of her character, her inner life, which sought social betterment? Performance, down to the level of the slightest facial or physical gesture, has a crucial role in characterisation. Not all movements, gestures or actions of a character have direct effects on narrative development as it is often defined, but all have something to say about their inner life. Through close attention to elements of performance we can gain the greatest amount of information about their interiority, and in turn come to a greater understanding of their function within the film's world.

Film's ability to become intimate with the human form and face allows many different aspects of expressivity to be conveyed by actor performance, often through the smallest of gestures. Several performance elements characterise Madeleine's troubled state of mind as the Elsters leave the restaurant. When she is left stranded by Elster in profile (shot 3 above), Madeleine swallows and also blinks fitfully as she turns her head. These tiny actions convey nervousness and vulnerability that seem to contradict her overall poise and confidence. We also see that her eyes are cast downwards, which further reinforces her insecurity. Her husband's description of her curious, detached and distracted trances is still fresh in the memory from the previous scene at Elster's office. When his description is echoed in Madeleine's behaviour during this scene, it supports his version of the truth about her. This in turn strengthens the impression of their mutual love and his genuine concern for her.

But the signifiers of nervousness can fit the situation of both Madeleine and Judy in this scene and the conclusions we draw from her behaviour depend whether this is our first viewing of *Vertigo* or a subsequent viewing. On a first viewing, the aspects of the restaurant scene which align us with Scottie's interiority are part of the film's structure of his and our deception. We never suspect that Madeleine and Gavin Elster are duping Scottie and that the film is duping us during this scene. On later viewings, Novak's performance is complicated by our knowledge of her collusion in Elster's deception. Although the nervous behaviour of Novak as Madeleine is consistent with Elster's description of her troubled mind, we can also recognise that Novak's performance of Madeleine is inextricable from her performance of Judy pretending to be Madeleine. Where does Judy's performance of Madeleine's nervousness begin? Are her insecurities demonstrations of Judy's fears as she plays her role? Is the nervousness the Madeleine mask itself, or a sign that the mask is slipping? It is undoubtedly both. The key point is that Novak's performance and Hitchcock's presentation of her performance are consistent with both of Novak's roles. In this among many other ways character interiority is crucial to the film's narrative.

Two major aspects of Hitchcock's movie reputation are raised by this analysis. One is supported by it, the other called into question. Firstly, this fragment of *Vertigo* bears witness to Hitchcock's mastery of POV structures and his understanding of their implications for audience experience and our understanding of his films and characters. Hitchcock's complex manipulation of POV, and the stretching of its conventions, creates a range of possible interpretations which improve with repeated viewing. Secondly, this film scene contradicts the frequently expressed view that Hitchcock's films are inhabited by ciphers, not rounded characters.[6] This is a misguided oversimplification of Hitchcock's achievement. Hitchcock presents Madeleine to the virgin *Vertigo* viewer as the damaged, nervous and troubled young woman described by her husband. He also provides the experienced viewer with Madeleine/Judy, an even more complicated character. And yet subsequent viewings do not act to rupture the veracity of the innocent Madeleine role. The context of audience knowledge may change, but Hitchcock's masterful handling of performance and camera ensures that the multi-faceted Madeleine/Judy is not turned into a flagrant cheat by that knowledge. Like all great works, *Vertigo* is made to sustain multiple viewings, and our experience can be enriched by returning to it.

Notes

1 In discussion with V. F. Perkins, June 1997.
2 This chapter spoils the plot for those who have not seen *Vertigo*. It should only be read once the reader has viewed it.
3 Hitchcock manufactures this fact (through editing, the ordering of information and events) to imply certain traits, emotions, thoughts or intentions relating to Scottie. His presence at the restaurant, arriving before the camera, signals his curiosity, eagerness, professionalism, maybe even his boredom with his current life.
4 Green becomes her colour (as Madeleine and Judy) for the whole film: her Jaguar car is green, she wears predominantly green clothing and Judy's hotel room is swathed in the green neon light of the 'Empire Hotel' sign. These costume and set choices are further enhanced by fog filter effects during the cemetery scene, which Hitchcock noted 'gave us a green effect'; the green light in the hotel 'gives her the same subtle, ghost-like quality' (in Truffaut 1969: 306). In her first appearance, Madeleine/Judy is carrying the connotations of ghostliness which her resurrected character comes to represent to Scottie. See also Wood (1989: 235 n. 18 and p. 384).
5 For the knowledgeable viewer, the tragedy of this multi-faceted character does not end there: as Judy, she is also cast aside by Elster and becomes desperate for Scottie's love.

6   As one example of this tendency Raymond Durgnat, responding to Raymond
    Chandler's notes on his collaboration with Hitchcock on *Strangers on a Train*
    (1951), remarked: 'the situations and the settings determine the actions, to which
    character is made to fit. Character is passive to the overall action, to the mach-
    inery of dream which is like the machinery of predestination. Character[s] [are]
    merely smoke figures' (Durgnat 1970, in LaValley 1972, 92).

References

Barr, C. (2002) *Vertigo* (London: BFI).

Bellour, R. (1977) 'Hitchcock, The Enunciator', *A Journal of Feminism and Film
    Theory*, Fall, 67–91.

Cavell, S. (1984) 'What Becomes of Things on Film?', in *Themes Out of School* (San
    Francisco: Northpoint Press), pp. 173–83.

Durgnat, R. (1970) 'The Strange Case of Alfred Hitchcock, Part Three', in Albert J.
    LaValley (ed.) (1972), pp. 91–6.

Keane, M. (1993) 'Dyer Straits: Theoretical Issues in Studies of Film Acting', *Post
    Script*, 12, 2, 29–39.

LaValley, A. (ed.) (1972) *Focus on Hitchcock* (Englewood Cliffs, NJ: Prentice Hall).

Modleski, T. (1988) *The Women Who Knew Too Much: Hitchcock and Feminist Theory*
    (New York, London: Methuen).

Perkins, V. F. (1990) 'Must We Say What They Mean? Film Criticism and Interpre-
    tation', *Movie*, 34/5, 1–6.

Smith, M. (1995) *Engaging Characters: Fiction, Emotion, and the Cinema* (Oxford:
    Clarendon Press).

Truffaut, F. (1969) *Hitchcock* (London: Panther Books).

Wilson, G. M. (1986) *Narration in Light* (Baltimore, London: Johns Hopkins Univer-
    sity Press).

Wood, R. (1989) *Hitchcock's Films Revisited* (New York: Columbia University Press).

6

Narration, point of view and patterns in the soundtrack of *Letter from an Unknown Woman* (Max Ophuls, 1948)

Steve Neale

I want in this chapter to draw attention to an aspect of *Letter from an Unknown Woman* that has rarely been discussed – its soundtrack. To be more precise, I want to draw attention to *Letter*'s diegetic music, its noises and sounds, and the timbre, tone and content of some its dialogue. In doing so, I want to consider the relationship between these elements and their organisation and two different areas or fields of debate. The first is the debate, specific to the film, concerning the extent to which there are differences between the point of view of Lisa (Joan Fontaine) as a character and the point of view constructed in and through the narration of the film as a whole. The second is the extent to which such currently ubiquitous terms as 'interpretation', 'meaning' and 'reading' are appropriate to describe the issues at stake either in considering this topic or in considering what for the moment I would prefer to call the 'perception' or 'ascription' of those patterns in *Letter*'s soundtrack that prompted this chapter in the first place and whose limit case – the repeated presence of the sound of ringing bells at various points in the film – I discuss later on as an example. I shall turn to the soundtrack in a moment. Before doing so, though, I need to outline the nature of the debates about *Letter*, point of view and narration.

Point of view and narration

Large sections of *Letter* are flashback sequences purporting to illustrate or embody the account of events contained in Lisa's letter to Stefan (Louis Jourdan). In part because they are cued and accompanied by passages from the letter and in part because these passages are voiced on the soundtrack by Lisa herself, these sequences are set up as Lisa's narration and thus might logically be expected to convey her knowledge of events and her point of view. However, most commentators have noted that they contain details, characters, even 'minor' events of which Lisa herself is unaware. They have gone on to argue that the cinematic presentation of these and other sequences in the film organises these discrepancies, details and events in such a way as to generate from them a series of ironies and hence on the one hand to 'locate' Lisa's point of view as a character and on the other to construct a distinct point of view of its own. Robin Wood, for instance, both in his chapter on the film in *Personal Views: Explorations in Film* (1976) and in his essay '*Letter from an Unknown Woman*: The Double Narrative' (1993), notes the extent to which 'our intimate involvement' with the film's central characters 'is consistently balanced by the fact that we always know more than they do' (1976: 127). He identifies a 'pervasive tension between subjective narrative and objective presentation' (1976: 127). And as an example, he notes that throughout the fairground sequence in Prater

> we see that Lisa is completely enclosed in the world of her dream, aware of nothing except Stefan and the apparent realization of her fantasies. Ophuls, however, shows a lot that is outside this world: the old man who works the levers that operate the backdrops, the old woman Stefan pays for the entertainment. While Lisa and Stefan dance together, Ophuls cuts in a bit of dialogue between the singularly unromantic women of the ladies' orchestra, who drink beer, chew sausage and complain of being kept late. ... All this is clearly outside Lisa's consciousness, and could not have been described in the letter. Despite the subjective narrative, Ophuls does not restrict us to Lisa's viewpoint. (1976: 127)

In a similar fashion, George M. Wilson refers to the shot of Lisa and Stefan, viewed from the top of stairs as they return to Stefan's flat after their evening at the Prater. This shot recalls one earlier in the film in which the camera had taken the same position and Lisa, positioned in the foreground, had watched Stefan come home with one of his female conquests. The 'visible absence of Lisa as observer' in the later shot, Wilson writes, 'makes salient that she is now merely the subject of *our* perception and is utterly removed from the perspective that earlier she had held' (1986: 103, emphasis in original) – and this despite both shots occurring during what purports to be segments of Lisa's letter, hence of Lisa's account. V. F. Perkins, too, refers in his analysis of the sequence in Linz to the fact that the principal characters, including Lisa, fail to notice 'the peasant cart which interrupts our view' of Lisa's introduction to Leopold (1982: 66).

Of the principal commentators on *Letter*, only Tony Pippolo (1979) attempts to argue that there is a seamless fit between Lisa's account, Lisa's point of view and the presentation of the sequences she purports to narrate; only he attempts to motivate the discrepancies, to which he nevertheless draws attention, as consonant in one way or another with Lisa's consciousness, Lisa's sensibility or Lisa's state of mind. The others all argue that such

discrepancies help mark a difference between Lisa's point of view and that of
the film. Discrepancies of one kind or another are common, indeed conventional, in flashback sequences of the kind used in *Letter* because, as Wilson
points out, such sequences always contain 'far more information than the
speaker's statements could convey' (1986: 106; see also Wood 1993: 6). What
happens in *Letter*, it is argued, is that these discrepancies are exploited in
a systematic way, used to highlight the issues, conditions and limitations of
awareness, point of view and perception that Wilson, Wood and Perkins all
discuss.

In making such arguments, logical or literal inconsistencies in presentation, such as the shot from the viewpoint of Lisa's husband, and logical or
literal instances of perceptual unawareness, such as the lack of awareness of
the peasant cart, are treated not just as evidence of this difference, but also as
evidence that the film is concerned, in a more metaphorical way, with 'views
of the world' and their blindspots. This concern is as manifest in the film's
presentation of Stefan as it is in its presentation of Lisa. (It is Stefan who fails
to recognise Lisa until the end of the film; it is Stefan who has failed to fulfil
his potential as a pianist; it is Stefan who, as Lisa points out, does not know
himself. In this respect Stefan's lack of awareness is contrasted not just with
Lisa's knowledge but also with the knowledge possessed by his servant, John.)

However, in part because Lisa's letter is the means used to set up the
presentation of so many key events, in part because she herself often passes
judgement on their significance, and in part because, to use Murray Smith's
terms, we are 'aligned' with her and granted 'access' to her thoughts and
feelings for so much of the film (see Smith 1995), commentary has tended to
focus on Lisa and on her 'romantic' view of the world.

Thus, following his discussion of the Prater sequence, Wood underlines
the extent to which '[t]he tendency of the film to draw us into her vision is
balanced and counterpointed throughout by a conflicting tendency to detach
us from the "dream" and comment on it ironically, hinting at some prosaic
reality that Lisa excludes, exposing some of the very unromantic mechanisms
upon which the dream depends' (1976: 127). And Perkins, referring initially
to the work of music-making performed by the bandsmen at Linz, writes:

> The foregrounding of servitude and menial labour ... as the condition and cost
> of 'splendour' is a constant of Ophuls's later work, but it has a particular role
> in *Letter from an Unknown Woman*. As the disregarded support for an often
> dazzling way of life, servitude is the skull-beneath-the-skin both of elegance
> (achieved or attempted) and of romance. For if the bandsmen are conscripted
> into Leopold's attempt to pass off a parental scheme as his heart's vocation,
> Lisa, too, will avoid recognising the mechanics that construct and maintain the
> fabric of her idyll with Stefan – for example, the tired 'railway' workers and,
> most notably, the bandswomen of the Prater whose mock-military garb stresses

their correspondence to the Linz cadets. What Lisa cannot see, and this relates to her misreading of Stefan himself, is the substructure of routine on which she elaborates her fantasy of the unique and the ordained. (1982: 65–6)

It seems to me that these particular observations are correct. (Wood's perspective and the emphasis he places on the 'tragic' consequences of Lisa's attitudes and actions lead him to discuss the possibility of a film '*against* Lisa' (1976: 130, emphasis in original; see also 1993: 7–8).) But both Perkins and Wilson make it clear that she remains, throughout, the film's centre of sympathy even as the film itself lays bare the conditions of existence, the logic, and the limitations of her 'fantasy' and the destructive nature of the events to which it gives rise. To use the terms proposed by Julia Hallam and Margaret Marshment in *Realism and Popular Cinema*, we are 'aligned' with her in terms of 'interest', 'concern' and 'emotion', but not necessarily in terms of her perception, evaluation or understanding of events, other characters, or even herself (2000: 130–7). One can easily add to the list of figures and instances of 'servitude' and 'menial labour' in the film (the flower sellers, the street musicians, the railway workers, the removal men). One can point as well to specific instances of the 'prosaic' (the peasant cart) and the 'routine' (rug-beating day). What I want to highlight here is the extent to which nearly all of them involve or generate heavily marked and carefully organised instances of diegetic music, noise, speech and sound, and the extent to which, as a consequence, they expose the limitations inherent in a vocabulary dominated by visual metaphors, figures and terms – 'point of view', 'viewpoint', 'view of the world', and so on. The vocabularies proposed by Smith and by Hallam and Marshment are in this respect much more useful, though even they find it difficult to find synonyms for the cluster of attitudes and beliefs to which terms like 'point of view' or 'worldview' can allude. This is not, or not just, because of a historical overemphasis on the visual nature or aspects of film. The same problems – and the same terms – bedevil discussion of these topics in literature too.

Music, noise, speech and sound

Consider the initial segment in the first flashback sequence. As a dolly-in to a medium close-up of Stefan reading the letter begins to blur and to dissolve into an equally blurred image of the interior of a removal van, Lisa's voice can be heard on the soundtrack. 'I think everyone has two birthdays', she says, 'the day of his physical birth; and the beginning of his conscious life'. As these words are spoken, the image of the van's interior comes into focus to reveal some books, a chandelier, a harp and the legs of a removal man. At the same time, music from the streets can be heard. (It continues to be heard throughout the segment.) As soon as Lisa's words are spoken, the removal

6.1 *Letter from an Unknown Woman* (Max Ophuls, 1948)

man picks up the harp. As Robin Wood has pointed out, it produces a loud 'discordant "twang"' as he does so (1993: 6). As the camera pans left, Lisa as a young teenage girl is shown looking in wonderment at what is going on and in particular at what on the soundtrack she calls 'such beautiful things' (Figure 6.1). As she begins to finger the harp, which has now been moved to the pavement, a stern female voice can be heard off-screen: 'Lisa!' Lisa turns and the camera tilts to reveal Lisa's mother at an upstairs window. 'Come in, Lisa! Come in this minute, you hear! Lisa!' 'Yes, Mother', says Lisa, as she turns somewhat reluctantly to enter the apartment block.

Inside, she is greeted as she moves across the entrance hall and up the stairs not only by sights, but also by the sounds and words, of the removal men at work: the noise of the pulley used to lift the piano up the stairs (something we hear before we see); the dialogue of the removal men: 'Who's going to clean that up? Me I suppose. As if I haven't got enough to do.' 'This is the last time I move a musician!' 'Why does he have to play a piano? Why not the piccolo?' Lisa reaches the top of the stairs as one of the removal men asks John where to put the books he is carrying. John cannot speak. He writes down the instructions. Lisa has dropped her scarf. John picks it up for her. 'Thank you', she says. As Lisa and John stand looking at one another, we hear once more the off-screen voice of Lisa's mother: 'Lisa! What are you doing out there? Come inside!' Lisa, still looking at John (and with the music from the street still playing on the soundtrack), opens the door to her apartment then closes it with an audible click. There follows a dissolve to a shot of Stefan's hands playing Liszt's 'Un Sospiro' on the piano as we move into the flashback's second segment.

Throughout this first segment, the film presents us with the sounds produced by the work – the menial labour – of the removal men. One of these sounds, the twang of the harp, is marked out not only by its early occurrence in the sequence, but also by the fact that it occurs immediately after Lisa's romantically philosophical words about having two birthdays. (Wood makes the sound part of his argument about the 'double narrative': 'What we have here is not the addition of "neutral" detail but a contradiction in *tone*: from the outset, Lisa's narration and Ophuls' narration are set in partial conflict, and that out first intimation of this is stirred by the notion "discord" can hardly be accidental' (1993: 31).) It is marked out, too, by the fact that it is 'noise', so to speak, not music. This distinction is reinforced once the second segment begins. We hear as well as see Stefan playing 'Un Sospiro'. We witness Lisa's dreamy reaction. But we are also presented with the reaction of Lisa's female companion, Marie: 'I wish he'd stop that noise.'

Diegetic music and the labour it involves is an important element not just here but throughout the film. It is noted in Perkins's comments on the bandsmen at Linz. It is implicit in the comments, cited above, on the role of the female musicians at Prater. And it is explicit in Wood's discussion of the role and significance of Mozart's 'Magic Flute' in the scene at the opera (1976: 127–8). (It is also explicit in the nature and trajectory of Stefan's career. The labour involved here, which is menial in the literal but not in the social sense, is highlighted during the course of the second sequence: Stefan is unable to complete 'Un Sospiro' successfully; his frustration, and his unwillingness to work or to practice further, are underlined when he slams down the lid of the piano with a loudly audible 'bang' – another instance, it should be noted, of noise.)

The street music that plays throughout this first sequence is a further example. We are not here shown the musicians who play it. But we see as well as hear the playing (and singing) of similar music later on (just prior to Lisa's first encounter with Stefan following her return to Vienna from Linz; as elsewhere in the film, the involvement of labour in music-making and in other forms of leisure, entertainment and amusement is here marked in and through the paying of money). The 'prosaic' nature and the 'low' cultural status of the music are marked. But like the waltzes played by the female orchestra and the marches played by the bandsmen at Linz, it is not just contrasted, as the film proceeds, with the nature and status of 'Un Sospiro', 'The Magic Flute' and the other instances of classical music that Lisa associates so strongly with Stefan and that so stimulate her romantic imagination. It is also part of a multi-faceted musical continuum dependent for its impact and status on perception and context: in the Prater sequence, Stefan, after all, plays waltz music too; and in the second segment, it is Stefan's playing, not his slamming of the piano lid, that Marie refers to as 'noise'.

Once inside the apartment block we are presented not just with the sardonic words of the removal men but also with the sardonic tones in which they are spoken. The tenor of these words and tones contrasts strongly with that of Lisa (who speaks softly and sincerely of 'beautiful things'). So too, in a different way, does the tenor of the harshly shouted commands and admonishments of Lisa's mother. It is hard to convey the effect of these contrasts in writing. But along with the different accents of the performers (Joan Fontaine's unmarked 'English' accent takes its place alongside the heavily marked 'Mittel European' of nearly all the 'minor' characters, and, of course, the equally marked French of Louis Jourdan), tenor and tone are extremely important. The world-weary tones of the workmen are as much an index of their perspective on events as their words. The harshness of Lisa's mother's voice is as much a sign of her role as unwitting obstacle or counterpoint to Lisa's romantic imaginings, designs and plans as what she says. John's silence, meanwhile, is as much a means of highlighting his special role as the person who sees, who recognises, who knows and who understands as his visual presence in this and in other key segments and scenes.

Sound and music figure in similar ways elsewhere in the film. Rug-beating day begins with the sounds as well as the sights of the labour performed by Lisa and others in the courtyard. As the scene proceeds, and as Lisa makes her way to Stefan's music-room, the noise produced by the beating of rugs recedes, to be replaced on the soundtrack by one of the motifs from Daniele Amfitheatrof's score, played gently on a small group of strings. The mood is enhanced by the gentle creaking of the door as Lisa enters the room. It is also enhanced by the barely perceptible sound made when she brushes against the harp, which is now located near the wall in Stefan's room. It is only broken by the noise she makes knocking over some sheet music stacked on a shelf. The first scene at the station is filled with sounds of 'routine' activity. And the sequence at Linz is marked not just by the music of the bandsmen, but also by the rumbling of the cart to which Perkins refers and the clip-clopping of the horses that draw a carriage in the background as the characters make their way toward church.

Both the station scene and the sequence at Linz are also marked by the sound of ringing bells. The ringing of bells – of various kinds – can be heard thirteen times during the course of the film: church bells can be heard as Stefan gets out of the carriage in the opening sequence, during the first half of the sequence at Linz, then again, near the end, as Stefan holds his head in his hands on reaching the end of the letter; a passing cyclist rings his bell as Stefan pauses at the entrance to the apartment block to look back at Lisa, who has opened the door for him; the streetcar bell rings as Lisa steals a look at another passenger's programme for one of Stefan's concerts; a streetcar bell rings again once Lisa steps off on her way back to the apartment block after running away from the station; on arriving at her destination, she rings the bell on the gate; she rings it again, later on, when she decides to visit Stefan after meeting him again at the opera; during the course of this sequence she rings Stefan's doorbell as well; handbells ring throughout the station scene mentioned above and throughout the two subsequent scenes at the station (when Stefan leaves for Milan and when Lisa sends puts her son on the train); finally, as Stefan's seconds arrive, his doorbell is rung once again. These instances are intriguing for a number of reasons. They seem to constitute further evidence of sonic organisation. Yet their function is not immediately clear. Do they constitute a pattern, a motif? If there *is* a pattern, can it be said to serve a semantic purpose? To what extent do answers to these questions entail notions of 'reading' and 'meaning'? This is the second area of discussion prompted by aspects of *Letter*'s soundtrack to which I would now like turn.

Motifs, reading and meaning

In *Making Meaning: Inference and Rhetoric in the Interpretation of Cinema*, David Bordwell discusses the protocols and practices that govern what he calls 'interpretation'. He points out that interpretation – the ascription of meaning to films and their constituent elements – involves the mapping of 'semantic fields' onto as many as three sets of textual features: characters and their traits, actions and relationships; 'the characters' surroundings – setting, lighting, objects, in short the "diegetic world" they inhabit'; and such nondiegetic 'representational techniques' as camerawork, editing and music (1989: 170). Elements within these sets are hypothesised as meaningful and correlations are made, as far as is possible, with elements in other sets across the span of the text as a whole. In making these points, Bordwell notes that 'Theorists of criticism have ... generally identified interpretation with the ascription of pattern to a text' (1989: 187). He also notes that 'all schools of criticism' have assumed that motifs 'carry meaning' (1989: 187). But what is 'pattern'? What constitutes a motif? Do motifs always, in fact, 'carry meaning'?

As Bordwell points out, repetition and variation are generally considered to be one of the hallmarks of meaningful motifs. To that extent, the ringing of bells in *Letter* clearly counts as a possible motif. As noted above, ringing bells can be heard more than a dozen times during the course of the film. As also noted, different kinds of bells – producing different kinds of sounds – can be heard at different points in the narrative: church bells at the beginning, at the end, and during the course of the sequence at Linz; handbells in the station scenes; a doorbell and gate bell at points in the narrative at which Lisa plans to visit Stefan; and so on. They can thus be grouped into sub-sets according to various criteria (pitch and tone, diegetic location, the types of narrative action they accompany, and so on). But there are factors in their distribution that might be said to militate against their status as components in a meaningful motif. The ringing of bells occurs unevenly. There are large stretches of film during which bells cannot be heard ringing at all. The most notable of these is perhaps the sequence during which Stefan and Lisa spend the evening together, when Lisa's dreams of romance with Stefan appear to come true. This might itself help mark the points at which bells actually do ring as indices of the failure, the lack or the mere hope of romance. However, this would in turn entail the assumption of a single 'semantic field' – that of 'romance' or '*the* romance' – to which each instance of ringing can be linked, and the problem here is that this not always easy to do. This is especially true of the ringing of church bells during the course of the opening sequence, at a point prior to any hint of romance. Here, if anything, culturally coded associations between tolling church bells and 'fate' or 'doom' are more likely to be evoked instead, especially as all we know at this point is that Stefan has been challenged to a duel. Moreover, whether associated with 'fate' or (retrospectively perhaps) with the romance (and its fateful course), how do the church bells that ring in this sequence relate semantically to the church bells that ring in the sequence at Linz?

With sufficient ingenuity, it might possible to make semantic links between all of these instances, thus to provide an 'interpretation' or a 'reading' of the bell motif as a whole. However, I would prefer to suspend the issue of mean-ing (or at least 'a' meaning) and to treat this motif (or this quasi motif) in terms of its possible functions and effects. It seems to me there are at least three of these. Firstly, the ringing of bells adds 'aural texture' to the fictional world, thus taking its place alongside the other aural elements mentioned above. Secondly, insofar as any of its moments or manifestations remain unremarked by any of the characters, it is further evidence of an organising instance (and hence of a point of view) that exists in excess of the characters themselves. And thirdly, precisely because it remains unremarked, hence pre-cisely because appropriate semantic cues are provided neither in the dialogue nor in any other evident way, the construction of an appropriate semantic field, and the ascription of an appropriate label to it, remains a problem. (To put it another way, it is difficult to locate elsewhere or in other aspects of the film a marking of the bell motif as significant. If the bell motif is a motif it appears to lack the 'codic doubling' that Ben Brewster discussed as a condition of semantic pertinence in 'Notes on the Text "John Ford's *Young Mr Lincoln*" by the Editors of *Cahiers du Cinema*' some years ago.)

The interest, for me, lies not in resolving this problem, not in finding the appropriate label, but in drawing attention to the questions it raises. These questions centre on the nature of motifs and on the conditions that govern their perception. Much has been written about 'reading' and 'meaning', about the semantic nature of texts, and about the extent to which conditions of reception govern their 'interpretation'. But very little has been written on the topic of motifs and other types of formal or stylistic organisation. In one of the most recent books to argue for the importance of studies of reception, Martin Barker and Kate Brooks refer to the methodology used by art historian Michael Baxendale. They identify 'three separate elements: the principles governing the making and placing in public places of the paintings; the patterning of elements within the paintings; and the ways in which these provided specific kinds of opportunities for use and response' (1998: 138). While attention has been focused on the first and third of these elements, the second has been somewhat neglected. (Is patterning simply an objective property of texts which audiences respond to and use? Or is its perception bound up with use, with response, and with the circumstances and conditions in which they occur?) The same might be said of the topic of sound (particularly sound in non-musical films of the studio era). The fact that these topics coincide in this particular instance makes it, for me, all the more intriguing.

References

Barker, M. and K. Brooks (1998) *Knowing Audiences: Judge Dredd, Its Friends, Foes and Fans* (Luton: University of Luton Press).

Bordwell, D. (1989) *Making Meaning: Inference and Rhetoric in the Interpretation of Cinema* (Cambridge, Mass.: Harvard University Press).

Brewster, B. (1973) 'Notes on the Text "John Ford's *Young Mr Lincoln*" by the Editors of *Cahiers du Cinema*', *Screen*, 14, 3, 29–43.

Hallam, J. and M. Marshment (2000) *Realism and Popular Cinema* (Manchester: Manchester University Press).

Perkins, V. F. (1982) '*Letter from an Unknown Woman*', *Movie*, 29, 30, 61–72.

Pippolo, T. (1979) 'The Aptness of Terminology: Point of View, Consciousness, and *Letter from an Unknown Woman*', *Film Reader*, 4, 166–79.

Smith, M. (1995) *Engaging Characters: Fiction, Emotion and the Cinema* (Oxford: Clarendon Press).

Wilson, G. (1986) *Narration in Light: Studies in Cinematic Point of View* (Baltimore: Johns Hopkins University Press).

Wood, R. (1976) *Personal Views: Explorations in Film* (London: Gordon Fraser).

Wood, R. (1993) '*Letter from an Unknown Woman*: The Double Narrative', *CineAction!*, 31, 4–17.

7

Revisiting Preminger: *Bonjour Tristesse* (1958) and close reading

John Gibbs and Douglas Pye

This chapter centres on the detailed analysis of a short section from Otto Preminger's film *Bonjour Tristesse* (1958), an adaptation of the 1954 novel which had been a *succès de scandale* for its eighteen-year-old author, Françoise Sagan. In choosing *Bonjour Tristesse* one intention is to celebrate the achievements of an extraordinary and neglected film. We also want to revisit the writing about Preminger in the early issues of *Movie*, published in 1962, and to link the ways in which *Movie* writers characterised Preminger's style and its effects to a discussion of the film's narrative method. The adaptation is basically faithful to the events, characters and relationships of the novel but the film's narrative organisation and various levels of narration change the telling of the story very significantly. We will be concerned especially with the epistemological restrictions within which the spectator is held and the film's use of what we will characterise as a form of unreliable narration. The narrative and stylistic choices which focus these issues are also inseparable from questions raised by performance and the construction of character. All these strands come together around close reading of a kind which has tended to be out of favour within the various theoretical approaches which have dominated film studies since the 1970s, and a major purpose of the article is to show how close reading, involving interlocking levels of interpretation, is an indispensable basis for understanding the distinction of *Bonjour Tristesse* – and, by extension, many other movies.

'It was very hot the day Anne was due to arrive. My father and Elsa had gone to meet her at the railway station.' As we hear the words in voice-over, there is a dissolve from the black-and-white images of the Paris night club in which Cecile (Jean Seberg) is jiving, to the vivid Technicolor of the film's flashbacks to the south of France the previous summer. Cecile is on holiday with her widowed father, Raymond (David Niven), and his current mistress, Elsa (Mylene Demongeot). Anne, an old friend of Cecile's mother, has accepted an invitation Raymond issued only half seriously months before and

7.1 *Bonjour Tristesse* (Otto Preminger, 1958)

had forgotten when he invited the much younger Elsa for the summer. Responding to a car horn which she takes to signal the trio returning, Cecile runs from her boyfriend's embrace towards the house. The camera picks her up as she scrambles over a rise in the left of the frame and tracks left to right, viewing her movement from a distance and from a slightly elevated position. She runs past the house and up a short flight of steps, a large spiky agave momentarily blocking our view of her as she calls, 'Anne!' before saying 'Welcome' and stopping hesitantly at the front of a car, the camera finally coming to rest as it frames Anne (Deborah Kerr), alone, facing Cecile (Figure 7.1). The camera's static position is then held as the rest of the greeting scene is played out.

There is nothing obviously 'striking' about Otto Preminger's visual treatment of this moment. Within the infinite possible permutations of how to film Anne's arrival and Cecile's response to it – key elements in the narrative – Preminger's decisions seem almost minimal, the camera seeming to offer us little more than clear and continuous access to the unfolding action. This is not to overlook the skill which lies behind the unobtrusive elegance of the camerawork or the aesthetic pleasure we can derive from the play of movement, colour and composition in the CinemaScope frame, but to indicate how the intricate levels of decision making involved in presenting this brief passage of action seem rendered almost natural and obvious, the problems Preminger is solving absorbed seamlessly into the single extended take.

One of the problems posed by this narrative moment is how to introduce Deborah Kerr, the only one of the film's stars we have not yet seen. This intersects with major narrative questions for the spectator: what will Anne be like; how will she interpret and respond to the presence of Elsa; how will Cecile (and then Raymond) negotiate the anticipated embarrassment brought about by his careless scattering of invitations? That Françoise Sagan's novel and Preminger's film are narrated by Cecile provides an apparently straightforward justification for anchoring our access to the action in Cecile's experience, and in the film as a whole Preminger accepts this logic by maintaining a pattern in which the spatial dimension of the film's point-of-view structure tends, with some significant exceptions, to follow Cecile. So in this sequence, as so often in the film, we begin with Cecile – rather than, for instance, cutting to Anne arriving in the car to find no welcoming party and then intercutting Cecile and Anne as they prepare to meet.

Introducing the scene via Cecile would still, however, be perfectly compatible with a highly edited treatment of the meeting. In choosing a single take, combining moving and static framing, and an elevated, somewhat distanced view, Preminger elaborates other dimensions of point of view, much less tied to Cecile. We observe from a distance rather than being taken into the space between the characters. Preserving spatial distance and holding the camera's static view for the greetings precludes the interpretative force a fragmented treatment could provide – where details of facial expression and gesture could be isolated for us. We observe the characters at full length within the location setting, watching them negotiate a meeting very much at odds with what they had expected. What we observe becomes the basis for inferences we draw about the characters' feelings and motives.

Such methods were central to the accounts of Preminger's work published in *Movie* in the early 1960s. Analysing Preminger's long takes, *Movie* writers celebrated his eschewing of overt 'direction', his avoidance of rhetorical devices, the complex balance of perspectives achieved by refusing – for example – the emphasis a close-up might provide. In Preminger's work staging the action was revealed as an area of creative decision making as much the domain of the director as editing or the pictorial qualities of the image. Observing the action, the spectator, as Ian Cameron wrote of *Bonjour Tristesse*, 'must actively make choices rather than passively accept those of the director' (1962: 22). Terms such as 'detachment', 'impartiality' and 'objectivity' were used to describe effects of Preminger's style.[1] Robin Wood even compared the strategies of *Exodus* to Brecht's *Verfremdungseffekt* (1962: 25).

Why return to Preminger and early *Movie* now? One reason for reassessing Preminger is provided by the appearance of *Bonjour Tristesse* and an increasing number of other Preminger movies in restored widescreen versions. The absence of good prints may be one reason why Preminger's major films of the later 1950s and 1960s – a number of them adaptations and most made in CinemaScope – which were at the heart of *Movie*'s discussion, are, as far as one can tell, rarely taught on film courses, and certainly rarely written about. Of the directors championed by *Movie*, Preminger is the one who has most completely disappeared from curricular and critical interest. Insofar as he is present in film courses and film criticism it is as a director of *films noir*.

Returning to Preminger and *Movie* together is also to reconnect with methods of critical analysis which were crucial in establishing serious and systematic English-language film criticism, especially of Hollywood cinema, in the 1960s, and which were initially attacked and then widely ignored in the elaborate political and methodological debates that characterised film studies in the decades following *Screen*'s transformation into a journal of high theory in the early 1970s. In particular, it seems important to argue for the continuing relevance of a detailed criticism which is attentive to the nuances of action, performance and setting, the constantly shifting texture of the drama in which tone, vocal inflection, gesture and posture combine significantly with the words spoken and the multiple elements of mise-en-scène. In film theory, one of the saddest effects of David Bordwell, Janet Staiger and Kristin Thompson's monumental work, *The Classical Hollywood Cinema*, has been to create an influential paradigm of causality (as the 'armature of the classical story') which tends to make such complex dramatic and human interaction little more than incidental detail to the main event of driving the narrative machine (Bordwell, Staiger and Thompson 1985: 13). Preminger is one Hollywood director among many who can offer a corrective to these views. Returning to *Movie* as a crucial reference point in this work is not about trying to turn back the clock, but about staking a claim for these forms of analysis as an indispensable basis for reasoned film criticism. As the analysis of the sequence develops, a further range of issues provoked by Preminger's methods will emerge.

Cecile's movement, the tails of the open shirt she is wearing over her swimsuit flowing in her wake, is brought prematurely to a halt at the front of the car as she realises Anne is alone. Anne, more formally dressed in a highly fashionable, pale cream bucket dress, pauses at the edge of the shade by the car's rear wheel. Her appearance is striking and hints, without offering insight or information, at the drama played out as she prepared for her journey and her arrival. We already know that Anne is a fashion designer, and her costume invites speculation about the impression she wishes to make by arriving in a dress made more for city than country and which is in marked contrast to the informal daytime wear of the other characters. After the long drive from Paris we might expect a little crumple or fatigue. Does her impeccable appearance signal that she has changed for the final stage of the journey? Preminger's method requires us first to find Anne's costume significant, then to connect it to what we have been told about her and to our understanding of the broader situation – processes of observation, inference and speculation that are crucial to his development of our point of view on the action.

'Thank you, Cecile', replies Anne to Cecile's greeting, posing briefly, with a smiling inclination of her head, half a bow, in a humorous but slightly awkward response to the air of formality in Cecile's sudden halt and 'Welcome'. Both women seem to be improvising ways of dealing with a one-to-one meeting that neither of them anticipated but which for Cecile alone is informed by the prospective embarrassment of the situation. Cecile's dilemma is wonderfully dramatised in the exuberance of her rush to welcome the three people she is expecting (a child welcoming the grown-ups back), suddenly deflated as she sees Anne alone, and her struggle to adopt a more 'proper' mode of welcome. Behind this we might interpret her immediate recognition that Anne doesn't yet know about Elsa (she would if she had been met at the station) and that Cecile doesn't quite know what to do. This seems a major determinant of the way she acts over the next few minutes but there may be other reasons, signalled to us by Anne's appearance, why Cecile would not feel comfortable greeting her with puppy-like enthusiasm. Anne, on the other hand, is expecting Raymond to be there to meet her and is faced with his teenage daughter. Nor can the women mediate any unease in their first meeting through the presence of Raymond. These things crucially inflect the expression of pleasure – which may still be genuinely felt – in their meeting.

They pause. Then Anne half laughs, opens her arms, trips across the distance between them and hugs Cecile. 'Ahh ..., are you that grown up?' she rhetorically enquires, holding Cecile by the shoulders.

Our view enables us to see that the warmth and spontaneity being reached for, a little uneasily, by Anne are met by Cecile with legs rooted to the ground rather than moving forward, only her upper body angling towards Anne to respond to the embrace. Then Cecile becomes more animated, perhaps an acknowledgement of the reticence of her behaviour so far. 'Really welcome,' she says and kisses Anne on one cheek. 'And really thank you,' replies Anne, picking up playfully on the language in which Cecile enacts her self-consciousness in having to play the hostess, before kissing Cecile on the cheek in return.

The kisses have nothing of the conventional ease of a continental greeting, a mode readily available to Preminger since both characters are French. Anne even makes an audible 'mwah' when she kisses Cecile, as if she is negotiating the twin perils at this moment of the merely conventional gesture and overemphatic affection. The willed sincerity of Cecile's 'Really welcome' and of Anne's reiteration of the word also colours our sense of the attempted warmth of the exchange.

This tiny encounter is much more difficult to describe than to understand as we watch the film. Even at a first viewing we are likely to register the undercurrents that shadow the meeting and which find expression in the details of performance. We bring to bear our everyday skills of interpreting social situations, body language, tone of voice, in a largely intuitive process of moment-by-moment interpretation. The point of a detailed account is not therefore to bring out hidden meanings but to make explicit what Preminger's performers enact and what his direction presents to us without interpretative emphasis. We are scarcely aware of the skill involved in creating what we see and hear. Equally, we are barely conscious of the intricate processes of interpretation in which we engage as we attempt to understand the drama being played out.

In this account, we have taken qualities of performance to be central to the meanings generated by Preminger's staging of the scene, and one informing issue about performance in the film can usefully be taken up here. We have emphasised an undercurrent of unease in the character's responses to each other and indicated aspects of the wider situation that might lie behind it. We have wanted to avoid simple binary ways of understanding what is going on – as in spontaneous warmth and pleasure vs. insincere expressions of the same – in favour of a less rigid interpretation of the women's feelings and motives. In putting considerable pressure on the details of performance we have tacitly assumed these to be precise and meaningful. What might be thought of as the somewhat 'stilted' nature of the exchange we have attributed to the characters, not to inadequately realised performance.

This is a fundamental matter for our understanding of the film as a whole. Perhaps most obviously in Deborah Kerr's and Jean Seberg's vocal delivery, there are qualities that might more generally be described as 'stilted', an apparent lack of ease, something willed and lacking the fluency of thought or feeling directly and confidently expressed, that could be mistaken for deficient acting. A number of reviews were in fact very critical of the actors and particularly of Jean Seberg, taking the signs of unease or awkwardness to be symptoms of inadequate performance and, by extension, of Preminger's insecure grip on his project.[2] On the other hand, thought of, as in our account of Anne's arrival, as mannerisms of the characters rather than the actors, these things can be understood as signifying precisely a *performance* of roles and feelings – not exactly insincerity, but an assertiveness, as of feelings and ideas not entirely internalised or not conveying complete conviction. As Anne and Cecile meet, the hesitancy of the moment might suggest an initial desire for intimacy (or a desire for at least a convincing performance of intimacy) that can't quite be willed into realisation.

These thoughts are also relevant, though in a very different register, to David Niven's Raymond, but significantly *not* to Mylene Demongeot's Elsa, a performance used very precisely by Preminger to contrast with the those of the other stars. Elsa acts and expresses feelings in ways that carry the conviction of spontaneity. Cecile, Raymond and Anne are acted in registers that richly imply characters who are, much if not all of the time, performing to each other and to themselves, performing happiness, performing confidence, performing affection, so that this becomes an informing feature of the drama and a major subject of the film. This is particularly crucial for an interpretation of the film's construction of Cecile and an understanding of how Preminger directs Jean Seberg. In her characterisation suggestions of awkwardness are perfectly attuned by Preminger to the expression of the performative qualities in a character whose assertions of feeling and understanding, and whose self-dramatising responses to events, are central to the film's structure of point of view.

As with so many aspects of the film, however, these qualities of performance are present but not insisted upon. We may barely recognise the skill of the performances or even, like some reviewers, take it for an absence of skill. Preminger's unwillingness to provide signposts for the spectator inevitably allows the possibility of such varied interpretations, the discretion involved here intimately bound up with Preminger's direction of the camera, notably the frequent use of long takes and framings that often keep us at some little distance from the action.

Following their greeting the pair walk to the terrace to see the view, moving to the left of the static frame. After a cut, the camera tracks alongside them, right to left, again our view partially interrupted by three smaller agaves, until they reach the front of the terrace where characters and camera come to rest. As they move and talk, both women are still carefully negotiating their unexpected situation.

(As they walk.)

CECILE: How did your new collection go?

ANNE: Oh extremely well, but I wish I could have found some material the colour of this water, Mmm! D'you know I spent my honeymoon by the sea, twelve years ago.

CECILE: Did you like it? *(Laughs, they look at each other.)* I mean the place.

(They stop.)

ANNE: Yes, I liked both it and the place, although it wasn't nearly as lovely as this. *(Anne removes a cigarette case from her pocket.)* Do you know, I had quite a debate with myself before coming down here. I'm delighted I lost.

CECILE: I'll fetch your things. *(She attempts to walk past Anne, but Anne catches her arm and returns her to her original position.)*

ANNE: What's the matter, Cecile?

CECILE: Nothing. Why?

ANNE: You're embarrassed.

CECILE: There's nothing, Anne. (*Anne lets go of Cecile's arm and continues playing with her cigarette case, eventually removing a cigarette.*)

ANNE: All right, may I take a guess? You're annoyed that Raymond isn't on hand to spread a red welcome carpet. (*Cecile ties the two ends of her shirt together.*)

CECILE: Oh, he's spreading it, with flowers, only he's spreading it at the station.

ANNE: But I wired I was driving.

CECILE: You wired?

ANNE: Oh yes, you know I wouldn't decide to drive and not send word. Now where do you suppose that telegram is?

CECILE: In one of his pockets, unopened. (*Calls.*) Albertine ... I mean Leontine. (*To Anne.*) Slight maid problem – some weird sisters rotate working for us.

ANNE: Weird? How?

CECILE: Every week one or the other is suddenly stricken with some odd malady. Maybe it's us. (*Anne finally lights her cigarette, although we don't see her draw upon it until much later. There is a cut to a view of the maid approaching in the shadow of the house. The camera pans right with her until all three are in frame, Anne in the middle, and the camera's position offers a reverse angle to the previous shot.*)

CLAUDINE: Yes, Mademoiselle.

CECILE: Oh, Leontine ...

CLAUDINE: (*Appearing out of the shadow.*) Leontine has the bad liver. I am her sister Claudine.

CECILE: Oh, well, Claudine, did a telegram come today?

CLAUDINE: I handed it to Monsieur himself.

ANNE: Didn't he read it?

CLAUDINE: Do you know him, Madame?

ANNE: There are some bags by my car, will you please take them to my room.

CLAUDINE: Yes, Madame. (*She withdraws.*)

ANNE: Where is my room?

CECILE: We can go this way.

(*The shot continues, as does the conversation, with the camera tracking in front of the characters as they walk down the terrace along the front of the house, and then panning left to follow them until they reach the door to Anne's room.*)

What Anne finds to talk about immediately is her honeymoon, perhaps inno-
cently put in mind of it by the place, or more complexly, put in mind of it by
her situation. The association between the view and her honeymoon might be
understood to suggest, despite her very proper appearance, that she understands Raymond's invitation as implying a sexual relationship, but that this is
immediately associated in her mind with marriage. With a little hindsight her
conversation can also be interpreted as a veiled announcement to Cecile that
what has brought her here is the thought of marriage. Such connotations find
some support in the lines about being glad that she lost the battle with herself,
in which Anne identifies herself with her super-ego ('I'm glad I lost'). If this
were no more than a holiday, why would it generate such an internal debate?

As Ian Cameron observes, 'almost every action in the film is capable of at
least two interpretations on the level of motivation' (1962: 22). Moments of
business and details of performance are often enigmatic but richly suggestive.
Why, for instance, does Anne play with, and eventually smoke, her cigarette?
Smoking might signify in this context relief at the end of a long journey, the
beginnings of relaxation. Here, she seems to need something to do with her
hands, so that preparing to smoke acts as a claim of bodily ease which instead
signals its absence. Several explanations could account for her actions, none
of which preclude the others: is she anxious, despite her assertion, that
she has lost the battle with herself; or disturbed that Raymond appears less
engaged in the fact of her visit than she would like; or nervous because she is
announcing her intentions to Cecile?

When Anne claims to understand that Cecile is embarrassed and proffers
an explanation it is one moment of many in the film in which characters
assert an understanding of the motives of others which is plainly not available to them. Cecile may be embarrassed or not, but we can also understand
Anne to be denying her own unease by projecting it onto Cecile. Again, what
lies behind this could be implied by her introduction of Raymond's absence
into the conversation: she won't ask where he is because that would be to
display concern, so she introduces the topic less directly and in relation not
to herself but to Cecile.

Crucially, Preminger's treatment of the scene makes accessible this complex of possibilities but we arrive at them, or others, by trying out hypotheses
based on what he presents. The action is filmed in another extended take
with a camera that moves with the characters but is again also static for
a considerable proportion of its length. It is a method that requires the performances to develop in relatively long stretches, preserving their continuity,
and that defines our relationship to the action and characters as one of
observation, requiring us to assess the characters as they act and react in real
time, keeping us outside the action while holding the characters in frame
together and without spatial bias towards either.

A related (and remarkable) decision is not to show us the view, the initial topic of conversation and evidently one of the glories of the villa. This could seem an obvious point at which to enable us and Anne momentarily to revel in Mediterranean sun and sea and for the filmmaker to make the most of the location setting. Preminger refuses the temptation, denying us the visual pleasure and, crucially, refusing to allow Anne's experience and ours to coincide. Instead, he invites us to observe and interpret the women's behaviour. Taking Anne to look at the view is perhaps Cecile's way of handling the tricky social situation but it is not the subject of the scene. By the end of these three shots we have travelled the length of the terrace without once being directly shown the prospect it provides, although distant views of the sea appear as background to the action at two different points in the third shot. Authenticity of location is important, especially *because* the evidently spectacular nature of the setting is not being exploited. But what is crucial for the scene is that our view of the characters' interaction should be minimally interrupted, their responses to the situation held within the continuous time and space of the long takes.

A further strategy employed in the shot that begins with the maid's entrance is the composition of the CinemaScope frame with three characters arranged across it, a method of staging which forms one of the film's key visual patterns. The composition favours the character in the middle and makes the central drama of the moment that character's response to the other two. In this example we see Anne first give a smile of complicity to Cecile as Claudine's identification of herself confirms Cecile's account of the weird sisters, but then fire a glance of genuine anxiety in her direction when Claudine questions Anne's knowledge of Raymond (Figure 7.2). Anne's response to this is to order Claudine to fetch her belongings from the car: she

7.2 *Bonjour Tristesse* (Otto Preminger, 1958)

regains her poise by exerting class privilege. The movement, though not the shot, concludes with Anne again looking to Cecile to join her in a shared superiority to Claudine. The shot itself continues with the track along the terrace, maintaining the uninterrupted scrutiny of Anne and Cecile until they enter the villa.

Much of what we have been arguing relates directly to what *Movie* calls Preminger's 'objectivity', his 'aim to present characters, actions, and issues clearly and without prejudice', 'to show events, not to demonstrate his feelings about them' (Editors of *Movie* 1962: 11). As we are seeing, the access Preminger gives us to his characters is in some ways extremely restricted. One way of putting this would be to say that Preminger places us epistemologically in relation to the characters in something of the way they are placed in relation to each other – except, of course, that for us they are characters seen through Preminger's direction, both of the actors and of the camera. But what we see of them is what they do. Another way of getting at this is that Preminger's method doesn't imply either a claim to *know* his characters, especially to know exactly what motivates them to act as they do, or an invitation to us to think that we can know them.

The scene continues without a cut as Cecile takes Anne along the terrace to her room (previously Raymond's). What follows inside the villa maintains and develops the sense of the characters struggling to appear at ease with one another and the associated sense of overinsistence in their behaviour (particularly Cecile's) which betrays its nature as a performance. But two issues so far implicit or unacknowledged – Anne's motherliness towards Cecile and the presence of Elsa – now become central. There is also a distinct difference between Preminger's handling of the interior action and his staging of the exterior shots, the increase in editing, in particular, marking a significant shift from the film's dominant visual strategies and a new dimension to the drama.

The scene in the bedroom is one of three between Anne and Cecile (and only four in the film) in which Preminger uses versions of reverse field cutting, which have the conventional (but in their context here highly expressive) effect of spatially separating and opposing the characters.[3] Selective use of the most familiar method of filming dialogue becomes a focused and self-conscious decision, given its specific significance by the wider context in which it is avoided, the visual separation between the two women enacting a central aspect of the drama.

In this scene, which lasts approximately two minutes forty seconds, there are fourteen shots, as opposed to the previous two minutes seventeen seconds since Anne's arrival in which there were just three. When the women enter the villa Preminger begins by maintaining the use of long takes, with two extended, mobile shots, lasting sixty-five seconds, in which Anne begins to explore the room, the maid brings in the luggage and Cecile opens the dress box containing the present Anne has brought her. Even here, though, the cut between these two shots is used to underline an early stage of the tension between Cecile and Anne that will be central to the rest of the scene. When Cecile announces that she has 'flunked' her exams she leaves the frame to open the door to the maid and Preminger cuts from Anne to Cecile as Anne repeats the word interrogatively. The cutting becomes more rapid when Anne responds sharply to the 'vulgarity' of Cecile's claim that she can 'always get a man to look after me', and 'you don't need a diploma for that!' From the first separate shot of Cecile (the fourth shot indoors), which shows her after Anne's 'vulgarity' speech, Preminger establishes a pattern in which every other shot is of Cecile alone, a total of six of the fourteen shots.

The introduction of this form of scene dissection obviously changes our orientation to the action. Instead of seeing the characters largely in the same frame and from a certain distance, Preminger now cuts into the space between them, guiding our attention much more emphatically than he chose to in the long takes. The key example of this is the very unusual close-up of Anne at the moment at which Cecile reveals that Elsa is also a guest at the villa. Preminger cuts to a close-up of Anne's head, initially with its back to us (and therefore to Cecile) but then turning into left profile and, briefly, almost into full face, before turning away again (Figure 7.3). Such tight shots, extremely rare in the film, are confined to Anne's crisis moments. (The later ones are used when Anne overhears Raymond making love to Elsa and making disparaging reference to Anne's age and when, seconds later, she is in her car, on the point of departure.) This is transparently a spatially privileged view, in which the scale and intimacy of the shot accentuate the intensity of Anne's reaction and the breakdown of the self-possession and control which have so

7.3 *Bonjour Tristesse* (Otto Preminger, 1958)

far characterised her appearance. It seems, more decisively even than the preceding scene dissection, to mark a break with the prevailing detachment and cognitive restriction of Preminger's presentation of the action.

Two issues about the spectator's position here seem important for a discussion of how this privileged moment fits into the film's overall control of epistemic access to motive and feeling. The first is that we witness Anne's reaction separately from Cecile. We are positioned in such a way as to make us more acutely aware of the effect of Cecile's words than she is herself. Our close association with Cecile as narrator and protagonist is inflected, here as elsewhere, by perspectives carefully differentiated from hers. The second is that the spatial privilege of the close up is not sustained. Preminger rapidly cuts back to Cecile, who continues speaking until brought to a halt by the off-screen smashing of a vase. Instead of returning to Anne's face, Preminger then cuts to the vase on the floor and follows Anne into the inner room by tilting up so that we see only her back as she disappears. Another shot of Cecile precedes Anne's return, framed in medium shot but seen only in partial profile, her face largely hidden from us. Rather than enabling us to register exactly what Anne might be feeling by providing sustained access to her facial expression following Cecile's words, our view is limited. The intimacy of the close-up vividly shows the collapse of Anne's apparent self-possession, but we still have to reach, on the basis of the limited view we are given, for what exactly lies behind her reaction and the outburst that follows.

Preminger's refusal to accompany the spatial privilege of the close-up with a lifting of cognitive restriction corresponds to his treatment of Cecile in this exchange. Cecile has been occupying herself with the new dress, but when Preminger cuts back to her, just before she mentions Elsa, we discover Cecile looking out of frame at Anne. The directness of Cecile's look suggests that she is aware of the significance of the moment, the attempted lightness of her tone belied by her posture. The implication may be that in choosing to make this revelation Cecile is going onto the attack, paying Anne back for her maternalism. But rather than using cutting to clarify Cecile's motive by showing us the moment at which she turns towards Anne, the movement is withheld from us, her decision taken when we are looking in the other direction. At the same time Seberg's performance does not offer us conclusive insight, its restraint requiring us to attend carefully to what might underlie Cecile's actions.

The ambiguity that Preminger has created for the spectator around Anne and Cecile's motives is paralleled by the predicament of the characters in the next scene, when Anne's reaction itself becomes the subject of exchange, seconds later, between Cecile and Raymond, talking across the baffled Elsa, as they trade enigmatic questions and replies about Anne, each claiming to know more than the other. The enigma intensifies, for them and for us, when

Anne, apparently perfectly composed, then reappears on the terrace, dressed for swimming, announcing she is 'fine' and 'delighted to be here'.

Anne's entrance further emphasises the prevalence of 'performance' as the way in which these characters present themselves and reinforces the sense that her outburst had momentarily fractured a very carefully controlled social image. Juxtaposed with her 'breakdown', her sunny reappearance intensifies the impression that Anne's persona may be a be a form of self-protection. But equally, it poses very starkly the problem that faces the characters and the spectator, of how to understand the surfaces people in the film present to others.

These restrictions are crucial but not flaunted. We can take what we see to be pretty straightforward. But it is through the limits that Preminger places on our access to the drama that we can connect the insights of early *Movie* to strands of work in contemporary film theory and criticism concerned with significant variations of narration in the Hollywood cinema of the studio period. One framework for thinking about Preminger's method is what George M. Wilson calls, in *Narration in Light*, 'modes of nonomniscience' (Wilson, 1986: 82). Preminger is not one of Wilson's examples, though he could easily be. It is often the case, as Wilson suggests, that we can too readily assume in watching Hollywood movies that the events we witness are explicable and that we understand or are meant to understand them (or that we understand them enough, as much as is necessary). The many examples of restricted narration in Hollywood cinema challenge this assumption and we share Wilson's view that an urgent task of criticism is to identify and interpret these versions of nonomniscience – the various ways in which our access to the fictional world can be meaningfully (but not always obviously) restricted.

The film's epistemic restrictions have no parallel in Sagan's novel – they are the result of Preminger's systematic approach to the realisation of individual scenes, set within an adaptation that significantly complicates narrative authority. The novel is narrated by Cecile, looking back (not very far) at events of the summer when she was seventeen. Cecile's narration means that we have access to the story only through her voice and therefore we have only her version and interpretation of the events and of the characters. It may be implied that Cecile's view is a partial one and that her understanding is limited but we have no other version to compare with hers. In the film Cecile narrates in voice-over, so that in one way the film still offers the story as her account; but, as we have seen, the visuals do not attempt to reflect Cecile's subjectivity. In fact, quite the reverse. Although the film's presentation of its events can seem unproblematic (even 'transparent') what we see offers an alternative to Cecile's account, so that we are shown both Cecile herself and the wider context independently of her view. Although we see few events at which Cecile is not present (there are isolated moments and one extended scene), our orientation to the scenes which we share with her is quite distinct from hers. Preminger establishes the basis, in other words, for a significant tension between verbal and visual narration. The 'objectivity' of Preminger's style acts as an implicit corrective to the claims of Cecile's voice-over.

Another decision in the adaptation which crucially affects the film's *placing* of Cecile and her account is the invention of sequences (photographed in black and white) representing Cecile and Raymond's life in Paris since Anne's death. This has no parallel in the book, in which only the last page or two deal with their lives after Anne. (Both book and film withhold the fact of Anne's death until it happens within Cecile's telling of the story.) Cecile's voice-over begins in Paris, but well before we hear her narration we have seen her apparent emotional disengagement from the luxurious but empty society existence she shares with her father. The film moves into the past from this colourless present and our guide is a young woman who offers herself to us as emotionally null, but who we see is perfectly capable of more or less convincing performances of enthusiasm and interest when the occasion demands.

The first transition from present to past can indicate something of what is involved. Cecile is in a night club with her father, his date and a young man who is romantically interested in Cecile. As Jacques and Cecile dance to the title song, Cecile's voice is heard.

> And after the races he'll take me to dinner and dancing again. And on Thursday to the tennis matches, the country. What a waste of time, dear Jacques, what a hopeless waste of time!
>
> . . .
>
> He's attractive and he's nice. And I'd like to warn him but he wouldn't understand. That I can't feel anything he might be interested in. Because I'm surrounded by a wall, an invisible wall made of memories which I can't lose.
>
> . . .
>
> (*Cecile is now dancing with Raymond.*)
> But even with my father it isn't the same any more. Nothing is. Will I ever be happy again, as I was at the beginning of that wonderful summer?

The assertion of emotional disengagement from the life around her and Cecile's dramatisation of her state of mind ('What a waste of time, dear Jacques, what a hopeless waste of time!') are clear from the lines themselves. But doubts about Cecile's reliability as a storyteller are implied here less by what she says than by qualities of performance, and notably tone of voice (the quality we identified in the earlier discussion as signalling the film's creation of characters who *perform* to themselves and others). The issue of performance is foregrounded in this scene by Juliette Greco's singing of the title song and the cutting back and forth from the singer *performing* melancholy to Cecile's blank face. When the voice-over begins, the language and the self-dramatising delivery of the lines are perfect complements to the song, performing 'tristesse' in another register. This is a young woman who sees herself as a character in a tragic drama, self-consciously creating and playing out a role. It is significant in this respect that on four occasions in the film, including three in the black-and-white scenes in the narrative present, Preminger stages moments of reflection for Cecile as she looks at herself in a mirror. As Ian Cameron observes in *Movie*, 'It is as if she were trying to explain her actions to a psychiatrist or a detective. We do not have to accept all her evidence' (1962: 22).

The film makes Cecile an unreliable narrator.[4] This is not to say that she is shown to be a liar or to be consistently wrong-headed but that the film enables us to question her account of events and her claims to understand herself and others. Remarks made both in the voice-over ('even the maids were happy') and in conversation ('Raymond picked the flowers himself, and cut them himself, and even arranged them himself. Isn't he sweet?') sound overinsistent and are sometimes directly contradicted by other evidence (the sisters are created in ways that do not seem intended to convey 'happy'). These are elements of a more general pattern in the presentation of Cecile. Preminger finds ways of suggesting that she copies the behaviour of the adults – not only Raymond, as Anne at one point suggests, but also Anne herself. Examples include the way that Cecile kisses Phillipe at the dance on the Quay, inspired by Raymond and Anne's embrace of moments before, and the way in which she works herself up into a frenzy of admiration for Anne before passionately falling to the ground with Phillipe. But again it is important not to overstate the emphasis these elements are given. They are part of the delicate balance that the film achieves – elements which we can observe and synthesise but which do not dominate – in its dramatic and thematic structure as well as in its mise-en-scène.

One other issue about the adaptation is also crucial as a framework for interpretation. The film's treatment of the father/daughter relationship is rather different to the book's. In the book, for instance, there is much less sense of the regularity with which Cecile and Raymond go on their summer holidays with Raymond's latest mistress. The film both accentuates this and makes clear in dialogue how crucial it is for Raymond that Cecile should be on holiday with him. This is one part of the film's presentation of Raymond as (in Ian Cameron's words) 'most unfatherly' (1962: 22) and of the relationship as bordering on the incestuous. The film makes much more readily available than does the book the interpretation that Raymond invites young women on holiday, in part, as a kind of cover for being with his daughter (though the film at no point suggests that either Raymond or Cecile is straight-forwardly conscious of this). This interpretation of the central relationship, and the (unconscious?) feelings for her father that it might imply in Cecile, is another element in the argument that we should understand Cecile as an unreliable witness.[5]

This has been a deliberately restricted approach to the film, focusing only on a handful of shots in one short episode. Clearly, our hope is that the detail analysed here is reasonably representative and that the motifs and methods discussed can be traced across the film. But the intention has also been to argue for an approach that begins with details, argues for the significant interrelationship of the film's decision making, and locates in this detail the route to the significance of wider decisions in the adaptation. There is no inevitable route or method to productive critical analysis but we have wanted to suggest that, as we organise our insights and responses and begin to develop an argument, rooting the process in observed detail is a way of ensuring that we respect both the choices made by the filmmakers and the way in which these have shaped our encounter with the film.

Central to the argument have been some observations about the film's relationship to the original novel. In a different context *Bonjour Tristesse* could be used to exemplify how in a skilful adaptation of a novel to the screen fidelity and transformation can go hand in hand. Preminger's film retells Sagan's tale but changes and enriches it, notably through the ways in which Cecile's narrating voice becomes subject to perspectives developed by Preminger's methods of creating and presenting the film's world and its people.

But we have also wanted to argue that Preminger does not substitute his own authority for Cecile's unreliability. His method maintains a crucial epistemic distance, showing us the characters but not implying that he can know them. There is no bedrock of secure insight into feeling or thought. Part of what is involved here may also be an implication that many of these characters do not (cannot?) know themselves. Even Cecile's narration, which could potentially offer access to an authentic inner life, is demonstrably a dramatisation of the self. These limits align the film with the scepticism which characterises a good deal of modernist narrative, a refusal to claim unrestricted knowledge of the world or the self.

One major consequence of Preminger's method is, therefore, to place huge importance on the ways in which character is presented to us through the actors' performances. They are all we have. We are placed in relation to char-acters in ways that parallel those by which in our lives the self is placed in relation to others. This is why we have laid so much emphasis on qualities of performance and on trying to draw out what they might imply. Preminger presents the interaction between these 'people' and we try to grasp the social and psychological complexities that underlie their actions and words. Recognition of the fundamental importance of character, and the human complexity that it can dramatise – ideas that have received little sympathetic attention in recent film theory – is therefore central to Preminger's cinema and to the response it invites.

In turn these thoughts underpin our sense that understanding the film is inescapably to be involved in very close reading. This is not only to argue that there is nothing useful that can be said about the film that does not rest on the detail of the world and events the film presents and on its way of presenting them, but also that these things only take on significance through interpretation. We have argued that interpreting the film involves recognising the play of action and reaction between characters, which in turn opens possible perspectives on various levels of motive and feeling. This process is also inescapably one of analysing and interpreting Preminger's direction – the material decisions that create characters and an inhabitable world.

But interpretation of this kind is also inevitably an insecure and uncertain process. If Preminger refuses to claim the traditional authority of knowing his characters, he does not intend to offer the spectator a more secure or unrestricted viewing position. As we do in our everyday lives, when we watch the film we have to rely on accumulated experience of ourselves and others to intuit what might lie behind what we see and hear. The insights and hypotheses we develop about the film's dramatic world may be supported or undermined by further evidence accumulated as the film proceeds. Such evidence, systematised, is also the basis of critical argument, the process of proposing and developing lines of interpretation. These are processes that involve possibilities, sometimes probabilities, but rarely certainties.

Notes

1   Mayersberg 1963: 31; etc.
2   For example, the reviewer in *Variety* (15 Jan. 1958) claims that 'Script deficiencies and awkward reading – some lines are spoken as though just that – they are being read – have static results', and that 'As the more conventional of the principal characters, Miss Kerr has looks and poise but there are instances when she, too, has difficulty with the stiltedness of the dialog.' Similarly, *Monthly Film Bulletin* opines, 'Jean Seberg, who speaks rather than acts her lines, turns in the least effective performance', *Monthly Film Bulletin*, 25, 292 (May 1958), 55.
3   The other occasions involving Anne and Cecile are when Anne talks to/at Cecile after she and Raymond have spent the night together and announced their engagement, and later when Cecile creeps onto the terrace after an illicit visit to the bedroom of her boyfriend Phillipe, a scene which answers Anne's arrival, and in

which it is Cecile who goes through the actions of smoking a cigarette. The fourth
example is the final scene in Cecile's bedroom, between her and Raymond.
4   Preminger's interest in unreliable narrators and untrustworthy protagonists goes
    back at least as far as *Laura* (1944).
5   A number of reviewers commented on the incestuous undercurrents in the film
    and it is also picked up in the more recent entry in *The Time Out Film Guide*,
    which begins: 'The flirtation with incest at the centre of this adaptation of Françoise
    Sagan's novel is tame by modern standards' (Milne 1993: 83).

References

Bordwell, D., J. Staiger and K. Thompson (1985) *The Classical Hollywood Cinema:
   Film Style and Mode of Production to 1960* (London: Methuen).
Cameron, I. (1962) '*Bonjour Tristesse*', *Movie*, 2, 22.
Editors of *Movie* (1962) 'Why Preminger?', *Movie*, 2, 11.
Mayersberg, P. (1963) 'The Trial of Joan of Arc', *Movie*, 7, 30–2.
Milne, T. (ed.) (1993) *The Time Out Film Guide*, 3rd edn (London: Penguin).
Wilson, G. M. (1986) *Narration in Light* (Baltimore: Johns Hopkins University Press).
Wood, R. (1962) '*Exodus*', *Movie*, 2, 24–5.

8

Meaning and value in *The Jazz Singer* (Alan Crosland, 1927)

Corin Willis

The Jazz Singer is not a film which generally features in discussions of cinema art. In the 2002 *Sight and Sound* poll of the 'ten greatest films' it failed to attract a single vote from the hundreds of directors and critics consulted. The meaning that the film has, its place in popular memory, arises from the material conditions of its production, from its status as the first talking picture. In more recent times the sense of *The Jazz Singer* as a film defined by its context has been compounded by the attention which has been paid to Al Jolson's use of blackface. The film is a key reference point in debates on Hollywood's representation of race. Rogin (1996), Taylor (1996) and Gubar (1997), for example, all establish the parameters of racial representation in early Hollywood by moving from a consideration of blackface in D. W. Griffith's *The Birth of a Nation* (1915) to its use in *The Jazz Singer*.

My research interest in blackface motivated my first viewing of the film. My PhD used textual analysis of blackface scenes as a means of understanding the textual formation of racial stereotypes in early sound film. *The Jazz Singer* confounded the expectations that I brought to it and presented a challenge to my methodology of 'reading' the nature of Hollywood's racial representation from its use of blackface. In contrast to the racial jokes and innuendo brought out in its subsequent persistence in early sound film, blackface imagery in *The Jazz Singer* is at the core of the film's central theme, an expressive and artistic exploration of the notion of duplicity and ethnic hybridity within American identity. Of the more than seventy examples of blackface in early sound film 1927–53 that I have viewed (including the nine blackface appearances Jolson subsequently made), *The Jazz Singer* is unique in that it is the only film where blackface is central to narrative development and thematic expression. It is for this reason that in spite of, or indeed *because* of, its employment of the primary racial signifier in American popular culture, *The Jazz Singer* should be valued as a film with its own distinct and rich meanings. This chapter attempts to uncover the long-overlooked expressivity and value of the film, showing how it retains the ability to challenge preconceptions and undermine prefabricated theory.

The blackface dressing–room sequence

Blackface first appears in the dressing-room sequence two thirds of the way through the film, at a time when the central narrative theme, the duplicitous identity of Jakie Rabinowitz/Jack Robin, is delicately poised. Jakie runs away from his cantor father and his ethnicity by taking on a non-Jewish name, Jack Robin, to pursue his show-business ambitions. He returns to New York as an adult to take up a chance in a Broadway show. Jack fails to reconcile with his father, who rejects him because of his new identity and life as a 'jazz' singer.

Jack's father falls ill and a synagogue elder, Yudelson, calls at the theatre and asks Jack to take the cantor's role and sing 'Kol Nidre' on the following day, the day of Atonement. Jack refuses because the show is due to open at the same time. The scenes before the dressing-room sequence switch between the Jewish world of the synagogue, Jack's parents' home and the secular world of the stage. Jack is alternatively referred to as 'Jakie' and 'Jack' and the film clearly sets up a dilemma: his identity is at the crossroads between his Jewish past and an American future as a stage performer.

The opening of the dressing-room sequence apparently resolves this enigma. Jack has told Yudelson that 'We in show business have our religion too ... the *show must go on!*' and we see that he is dressed in black and preparing for the final dress rehearsal before the show that evening.[1] His co-star, Mary Dale, enters the dressing room to show him her shimmering stage costume. Mary notes his lack of enthusiasm but Jack assures her that he has nothing on his mind but being successful in the show. He turns to his mirror and begins to black up, an action which confirms his intention to be baptised into the world of Broadway. Now he turns to face Mary so as to display his finished 'costume' to her. A close-up captures Jack breaking into a broad grin and we see, for the first time in the film, the famed Jolson minstrel mask. For added effect the score breaks out into the strains of Jolson's most famous song, 'My Mammy', which is later used to close the film.

The coming together of the Jolson blackface brand in the film is cleverly timed to enhance the narrative impetus of Jack's attempts to move on and create a non-Jewish identity for himself as a Broadway star, but the way that the film manipulates the Jolson minstrel mask into a visual expression of the futility of Jack's actions is brilliantly effective. Jack's smile fades and, as the score abruptly switches from 'My Mammy' to mournful slower notes, he moves forward and his expression becomes sad and serious as he looks sorrowfully off-screen. As he leans forward a slight pan positions Jack's face against a photograph of Mary which lies behind him. Her white costume and the black background of the photograph produce a striking graphic similarity with the black skin/white mouth of Jack's minstrel mask. Now there is a cut to close-up of a photograph of his mother which reveals the motivation for Jack's look off-screen and the force which pulls him away from the involvement in Mary's world that the graphic similarity would seem to imply. The simple arrangement of two photographs on Jack's desk works to express the gulf that surrounds him, his Jewishness and Americanness, his past and his future. And now, placed in the middle of these emblematic photographs, the film has introduced its central visual expression of the impossibility of Jack reconciling his different parts into a unified identity.

Not for the first time in the film, the extra-textual meaning carried by Jolson the performer is tightly woven here into the narrative of *The Jazz Singer*. The Jolson act tapped into the minstrelsy which had been one of the most popular American entertainment forms of the nineteenth century. The oversized white mouth of the minstrel mask was intended to be seen from a distance as the grotesquely marked out lips of an African-American. And yet at the same time its artifice meant that the minstrel medium was shot through with a complex duplicity, the site of much critical debate in minstrel studies, in the way that it conjured up an aura of stereotyped blackness whilst at the same time registering the white performance of this blackness, a complexity neatly captured by Eric Lott's description of minstrelsy as 'the seeming counterfeit' (1995: 111). *The Jazz Singer* channels the cultural complexity inherent in the minstrel mask into a specific expression of the uncontainable split developing in Jack Robin's identity.

As the initial performative smile fades and Jack's mood becomes solemn, the audience is invited to look beyond the Jolson blackface brand dominating the surface of the screen and continue to watch the emotions of the character that Jolson plays inside the minstrel mask. Here the close-up framing is crucial in that the audience is constantly aware of Jack's own mouth inside the minstrel mouth. As Jack begins to 'break up' emotionally the close-up shots in the dressing-room sequence work to shatter the illusion of Jolson's minstrelsy, an illusion later preserved in the longer shots used to film the on-stage blackface songs in the following scenes. In the close-up fracturing of the Jolson minstrel mask *The Jazz Singer* succeeds in finding a rich cinematic expression for internal duplicity in human identity. Jack's attempt to cover over his problems by taking on his stage identity simply serves to bring his internal contradictions to the surface of the film.

Whilst the minstrel mask is transformed into a complex expression of Jack's duplicitous identity, its crude racial markings retain a strong visual presence which is also exploited for narrative purpose. Still in close-up, Jack turns back towards Mary and says, 'I'd love to sing for my people but I belong here'. He glances back at the picture of his mother and continues '– but there's something after all in my heart – maybe its the call of the ages – the cry of my race'. Now there is a cut to a longer shot and we see the Jack and Mary in the same frame together for the first time since he completed his minstrel costume. Mary attempts to hold Jack together as she says, 'No matter how strong the call, this is your life'. Nonetheless, the earlier affinity suggested in the graphic similarity of her photograph with Jack's minstrel mask has been lost and at the very mention of 'race' the film moves to a striking visualisation of racial difference with the screen split between her whiteness and his blackness.

Any evaluation of *The Jazz Singer* has, of course, to contend with the absent African-American signified by the minstrel mask. Meaning in this dressing-room sequence clearly resides in a 1920s understanding of the racial difference of African-Americans and in more specific stereotypes, such as the notion of the childlike emotionality of black males. Adopting the now classic line on nineteenth-century minstrelsy, where immigrant groups are seen to have accessed a white American identity through the performative demonstration of what they were *not*, Michael Rogin writes, 'The jazz singer rises by putting on the mask of a group that must remain immobile, unassimilable, and fixed at the bottom' (1996: 92). And yet the visual splitting of Jack from Mary in this shot would seem to suggest his affinity with racially marked African-Americans rather than his assimilation into whiteness. If indeed Jack's intention is to mask his ethnicity by becoming a stage performer then he has only succeeded in cracking open his racial difference. For, as the next few shots confirm, the real power of *The Jazz Singer* lies in its remarkably positive exposition and examination of 'racial' identities.

In fact, the film's counter-hegemonic stance in relation to the dominant racial ideology of the time was not without positive potential for the representation of African-Americans on the Hollywood screen. An added dimension to the expressive and thematic duplicity that the film draws from the minstrel mask is the splitting of blackface from its more unambiguous racial use in silent cinema as 'realistic' stand-in for African-Americans. This is something that Jim Pines highlights when he notes that Jack's 'blackface image functions more like a clown – in the circus sense – than an "artificial Negro" in the traditional movie sense' (1975: 17). *The Jazz Singer* did largely end the use of blackface as an 'unselfconscious method of impersonating African Americans' (Rogin 1996: 167) and yet no other film followed its lead in using it as an expressive signifier at the core of a film narrative. That the subsequent persistence of minstrel-derived blackface reverted to racial type, primarily through the pattern of on-screen co-presence with actual African-Americans, only serves to underline the 'unique' (Stanfield 1997: 409) nature of its use in *The Jazz Singer*.

8.1 *The Jazz Singer* (Alan Crosland, 1927)

Returning now to the film, Jack seems reassured and he and Mary cross to opposite sides of the room to inspect their costumes in different mirrors. Jack is shown from behind as he looks into the mirror, although we do not see his reflection. Jack's attempts to 'pull himself together' would seem to have succeeded since his dark top, wig and black neck momentarily work to hold the illusion of blackness that his disguise aimed to project. But a cut to a closer shot and tighter angle reveals the reflection of his broken minstrel mask once again (Figure 8.1). This shot perfectly illustrates *The Jazz Singer*'s formal splitting of the blackface medium. Jack's back profile remains in the right side of the frame and it continues to play with the racial currency involved in the use of blackface as 'realistic' replacement for African-Americans in silent cinema. At the same time, however, the left side of the frame is now dominated by the reflection of the minstrel mask, with Jack's own mouth prominently visible inside the minstrel mouth. Now, in the most significant moment of the film – one which reverberates through its entire narrative structure – Jack's fractured minstrel mask fades and the mirror frame becomes a vision of Jack's father singing in the synagogue (Figure 8.2). The film's emblematic use of the minstrel mask to strip away Jack's attempts at concealing his inner self is complete. The source of Jack's difference, his 'blackness', is revealed as an irreducible Jewishness. It may seem at this point, as superimposition formally splits an already reflected and fractured minstrel image, that Jack is hopelessly divided. However, at the same time as cracking open the contradiction of Jack's identity crisis, the revelation of the synagogue in the mirror points towards its resolution, as I will explain in returning to the dressing-room sequence later on.

8.2 *The Jazz Singer* (Alan Crosland, 1927)

A critical impasse in film studies

The blackface dressing-room sequence, and the mirror shot in particular, confounded my anticipated understanding of *The Jazz Singer*. Expecting confirmation that the first sound film established the basis for the racialised nature of the persistence of blackface in the early sound era, I found myself, like Jack Robin, staring at his reflection in the film, confronted with images of profound depth and complexity. And far from functioning as an unambiguous racial signifier blackface itself was the centre point of the film's extraordinary unpacking of accepted understandings of 'racial' identity which hinted at tension and contradiction within the normative whiteness so universal elsewhere on the Hollywood screen. I could not help but conclude that *The Jazz Singer* carries a certain aesthetic value, that it is not just a historic film but a 'good' one.

Contemporary film theory makes it difficult to evaluate any film, let alone one so visibly marked by the social and economic conditions of its production as *The Jazz Singer*. In this, film studies has been influenced by a broad methodological shift in the humanities against the notion of the text as a determining site of meaning, something that Stuart Hall has neatly described: 'since the "cultural turn" in the human and social sciences meaning is thought to be produced-constructed rather than simply found' (1997: 5). Specifically the effect of the 'cultural turn' can be seen in the way that the core issues addressed in film studies have swung away from questions of the 'text' to questions of the audience, as Dudley Andrew notes: 'the most advanced cultural critics have sold their stock in auteurs and even in texts, buying heavily into audiences and the cultures they comprise' (1993: 80). Textual analysis methods have generally been discounted in favour of methods which investigate the meaning of films in terms of their reception. In describing how reception studies have successfully debunked the notion of film 'as a container, holding immanent meaning' (1992: 8–9) Janet Staiger notes how for some exponents, 'reception studies eliminates the need to examine production since, they believe, meaning is produced by the reader' (1992: 3). In short, notions of value in film texts have become so fraught that there is often what amounts to a complete refusal to evaluate films at all.

There is growing recognition that such a stance towards the evaluation of films is problematic. Ava Preacher Collins has attempted to address the way in which film theory has 'neglected the issue of evaluation' (1993: 87). Though aligning herself strongly with 'the British culturalist turn to audience studies that challenged the privileging of text as a locus of stable and transcendent meaning production' (1993: 93), she voices concern that 'a film theory that has concentrated on the material conditions of production and reception of texts within specific cultural contexts [...] [has] not produced a corresponding transformation in the way we evaluate those texts' (1993: 87). Others have been more forthright in identifying the absence of evaluation as a fundamental blind spot in the study of film: 'The time has come for evaluation to walk side by side with elucidation' (Sarris 1998: 7).

Interestingly, evaluation of *The Jazz Singer* has a long history because of its status as the film which launched the sound era. In the decades after it was made the film remained, as Andrew Sarris (1977: 39) has noted, a point of attack for most film aestheticians who saw the introduction of sound as causing the death of 'pure cinema'. Today, as the title of Sarris's recent history of sound film – *You Ain't Heard Nothin' Yet* – indicates, *The Jazz Singer* remains a film to steal a line from, an emblem of the industrial shift from silent to sound cinema, rather than anything of intrinsic value. *The Jazz Singer* is seen as a film which was overrun by economic determinants as Warner Brothers used perhaps the world's most famous singing voice to promote Vitaphone technology in feature films. Charles Wolfe encapsulates this position in describing the film as a 'hybrid text' (1990: 67) which is divided between its silent sections and its use of sound technology.

Wolfe pays special attention to Jolson's introduction to the film in the 'Coffee Dan's' Vitaphone sequence set in a San Francisco cafe. Jolson sings two songs, 'Dirty Hands, Dirty Face' and 'Toot, Toot, Tootsie!' It is his banter between the songs, 'Wait a minute! Wait a minute – you ain't heard nothin yet!', which has been celebrated as the first synchronised speech in cinema. Wolfe argues that the Vitaphone process, which amongst other aspects involved a static multi-camera set-up and the direct vaudevillian address of Jolson's performative style, subverts and disrupts the narrative that has been established in the silent sections of the film.

William Lhamon has offered a radically different reading of the Coffee Dan's sequence which is worth pursuing because it indicates that, far from being economic considerations which had been pasted onto the film, Jolson's presence and the use of Vitaphone are central to narrative meaning in *The Jazz Singer*. Rather than disrupting the narrative, the song 'Dirty Hands, Dirty Face', Lhamon explains, is an extraordinary revelation of the entire narrative structure of the film because of Jolson's/Jack Robin's dramatic depiction and *performance* of a split identity. The words of the song reflect back on what has happened so far in the film and also point towards future events. Jack performs the persona of fatherly acceptance of a transgressive son who has 'Dirty Hands, Dirty Face'. Lhamon suggests that Jack's performance works to 'chastise' his own father and 'remakes' his own past where he had been rejected by his father because of his transgressions (1998: 106). The lyrics of the song also predict Robin's later transgression in the dressing room, where he apparently denies his father's final request to sing in the synagogue by 'dirtying' his hands and then his face, as he prepares to give his blackface performance on stage instead.

In fact, as Lhamon's account reveals, the song 'Dirty Hands, Dirty Face' is in quite beautifully crafted and structured dialogue with that central image later on in the film where, hopelessly split by the contradiction of his existence, the blackfaced Jack gazes at the vision of his father in the mirror. And here the song's invocation of the son as 'dirty' and transgressive and yet at the same time an 'angel of joy' even points to the eventual resolution of Jack's split identity at the end of the film. At this stage in the film, however, as the audience is introduced to the adult Jack Robin for the first time, this resolution does not seem possible. The Vitaphone introduction of Al Jolson in 'Dirty Hands, Dirty Face' powerfully captures the depth of *The Jazz Singer*'s depiction of the adult Jack Robin's split identity, which intensifies from this scene until it cracks open in the mirror shot later on: 'He is not an integrated personality but a mob of conflicts. He impersonates one character, then another. He is frankly speaking the contradictions within one self' (Lhamon 1998: 106). In noting that the cantor's presence is 'visible' (1998: 108) in Jack's performance Lhamon's account highlights how the song subtly registers what is so strongly visualised later in the mirror shot, the Jewish cantor 'inside' the jazz singer.

And yet Lhamon refuses to engage in any positive evaluation of the film itself. He attributes the rich meaning that he encounters in the number 'Dirty Hands, Dirty Face' and elsewhere in the film to the presence of a blackface performer. In Al Jolson Lhamon finds a particularly rich vessel for the socio-historical meaning of blackface performance: 'With helpful spurts from Vitaphone's synchronized sound, the lore Jolson enacted was overwhelming. It took over the film's weak screenplay and filled the vacuum of its weak direction' (1998: 103). As the last great exponent of minstrelsy, Lhamon argues, Jolson carried all of its complex and contradictory history. Jolson, 'at the bottom of the waterfall of gestural identity each earlier wave of immigrants had concocted' (1998: 103), carried the uses and effects that various groups, including African-Americans, had historically extracted from blackface minstrelsy. It is Jolson as blackface performer then, and not the film, which is the site of a richly complex depiction of a split and hybrid human identity: 'There is no resolution. The scores of the past do not settle. They are all present at once in his work, without hierarchy, without erasure ... many pressures show themselves converging in his performances' (Lhamon: 103).

I would strongly argue, though, that Lhamon's account underplays the way in which the cultural complexity of Jolson's performativity is woven into the formal complexity of the film. The first shot of Jolson in the Coffee Dan's sequence, as the score switches briefly to a rendition of 'My Mammy', is accompanied by the intertitle:

Jakie Rabinowitz had
become Jack Robin –
the Cantor's son, a
jazz singer. But
fame was still an
uncaptured bubble –
... al jolson.

The film transforms its central character from Jewish boy into American adult through its introduction of Jolson. Then, as Lhamon has outlined, Jolson's first performance displays the fact that the Jewish boy and the cantor father retain a strong presence in Robin's hybrid identity. More than this, though, I would add that the very song that registers the central theme of Jack's split identity is itself the site of the formal splitting of the film into sound. Indeed the brief sound scenes which occur later are tightly woven into the film's exposition of Robin's split identity. The next Jolson song, the 'jazzy' version of 'Blue Skies' that Jack sings to his mother on his homecoming, is halted by the cantor's cry of 'Stop'. The film then remains silent until Jack finds his voice in the on-stage blackface sequences. If, as Wolfe notes, these bursts of sound produce a 'hybrid text' (1990: 67) then they further enhance the way in which I argue that form mirrors content throughout and at many levels of *The Jazz Singer*.

It would seem crucial, in determining the levels of creative control at work in *The Jazz Singer*, to note the final dimension to the formal splitting at work in the Coffee Dan's sequence where Jolson's blackface is deliberately withheld. Jolson's name appears at the bottom of the introductory intertitle and his appearance is underscored by his most famous blackface song – and yet fame, for his character in the film, remains an 'uncaptured bubble'. There is, then, a tension embedded in Jolson's appearance in the film where, despite these hints, the audience is 'split' from their expected sight of Jolson's famous blackface brand.

The mirror shot in close-up

There are several levels of complexity to the mirror shot which greatly enhance the expressivity of the film and carry out crucial narrative work at this key moment. Firstly there is the self-reflexivity of the 'frame within a frame' device as our discovery of the 'truth' about Jack, his irreducible Jewishness, is delivered through Jack's own introspective gaze into a 'cinema' frame. Secondly, form literally mirrors content here as in its depiction of the seemingly irresolvable split in Jack's identity the film's own imagery is split by the superimposed shot of the synagogue.

On its surface level the vision of the synagogue that Jack sees in the mirror would seem to confirm his racial difference and signify that he is out of place in the theatre and belongs in the Jewish community. However, close inspection reveals that the boy standing directly in front of the cantor appears to be dressed in black whereas the others are dressed in white. The effect is that a minstrel-type figure, matching the back profile of Robin, stands out from the rest of the congregation in the synagogue. The shot then has an extraordinary Russian doll complexity in that the sign of the synagogue which appears in the theatre dressing room contains the central sign of Robin's identity in the theatre world. The 'vision' that apparently warns Jack against rejecting his Jewish heritage in favour of a secular existence itself contains the evidence that Jack equally cannot 'belong' in the Jewish world.

In a single moment then, a single shot, the complexity of the film's entire narrative, the infinite circularity of Jack's hybridity, is powerfully expressed. At one level the shot renders Jack as hopelessly divided and yet it is central to the resolution of the contradictions that have been posed by Jack's split identity. The film trades beautifully on the duplicity of likely audience experience in this scene. As they watch the anticipated 'coming together' of the Jolson blackface brand the complexity of the minstrel mask is used to point Jack towards the healing of his divided self, towards an outward expression of all of the elements that lie within him. He inspects himself closely in the mirror, peering through the markings of the most duplicitous mask in the history of American popular culture, and discovers that he is pure hybrid. Jack gazes into his soul and gains self-knowledge. He sees that he cannot choose one world over another but that, instead, he belongs in both at the same time. Although at this point the competing pressures around Jack remain unreconciled, the minstrel mask, in exteriorising his hybridity, allows him to articulate it. Yudelson and his mother arrive but he denies their pleas to return with them to the synagogue and performs in the dress rehearsal instead. As his singing confirms to the producer that he will be the hit of the show Yudelson remarks, 'just like his papa – with the cry in his voice'. Mary tells Jack that his mother is 'reconciled', that he belongs in the theatre. In the next scene Jack does return home to visit his dying father. There he denies the pleas of Mary and the producer to return to the theatre and he agrees to sing 'Kol Nidre'. As she hears the song Mary inverts Yudelson's earlier recognition of the spiritual side of Jack's stage song by remarking 'a jazz singer singing to his god'.

One cannot but endorse Lhamon's rich account of the way in which blackface gives Jack self-expression in the divided world that he inhabits: 'When Jack Robin blacks up towards the end of the film he will be able both to realize and to combine the various senses of himself, the pressures from his mother, his father, the kibitzer Yudelson, from Mary Dale and the show's producer, all these pressures simultaneously. He will be able to sing *kol nidre*, star in *April Follies*, and go on with his life' (1998: 108). And yet Lhamon's insistence that this meaning arises from the social text of blackface minstrelsy ignores the way in which the film specifically draws out complexity in the minstrel mask in service of narrative development. It ignores the creative control which is exercised throughout *The Jazz Singer*, where its duplicitous form, whether minstrel imagery or silent/sound sections, is an expression of thematic content. It overlooks the specific power, the art, of that central mirror shot which encapsulates the meaning of the whole in a single moment, a shot which visualises what has resonated through the film since the appearance of Jolson singing 'Dirty Hands, Dirty Face', the idea of a Jewish cantor *inside* a jazz singer.

Lhamon captures some of the distinctive expressivity of *The Jazz Singer*'s portrayal of hybrid ethnic identity when he notes that the blackface in the film 'contradicts one ready interpretation of the film: that it is about eager replacement of ethnicity or Jewishness with whiteness' (1998: 107). Indeed it is hard to reconcile the film with Michael Rogin's assessment that 'Blackface is the instrument that transfers identities from immigrant Jew to American' (1996: 95). In fact, as Sarris highlights in noting its 'very sectarian Jewishness' (1977: 40), *The Jazz Singer* was perhaps the strongest affirmation of a non-white/American ethnicity in classical Hollywood film. In the penultimate scene a doctor opens the bedroom window so that the cantor can hear his son singing in the synagogue. As the window frame crosses over the star of David on the synagogue window a cut inside reveals Jack singing 'Kol Nidre', 'a prayer specifically about reaffirming Jewish identification' (Lhamon 1998: 109). On the return cut to the bedroom his father says,

8.3 *The Jazz Singer* (Alan Crosland, 1927)

'Mama, we have our son again', and then dies. The fatherly acceptance
that Jack has yearned for throughout the film is finally confirmed when a
vision of his father appears behind Jack in the synagogue (Figure 8.3). The
cantor touches his son's shoulder and then disappears again. Jack raises his
hands to the heavens and, as the film draws on the extraordinary emotional
power of Jolson's singing, he ecstatically embraces his Jewishness. The superimposition which divides Jack earlier in the mirror shot now brings healing
and resolution whilst at the same time maintaining the general theme and
ambience of duplicity which surrounds Jack throughout the film until its
famous closing shot.

What are we to make of the ending of the film, the jump forward from
'Kol Nidre' to 'My Mammy', as the blackfaced Jack takes up a starring role
on the Winter Gardens stage and the film fades on a Jolsonesque, arms
outstretched, finale? Does it, as Charles Wolfe argues, occur in 'a narrative
vacuum' (1990: 73) motivated by the 'extra textual demand for blackface'
(1990: 78) that accompanied the casting of Jolson in the film?

It is true that Jolson is finally seen singing the song that earlier echoed
through the score from when he first enters the film in the Coffee Dan's
scene to the first appearance of blackface in the dressing-room sequence.
Yet it is clear that the Jolson persona only comes to dominate the closing
moments of the film because of the narrative motivation provided by Jack
Robin's own ascent to stardom and, more importantly, because this fame
signifies the resolution of his identity crisis. As the camera stays just far
enough away to hold together the oscillating illusion of Jolson's minstrelsy,
blackface, the very core of the film, is used to give full expression to Jack's

complex existence. It functions, as Lhamon notes, to 'hold all [Jack's] identities together without freezing them in a singular relationship or replacing their parts' (1998: 110). Far from presenting an anomaly, the closing fade, suspending the minstrel mouth and collar in an enveloping blackness, expresses in a single shot Jack's irreducible, but now articulated, hybridity. Already an extremely rare example of a closing sequence upholding rather than resolving contradiction in a Hollywood film, *The Jazz Singer*'s final frame resonates with the concepts of hybrid identity and ethnic diversity that have so undermined notions of 'race' in our time. The film stands as a very early example of an all too rare Hollywood exposition of tension and contradiction within American 'whiteness'. Had the precedent of *The Jazz Singer* been followed up, the history of racial categorisation on the Hollywood screen might have been very different.

Note

1   *The Jazz Singer* is in fact predominantly a 'silent' film. All dialogue cited from the film, unless otherwise indicated, is from intertitles.

References

Andrew, D. (1993) 'The Unauthorized Auteur Today', in J. Collins, H. Radner and A. P. Collins (eds) *Film Theory Goes to the Movies* (London: Routledge, 1993), pp. 77–85.

Collins, A. P. (1993) 'Loose Canons: Constructing Cultural Traditions Inside and Outside the Academy', in J. Collins, H. Radner and A. P. Collins (eds) *Film Theory Goes to the Movies* (London: Routledge, 1993), pp. 86–103.

Gubar, S. (1997) *Race Changes: White Skin, Black Face in American Culture* (New York: Oxford University Press).

Hall, S. (1997) (ed.) *Representation, Cultural Representations and Signifying Practices* (London: Sage).

Lhamon, W. (1998) *Raising Cain: Blackface Performance from Jim Crow to Hip Hop* (Cambridge, MA: Harvard University Press).

Lott, E. (1995) *Love and Theft: Blackface Minstrelsy and the American Working Class* (New York: Oxford University Press).

Rogin, M. (1996) *Blackface White Noise: Jewish Immigrants and the Hollywood Melting Pot* (Berkeley: University of California Press).

Pines, J. (1975) *Blacks in Film* (London: Studio Vista).

Sarris, A. (1977) 'The Cultural Guilt of the Movies: *The Jazz Singer*, Fifty years After', *Film Comment*, 13, 39–41.

Sarris, A. (1998) *'You Ain't Heard Nothin' Yet': The American Talking Film, History and Memory 1927–1949* (New York: Oxford University Press).

Staiger, J. (1992) *Interpreting Films: Studies in the Historical Reception of American Cinema* (Princeton: Princeton University Press).

Stanfield, P. (1997) '"An Octoroon in the Kindling": American Vernacular and Blackface Minstrelsy in 1930s Hollywood', *Journal of American Studies*, 31, 3, 407–38.

Taylor, Clyde (1996) 'The Re-birth of the Aesthetic in Cinema' in D. Bernardi (ed.) *The Birth of Whiteness: Race and the Emergence of U.S. Cinema* (New Brunswick: Rutgers University Press, 1996), pp. 15–37.

Wolfe, C. (1990) 'Vitaphone Shorts and *The Jazz Singer*', *Wide Angle*, 12, 3, 58–79.

9

A Hollywood art film: *Liebestraum* (Mike Figgis, 1991)

Michael Walker

In *The New Hollywood* Jim Hillier recounts the troubled history of *Liebestraum*, Mike Figgis's second Hollywood movie: the resistance of MGM, its distributors, to the finished film; the hostile preview; Figgis's attempt to salvage the situation by excising the brothel scene which so disturbed the preview audience; the film's limited release on the art-house circuit (1993: 172). Critical reaction to the cut version shown in the USA was not enthusiastic and may be encapsulated in the response of *Variety*: 'Figgis's problem here is the confused script, which doesn't seem to have a point' (Kimmel 1991: 88). The film fared slightly better in the UK: the complete version was released in January 1992, and it did at least receive an intelligent review by Mark Kermode in *Sight & Sound* (1992). Nevertheless, although the film is now over ten years old, I have found only one other critical account which touches on the film's remarkable qualities (Orr 1998: 109–14). What is the problem with *Liebestraum*?

The problem lies in the film's distinctly un-Hollywood form: it is, in effect an art film. If it had arrived from Germany with subtitles – the title is, after all, German – MGM would surely have had a better idea of what to do with it. Leonard Maltin, author of the most influential US film guide, might not have been provoked to write of the film's 'truly insane title' (1998: 767). There might still have been hostility to the film's enigmas, but it would have been better 'positioned'. Two recent films by David Lynch – *Lost Highway* (1997) and *Mulholland Dr.* (2001) – which are even more 'quirky' (Hillier's phrase) than *Liebestraum*, indicate that it is indeed possible for Hollywood to countenance an occasional 'art-house' product (although it took Lynch years to reach this position). Seeing *Liebestraum* with the brothel scene reinstated, British critics have in fact pointed out its 'Lynchian flavour' (Orr 1998: 110; Feay 2001: 661). But the Lynch film that it evokes is the earlier *Blue Velvet* (1986), which is by no means as radical as these later examples. In 1991 Hollywood, *Liebestraum* was an aberration.

Beginning with David Bordwell's seminal article on the art cinema (1979), a number of critics have outlined the features – and influence – of the European art cinema, distinguishing the films from the mainstream Hollywood product in terms of concerns, aesthetics, audiences, distribution, etc. (for example, Neale 1981; Bordwell 1985; Siska 1988; Petley 1999). In particular, Bordwell's comment, 'the art film solicits a particular viewing procedure' (1979: 60) – in which we puzzle over the ambiguities in the text – is relevant to my argument here. If an art film is approached as a Hollywood genre movie, confusion will almost inevitably arise. With the honourable exceptions of Kermode and Orr, this seems to have been the fate of *Liebestraum* in the UK, too. An observation in a recent publication summarises the position: 'Critics complained that its plot was convoluted, bordering on the nonsensical' (Lay 2001: 92).

In arguing that *Liebestraum* is a Hollywood art film, I am challenging the view adopted by David Bordwell and Janet Staiger in Chapter 30 of *The Classical Hollywood Cinema*. Their argument is that the modern Hollywood cinema has only 'selectively borrowed from the international art cinema', and that the art film devices in these films are embedded in traditional generic forms (1985: 373). In other words, Hollywood films only go so far towards the ambiguity and elusiveness of the European art cinema. Scripted and scored as well as directed by Figgis, described by him as a 'personal' film (Figgis 1991: xxxvi), *Liebestraum* – I would maintain – is no less an example of art cinema than the films of the European directors cited by Bordwell and Staiger, i.e. Federico Fellini, Ingmar Bergman, François Truffaut, Luchino Visconti and Bernardo Bertolucci. Nevertheless, aspects of the film can still be located in relation to traditional generic forms – which could perhaps help explain the confused critical responses.

The essence of the film's plot is an unusual linking between past and present events. The credits occur during a five-minute prologue showing a violent incident from the 1950s. To the accompaniment of an Earl Bostic version of Liszt's *Liebestraum*, a couple make love after hours in the music room of a department store. During this, they are shot – apparently by the woman's husband – and a third shot signals that the man then shoots himself. The narrative then jumps forward thirty years as Nick Kaminsky (Kevin Anderson) arrives in Elderstown to visit his dying mother, Lillian Anderssen (Kim Novak), from whom he was separated at birth. A teacher of architecture, he is drawn to the department store, which is a rare surviving example of nineteenth-century iron-framed construction. Since the violent incident, the store has been sealed, its contents untouched, but it is now about to be demolished. Coincidentally, the man in charge of the demolition is an old college friend of Nick's, Paul Kessler (Bill Pullman). Nick meets Paul's wife, Jane (Pamela Gidley), and the two are immediately attracted to one another.

They begin an affair which, because of the role played by the building, comes to mirror the adulterous affair in the past, with Paul in the role of the cuckolded husband.

To some extent, *Liebestraum* has the structure of a modern *film noir*, with the past traumatic event functioning as a mystery which the young hero investigates in order to uncover his past – specifically, his parentage. Nick first learns about the violent incident from Jane, who tells him that the killer was Ralston, the department-store owner, and the couple his wife and her lover, Munssen. The men died from the shots, but Mrs Ralston, although shot in the head, survived, 'brain dead'. From his mother's medical records, Nick learns that her married name was Munssen; a photograph in the police file of the incident then confirms that Munssen was his father. But he gets no further than this. As the film moves to its climax, with Nick and Jane making love, like Munssen and Mrs Ralston, in the department-store music room, cross-cut flashbacks show us 'what really happened' in the 1950s: the shootings were carried out not by Ralston but by Lillian, heavily pregnant with Nick, and Ralston – watching the couple – was shot presumably because he was a witness. But Lillian dies immediately after this revelation – motivated as her flashback memory – and no one else in the film learns about it. The *noir* plot structure is present, but is handled obliquely.

The sense of a lack of resolution to the narrative is even more evident in Jane's case. Like Nick, Jane too was adopted, and Figgis stages an encounter between her and the still alive Mrs Ralston in a way which suggests that they could be mother and daughter. Then, at the film's climax, the flashbacks to Munssen and Mrs Ralston making love show their faces for the first time, and we can see that they are played by Kevin Anderson and Pamela Gidley. But, in intimating that Jane is Mrs Ralston's daughter, the film also raises the quite startling possibility – mentioned by Orr (1998: 113) – that Nick and Jane are brother and sister. Although this is no more than a possibility, it is a highly charged one, and not usually the sort of issue left unresolved at the end of a film, especially a Hollywood film.

In a series of articles in *CineAction!*, I have looked at the ways in which a 'past traumatic event' – which is usually either pre-narrative or, as here, occurs at the beginning of the film – echoes in the narratives of certain sorts of movie. I discuss two types of example. One, I believe, is relatively widespread: films in which such an event tends to generate what I call a melodramatic narrative. In these films, the ways in which the event echoes and re-echoes throughout the film gives the narrative the characteristic crises, climaxes and reversals of narrative in melodrama, and this melodramatic thrust continues until the trauma which initiated the action can be 'healed' by a changed set of circumstances (Walker 1993). All my examples of this type are Hollywood films. For *The Conformist* (Bernardo Bertolucci, 1970), an art film, I argue that the relationship of the past traumatic event to the narrative is a feature of the psychoanalytical slant with which Bertolucci views his hero: that here the event is part of the psychological baggage the hero carries around with him, and the echoes are like personal examples of the 'return of the repressed' (Walker 1996). Neither of these types of narrative structure fits *Liebestraum*. First, none of the three protagonists has any apparent awareness of a connection to the past events, i.e. this is not like *The Conformist*. But, equally, although there is a sense in which the opening incident echoes in later events, this is not in the compulsive manner characteristic of melodramatic narrative, but more obliquely and allusively. In *Liebestraum*, I will argue, we have a third type of example.

Condensing the points made in Bordwell's 1979 article, Bordwell and Staiger summarise the features they associate with the European art film: realistic settings; psychologically complex characters; an exploration of the nature and sources of psychological states; subjective sequences; the foregrounding of authorial expressivity; narrative enigmas; lack of closure; an ambiguity which encourages competing readings (1985: 373–4). Not all these features are confined to the art cinema, and some films of the European directors Bordwell and Staiger cite obviously possess more of the features than others. Nevertheless, the features serve as a useful marker of the territory of the art cinema; they can be seen as tendencies, found to a greater or lesser extent in a given film. Not only does *Liebestraum* include most of these features to a marked degree, but its overall form is articulated with the sort of artistic self-consciousness characteristic of the art cinema. The unusual way in which the past traumatic event echoes in the narrative is, I believe, another element of the film's 'art film aesthetic', and an observation of Siska's – that art films 'foregrounded visual symbols and often employed metaphor and allegorical action to communicate (their) themes' (1988: 354) – also seems relevant. By looking at selected aspects of the film, I will seek to argue that, if *Liebestraum* is approached as an art film, it is possible to answer the most frequent critical charge against it: that it is muddled, confused, incomprehensible.

My phraseology in the ensuing discussion is often auteurist (for example, 'Figgis dissolves ...'), since it is a part of my argument that Figgis is responsible for the crucial creative decisions in the film. This does not however mean that I do not recognise the contributions of key collaborators, notably Juan Ruiz Anchia as director of photography, Waldemar Kalinowski as production designer and Martin Hunter as editor.

The malevolent building

Nick and Paul first meet in the movie on the sidewalk outside the Ralston department store, where Paul is talking to his foreman, Buddy (Joe Aufiery).

At the moment when Paul tells Nick, to the latter's horror, that the building is about to be demolished, a series of events occur in quick succession. First, a chauffeur-driven limousine draws up and, as the man inside – Ralston's son (Zach Grenier), we later learn – winds down his window and looks up at the building, Paul is sufficiently perturbed by his presence to say, 'What the fuck is he doing here?' At this point, a bolt sheers on the roof, and the 'N' of the Ralston sign begins to fall. Nick looks up, sees what's happening, and rushes to push Paul and Buddy out of the way just before the 'N' hits the sidewalk. Ralston reacts with an intake of breath and the limousine pulls away.

Although it is possible that, prompted by resentment that his father's building was being destroyed, Ralston has arranged for this 'accident' to occur, I believe that something more unusual is being intimated. The 'accident' could be linked to both Ralston and Nick. Even though the former may not have planned it, it looks as if he at least *willed* it; equally, however, it could be seen as arising out of Nick's unconscious, an expression of his hostility at the idea of the building being demolished. (Later, Nick does indeed protest to Paul about the demolition.) There is a suggestion, then, that the building responds to the tensions between the characters. At the moment when Paul wonders what Ralston is doing there, he and Buddy are framed against a notice saying 'This building is in a dangerous condition'. Such notices are a familiar feature of derelict buildings, but the timing of its introduction suggests that it should be read anthropopathically.

Another feature of the building is that it seems to draw Nick and Jane back to it, as if compulsively. Some of this is motivated quite logically: Nick wants to write an article on the building; Jane, a photographer, accompanies him to take photographs. But it goes further. On one occasion, Nick goes to the building late at night to retrieve his hotel keys, which leads to an almost hallucinatory sequence in which a woman's (ambiguous) cries draw him to the music room – where, rather conventionally, he is frightened by a cat – and he then sees a man moving amongst the store's many mannequins. The man is in fact Ralston, but he looks like a ghost, and Nick flees in terror, hitting a wall and knocking himself out.

As Nick lies unconscious on the floor, Ralston looks at him with a puzzled expression, finally saying 'You're dead'. In retrospect, we realise that the comment arises from Nick's resemblance to his father as a young man. But its timing, combined with the mysterious sounds of what could be love-making (which can still be heard, faintly, as Nick flees), contributes to the sense that elements of the opening incident are beginning to echo in the narrative. In addition, there is a rapid montage of shots as Nick's head hits the wall. The moment of impact is marked by a white flash, like an echo of the flash of Lillian's gun. (It also suggests a photo flash, but Jane never uses one.) There is then a red flash, a flash frame of Jane in her underwear in her dark room. After Ralston's comment, Figgis dissolves from his face to the continuation of this shot, as Jane lifts Nick's photograph out of the developing fluid and holds it in up front of her. (This is the shot on the front cover of the script.) He then dissolves to the next morning as Nick, lying in a pool of blood, recovers consciousness.

In the Ralston building, then, Ralston's presence again causes an 'accident', but one which echoes both directly (Nick mistaken for his father) and indirectly (his lying unconscious) elements of the past traumatic event. But here the echoes suggest a third type of example of the device: one which evokes Freud's notion of the uncanny. In his essay 'The Uncanny', Freud refers to a cluster of features which help make something seem uncanny: when an object which is lifeless seems to be animated; encounters with a double, a ghost or 'the return of the dead' (1985: 364); the compulsion to repeat. The manikins scattered throughout the store have a spooky, almost life-like presence; Ralston appears like the ghost of his father; Nick, the double of his father, is mistaken for him; this scene is one of a number in which the characters in the present find themselves in some sense repeating the events of the past. Likewise, Nick's reaction of fleeing in terror from Ralston suggests the 'dread and horror' (1985: 339) associated with the uncanny. But the introduction of Jane at the end of the sequence also links Nick's experience with Jane's desire for him. Throughout the film, red lighting is used to suggest disturbing undercurrents of menace or danger: the brothel scene is a good example. The red lighting of Jane's dark room is another: it's as if the desire implicit in her holding up Nick's photograph in front of her is linked to his unconscious state on the floor.

Freud theorises the concept of the uncanny as arising from two basic conditions: 'either when infantile complexes which have been repressed are once more revived by some impression, or when primitive beliefs which have been surmounted seem once more to be confirmed' (1985: 372). Rather than being associated with an individual, here it is as if the repressed material which 'returns' is associated with the building. The building may indeed be seen as an impressive symbolisation of the unconscious, filled not only with dirt and material from the past, but also with representations of 'part-objects', such as the body parts of the mannequins (see Hinshelwood 1989: 373–6, on the psychoanalytical concept of 'part-objects'). The sealing of the building in the 1950s was thus the 'act of repression', and now it is as if the presence in the building of the descendants of those involved in the past traumatic event serves to trigger the 'return of the repressed'. Once more, it is as if the building were acting anthropopathically.

It should be apparent that, if this reading is valid, something very unusual is going on in the film, something which is rather different from the function of 'malevolent buildings' in the horror or ghost-story genres. Elements of certain films in these genres may indeed be readable in terms of notions of repression, the return of the repressed and the uncanny, but such elements tend to assume the form of more overt, dramatic psychic manifestations – as in *The Haunting* (Robert Wise, 1963) – rather than the more suggestive, enigmatic happenings here. The events in the department store in *Liebestraum* could possibly be explained rationally, but they invite more symbolic, allusive readings; the sort of readings that Siska indicates are typical of an art movie. And there is still more to be said about the building: the final example of the characters being drawn back to it in a way which echoes the past is when, at the end of the film, Nick and Jane make love in the music room and Paul watches them. But, before discussing this, I would like to consider other threads in the film.

Nick's dreams

Dreams may of course function in films in many different ways, and the Hollywood cinema no less than the art cinema has produced its share of overtly 'Freudian' examples; I have already discussed the nightmare in *Murder My Sweet* (Edward Dmytryk, 1945) along such lines (Walker 1992: 30). Nevertheless, if the dreams in *Liebestraum* are considered as a group, they too may be seen to contribute to its art-film aesthetic.

Nick has three dreams. The first occurs the night after he has met Jane: in it, she twirls in the dress she was wearing and – to camera – unveils a breast. During this, the camera pans to show the Ralston building through Nick's hotel-room window and on the soundtrack we hear both the Bostic record and the sounds of sexual activity. The film also links the dream to Jane: Figgis dissolves to her in bed with Paul, and she is holding the same breast. On the surface, the dream simply expresses Nick's (and Jane's?) desire, but the soundtrack and the pan to the Ralston building serve to connect this desire in some mysterious way with the building and its history.

The second dream is prompted by Nick's sight of a teenage girl and young boy in the foyer of his hotel. It would seem to 'refer to' his childhood: the two children appear in the dream in a small, fenced garden with a freight train silently passing by, and from their remarks we deduce that Nick is the boy. The girl won't give something back to him and, when he says that he will tell his 'mom and dad' (who suddenly appear in the garden in stylised poses), the girl says that they are not his parents: 'your mother's a crazy woman'. Her remark is accompanied by a shot of an unhappy Lillian, an unseen man's arm round her echoing that in a photograph Nick has of her as a (happy) young woman. Nick wakes up, and hears some vigorous lovemaking from the room next door, a room which he is later assured by the desk clerk has been empty all week.

In the script, Nick has this dream when he first arrives in Elderstown, but it becomes more resonant in its relocation, which is just after Paul has drunkenly – and threateningly – warned Nick about having an affair with Jane during his absence. First, the girl, with her long red hair, also now 'stands in for' Jane, who used to have long (red) hair, but who cut it off when she found that Paul had been unfaithful. Second, this is the only time that Nick dreams about his mother, so that the dissolve from Lillian to Nick waking and hearing the mystery love-making suggests an evocation of the primal scene. It is here that the name of the town is significant: Elderstown is the town of the elders, i.e. the parents, and Nick and Jane's experiences there are also like psychic encounters with the parental world. But the seemingly hallucinated love-making has another possible explanation as an anticipation (an aural flashforward) of Nick and Jane's future love-making in the same next-door room.

In this dream, too, there is an echo from the prologue, where we see a freight train through the window as Ralston Sr climbs the stairs (the train is emphasised by a slow zoom when Figgis replays this sequence in the cross-cutting at the end). Once again, the echo is mysterious, enigmatic. One might contrast it with the recurring image of a freight train at the bottom of the garden in the remake of *A Kiss Before Dying*, another film made in 1991 by a British director in Hollywood, James Dearden. The image there has its own charge, but it nevertheless has a clear function in the narrative as a clue in a murder thriller: it is generically determined. In *Liebestraum*, typically of an art film, the meaning of the image is much more elusive.

Nick's third dream is the most significant. Surrounded by black-and-white photographs from the police file which have just revealed to him that Munssen was his father, he dreams that he goes to Ralston's house. Inside, a mirror at the bottom of the stairs reflects the staircase so that the décor looks like that in the department store, i.e. the house suggests a displaced version of the store. Hearing a traditional version of Liszt's *Liebestraum*, Nick traces it to a ballroom, where Jane sits, the music coming from a record player: she is sobbing, her hands covering her face. As Nick asks her what is the matter, Figgis shows an empty wheelchair eerily turning in another part of the room. Jane then uncovers her face, revealing a bloody wound in her forehead (where Mrs Ralston was shot). She begs Nick, 'Help, please'. Dissolve to Nick fleeing once more through the mannequins, but here his flight is terminated with a very brief shot of Mrs Ralston's body as shown in the police photographs – except, linking it to the mannequins, the body is in colour. He wakes up screaming.

The image of Mrs Ralston's body is the 'clue' to this dream: in freeze frame it can be seen that, consistent with the shock revelation at the end, she is the double of Jane. Whether or not Nick consciously grasps this – and hence its

significance for Jane's parentage – the dream indicates that he has unconsciously realised, and Jane's wound could be seen as the confirmation. But
his dreaming that Jane has suffered the same fate as Mrs Ralston could also
be a guilt-image: his desire for her has resulted in the same 'punishment'.
This connects with the earlier implicit link between Jane's desire for Nick
and his suffering an injury. When Nick knocks himself out, the blow leaves
a bloody wound on *his* forehead, and when he wakes from this dream, the
wound is again bleeding. A pattern is being established: the two personal
injuries – one actual, one dreamt – both echo the past traumatic event and
both, it is hinted, could in some sense be linked to Nick and Jane's desire for
one another. It is as if Nick and Jane are caught up in a scenario of desire
which is increasingly coming to resemble that of Munssen and Mrs Ralston
thirty years ago. The wheelchair, at this point a mysterious dream-image, will
later 'make sense' when Mrs Ralston appears in one in the hospital.

After the prologue/credit sequence, Figgis fades in to Nick on a train: he
has been asleep, and wakes at that moment. It is as if the prologue, with its
stylised imagery and elliptical narrative, were Nick's dream. His encounter
with Ralston among the mannequins is likewise dreamlike, and the film ends
with Nick and Jane asleep in each other's arms. Nick's dreams are thus a part
of a wider strategy in the film, in which oneiric imagery blends with more
naturalistic sequences to suggest emotional and psychic undercurrents.

This blending, moreover, lacks the firm distinction between dreams, fantasy and 'reality' one would expect in Hollywood cinema. The film also fails
to follow a traditional cause–effect narrative logic. For example, it is puzzling
that elements of the opening sequence could find their way into Nick's first
two dreams, or that the wheelchair should appear in the third dream in
advance of its appearance in the hospital. Such details, I would argue, are
typical of an art film, which is not constrained by a conventional naturalistic
logic, but is more open, allusive, ambiguous.

Lillian's mindscreen?

Mark Kermode suggests that 'the events depicted (in the film) may be taking
place in the tortured mind of the dying Mrs Anderssen', and that Figgis's
use of the same actresses as both whores and nurses would support this: 'the
brothel scene could be a product of her twisted imagination' (1992: 47).
Likewise John Orr: 'this could be the mindscreen film of a woman on the
edge of death willing the repetition of the original sin which ruined her, like
father like son, in her demented and despairing mind' (1998: 113). The concept of mindscreen comes from Bruce Kawin, who uses it to describe images
which visualise what a character *thinks*, such as memories, dreams and fantasies (1978: 10), so that Orr's suggestion here is the same as Kermode's. The

concept can be applied to all forms of cinema, but I would argue that, when its functioning in a film is not immediately apparent, but has to be teased out, then we are in the terrain, not just of the art film, but of a particularly challenging example of the art film. *Liebestraum* is not like *Citizen Kane* (Orson Welles, 1941) or *Rashomon* (Akira Kurosawa, 1950), in which the subjective nature of the various narrators' visualised accounts (their mindscreens) is overt: one could indeed make a fair degree of sense of the film without even considering that any of it could be read as Lillian's mindscreen. Accordingly, in exploring this idea, I am extending my argument to claim that *Liebestraum* is an unusually ambiguous example of an art film.

The most significant sequences are all in the second half of the film, where cross-cutting between Lillian and other events is used to suggest a connection between the two. During Nick and Lillian's first conversation, Figgis intercuts shots of Jane exploring the Ralston building. Here there are several dissolves back from Jane to Lillian, as if the women were somehow psychically linked, and twice sequences of Jane in the building are accompanied by Lillian's voice-over. As Lillian mentions the moment she identified Nick from his photograph on his book, the shot of Jane foregrounds a pointedly phallic red vase, so that the imagery sexualises Lillian's shock of seeing Nick as the reincarnation of her dead husband. The phallic vase, like the recurring background silhouette of a couple beside the (phallic) Eiffel tower, indicates that the repressed of the building is also heavily sexualised: later, Nick will hear from the policeman who discovered the bodies that Munssen's 'pecker was still up like a pole'. Then, when Jane is in the music department, she steps on the records which were smashed when Munssen and Mrs Ralston were shot (that even these have lain undisturbed for thirty years is a mark of the completeness of the symbolic 'repression'). Lillian is talking here about the night when her husband came home late and she 'could smell the cunt' on his fingers. In other words, she is referring to the point when she realised that he was unfaithful, which resulted in her revenge – and the smashed records.

In later sequences where Figgis cross-cuts between Lillian and other events, (a) Lillian seems to be reacting to the events and (b) she does so as if Jane were a sexual rival. But in this sequence Jane seems more like Lillian's alter ego, exploring the Ralston building as if retracing her own past there. In other words, there is a shifting symbolic relationship between the two women – another example of the fluidity of meanings which characterise the art cinema. But Lillian also has conflicting symbolic associations with the building itself. Dr Parker (Thomas Kopache) tells Nick that he expects Lillian to last about a week; Paul informs him that he expects to demolish the building in a week: here, the dying woman and the doomed building are paralleled. But Figgis also uses the demolition of the building to express Lillian's hostility: her comment about smelling the cunt is followed by a shock cut to

Buddy's men smashing the fixtures and fittings, as if her anger has been translated into an assault on the building.

The later examples of cross-cutting to Lillian are more pointed. When Nick and Jane kiss in her pickup truck, Figgis cuts to Lillian writhing in pain (or distress). Her comment – 'Please don't take him away from me' – reinforces the symbolic connection. Likewise, when Nick and Jane begin to make love in his hotel, there are repeated cuts to Lillian writhing in pain, as if in response to this. And here Figgis goes further. Following the intercut shots of Lillian, the camera begins to withdraw from the couple, and the bedside phone rings. The call is from the hospital, informing Nick about the severity of his mother's condition: in effect, Lillian has contrived to interrupt the love-making by provoking the call. The camera, meanwhile, tracks laterally into the room next door, which had originally been Nick's room, but which now – a consequence of rewiring – looks like a building site. Indeed, the room looks in the same sort of mess as the Ralston building under the blows of the demolition crew, as if Lillian's destructive anger were symbolically spreading to 'threaten' even her son. (It is when Nick returns to his hotel room with the police file on the Ralston killing that he first finds the room like this; like a warning that he is probing too far.)

Although aspects of the film may indeed be read as if they were Lillian's mindscreen, I would argue that this is only one of a number of interlocking readings. Nick and Jane are not merely re-enacting, in some sense, Munssen's past relationship with Mrs Ralston: the scenario of desire in which they are caught up is much more charged than this. This begins to emerge when Jane visits the hospital with Nick, and comes face to face with Mrs Ralston (Taina Elg), sightless, with the scar of a bullet wound in her forehead. Because we have seen a similarly wounded Jane in Nick's dream, we experience the encounter as Jane being confronted with an older version of herself. Frightened, she backs away, and goes into Lillian's room. But Lillian has just smelt Jane's vaginal fluids on Nick's hand and she climbs out of bed in a frenzy of hatred to attack her, shouting 'I've seen you with your legs spread'. Jane flees from the room in terror, and runs into Ralston in the corridor: he has come to see his mother.

In effect, Lillian's hysterical reaction to Mrs Ralston as sexual rival is being restaged, mediated through Jane. But the suggestion that Mrs Ralston could be Jane's actual mother is far more subversive. Lillian's identification of Nick because of his likeness to his father is echoed in her seeing in Jane the likeness of her mother. The past scandal concerned a patriarch who was unable to control transgressive female sexuality. But the secret which threatens to surface here is even more disruptive of patriarchy: incest.

The climactic scene in the hospital also marks Lillian's regression into the past which, consistent with the mindscreen reading, leads to a restaging of the past traumatic event. For no apparent reason, Jane returns to the department-store music room. Nick follows her. As they begin to make love, Figgis cross-cuts this with (1) flashbacks to the original incident (now revealing Lillian as the killer) and (2) Lillian in hospital going through the last painful moments of her life. We also see that Paul, holding a gun, is watching Jane and Nick make love. These threads are edited together extremely skilfully, so that three separate climaxes – young Lillian's shootings, Jane's sexual climax and Lillian's death throes – are condensed into a few moments of screen time. Only after Lillian has died does the film return to Paul. Jane and Nick are now lying on the floor in a post-coital sleep. A piano rendering of Liszt's *Liebestraum* begins on the soundtrack. Weeping, Paul turns and walks away, leaving a black screen. On the left-hand side, we see the teenage girl from Nick's dream playing *Liebestraum*; on the right, the credits come up.

Some critics, including Mark Kermode, seem to think that the ending is ambiguous, and that perhaps Paul shoots Nick and Jane. But there is no blood, and the final image of Paul is surely telling us that he did not shoot them, but simply left. Indeed, one of the points which emerges from this final sequence is how Lillian's rage in the past is not repeated in Paul in the present; he is upset, but he is not, ultimately, murderous. It is as if, with Lillian's death, the forces which have brought about this restaging of the past suddenly lose their power. There is also the structural point: Paul stands in for Ralston Sr in this restaging, and Ralston Sr, we now learn, was not the killer. Following the model I proposed for melodramatic narrative, there is even a sense that Nick and Jane's love-making – the final echo of the past traumatic event – is serving to heal the trauma of the original event. The mood of the final playing of *Liebestraum* (love dream), and the use of the girl – who in the dream teased the young Nick – as, here, a soothing presence, combine with the image of the lovers asleep to suggest that Nick and Jane, at least, have found peace.

In a sense, the reading of the film as Lillian's mindscreen competes with Nick's encounters with the 'ghosts of the past', which is where the sense of the uncanny mainly lies. However, even though the film's climax is the most obvious echo of the past traumatic event, it is scarcely uncanny. Is something else going on?

By way of an answer, I would like to suggest that there is another reading of the film. Perhaps it is the doomed building which has drawn the protagonists, including Lillian, back to the town, and which is exerting a mysterious power over them, even invading Nick's dreams. Like the unconscious, the building only yields up its secrets in a coded form, symbolically. In Nick's case, he discovers something about his parentage, specifically about his father's death. But what about Jane, whose photographs show that her interest in the building pre-dates Nick's arrival? The sequence in which she wanders alone in the building is, I believe, the key. In taking her from the phallic vase (the symbolisation of Munssen's pecker) to the site of the murders, it is as if the film is hinting at the secret of her conception. Rather than 'three separate climaxes', we should really speak of four, with the fourth – Munssen's orgasm as he is shot – resulting in Jane's conception. (If she was Ralston Sr's daughter, why was she adopted?) The shock meeting with Mrs Ralston in the hospital is thus also like Jane's encounter with a trace of this secret: the transgressive woman, unable to speak, her secret locked inside her. After Jane flees from the hospital we don't see her until the final scene in the music room. And, mysteriously, all the dirt which has until now covered every part of the building has been cleared away from this room. It is as if Jane has done this, and in so doing has also removed all the signs – such as the broken records – of the past traumatic event. This functions like a symbolic re-repression: repressing the details which, however obliquely, intimate that she and Nick could be brother and sister. The closing image of the teenage girl playing *Liebestraum* may now be seen to have an additional resonance: she represents the future, the daughter of Nick and Jane conceived at this moment, in the same place where Jane was conceived, but a daughter conceived out of love, not violence.

My argument in this chapter is that to approach *Liebestraum* as an art film opens it up, suggesting that its meanings are layered, and that it is not so much confused as complex. In particular, the film invites competing readings, perhaps the key feature which Bordwell and Staiger use to distinguish between classical film ('which solicits a univocal reading') and the 'ambiguity' of the art cinema (1985: 374). I have concentrated mainly on the film's characters and narrative – including its editing strategies – but it could equally productively be examined from the point of view of mise-en-scène. Viewed as a genre movie, *Liebestraum* will almost certainly disappoint; viewed as an art film, it seems rich and resonant.

I would like to acknowledge some very helpful feedback from Leighton Grist in the drafting of this chapter.

References

Bordwell, D. (1979) 'The Art Cinema as a Mode of Film Practice', *Film Criticism*, 4, 1, 56–63.

Bordwell, D. (1985) *Narration in the Fiction Film* (London: Methuen).

Bordwell, D. and J. Staiger (1985) 'Since 1960: the Persistence of a Mode of Practice', in D. Bordwell, J. Staiger and K. Thompson, *The Classical Hollywood Cinema: Film Style and Mode of Production to 1960* (London: Routledge), pp. 367–77.

Feay, S. (2001) '*Liebestraum*', in J. Pym (ed.) *The Time Out Film Guide* (London: Penguin).

Figgis, M. (1991) *Liebestraum* (London: Faber & Faber).

Freud, Sigmund (1985) 'The Uncanny' (1919), trans. J. Strachey, in *The Penguin Freud Library*, vol. 14 (London: Penguin), pp. 339–76.

Hillier, J. (1993) *The New Hollywood* (London: Studio Vista).

Hinshelwood, R. D. (1989) *A Dictionary of Kleinian Thought* (London: Free Association Books).

Kawin, B. (1978) *Mindscreen: Bergman, Godard and First-Person Film* (Princeton: Princeton University Press).

Kermode, M. (1992) '*Liebestraum*', *Sight & Sound*, 1, 9 (NS), 46–7.

Kimmel, D. M. (1991) '*Liebestraum*', *Variety* (26 Aug. 1991), 88.

Lay, S. (2001) 'Mike Figgis', in Yoram Allon, Del Cullen and Hannah Patterson (eds), *Contemporary British and Irish Film Directors* (London: Wallflower), pp. 91–3.

Maltin, L. (1998) *Leonard Maltin's 1998 Movie & Video Guide* (London: Penguin).

Neale, S. (1981) 'The Art Cinema as Institution', *Screen*, 22, 1, 11–39.

Orr, J. (1998) *Contemporary Cinema* (Edinburgh: Edinburgh University Press).

Petley, J. (1999) 'Art Cinema' in P. Cook and M. Bernink (eds) *The Cinema Book*, 2nd edn (London: British Film Institute), pp. 106–11.

Siska, W. (1988) 'The Art Film', in W. D. Gehring (ed.) *Handbook of American Film Genres* (New York: Greenwood Press), pp. 353–69.

Walker, M. (1992) 'Film Noir: Introduction', in Ian Cameron (ed.) *The Movie Book of Film Noir* (London: Studio Vista), pp. 8–38.

Walker, M. (1993) 'Melodramatic Narrative: *Orphans of the Storm* and *The Searchers*', *CineAction!*, 31, 62–73.

Walker, M. (1996) 'Style and Narrative in Bertolucci's *The Conformist*', *CineAction!*, 41, 33–42.

10

Swimming and sinking: form and meaning in an avant-garde film

Jim Hillier

Avant-garde or experimental films tend not to pose the same kinds of problems for reading and meaning as narrative films do. This is not to imply that avant-garde films cannot be narrative: some are not, but in practice it is quite difficult for most films to abandon any traces of narrative (and equally difficult for most spectators to abandon the familiar conventions of reading films narratively). Nevertheless, narrative in avant-garde films does often work in very different ways than in more 'conventional' narrative films (though 'conventional' here still covers a very wide range of practices). Such films are much more likely to explore organising structures other than narrative ones or, when narrative-based, to explore different processes and possibilities. Outside of narrative concerns, avant-garde films can be interested in questions which conventional narrative films would not even remotely consider, such as questions about the nature of the photographic image, or related questions about the tension between representation and abstraction in film – questions which are at the very centre of work by, say, Stan Brakhage or Michael Snow.

Sink or Swim is a forty-eight-minute, black-and-white (often grainy, shot on 16 mm) US independent/avant-garde film made by Su Friedrich in 1990 and concerns itself with a young girl's/the filmmaker's relationship with her father. Probably Friedrich's best-known film remains *The Ties That Bind* (1984), which concerns itself primarily with the filmmaker's mother's life story, but also with its relationship to the filmmaker's own life. These strongly autobiographical elements help to situate the film in the wider field of late twentieth-century experimental US filmmaking. Catherine Russell has grouped Friedrich's work with that of Peggy Ahwesh and Leslie Thornton around the idea of an 'ethnographic impulse', linking their work to earlier ethnographic documentary filmmaking and more obviously subjective personal documentaries (Russell 1998). The fact that the three filmmakers are all women also relates back to earlier avowedly feminist filmmaking such as Michelle

Citron's *Daughter Rite* (1979), where the filmmaker uses home movies and fabricated *cinéma vérité* documentary to explore both her own relationship to her mother and the relationships of many others to their mothers, and there are clearly links to a vital – dominantly male – tradition of experimental autobiographical work around filmmakers such as Jonas Mekas and Stan Brakhage dating back to the 1940s and 1950s. Certainly, Friedrich draws very openly on her own life: 'Whenever I set out to make a film, my primary motive is to create an emotionally charged, or resonant, experience – to work with stories from my own life that I feel the need to examine closely, and that I think are shared by many people ... I think you have to start at home.' But she is nevertheless anxious about her work being labelled 'personal' in any simple way: '*Sink or Swim* is personal, but it's also very analytical, or rigorously formal' (MacDonald 1992: 308–10).

Sink or Swim poses its viewers with problems both about overall structure and about the relationship of local sequences to each other and the structure as a whole which are rather different from those posed by more straightforwardly narrative films. I say 'more straightforwardly narrative films' because, as we shall see, narrative elements are very important in the film, albeit in some unfamiliar ways (just as they are in *The Ties That Bind*). Perhaps we should say that a structure of narrative is laid over – or beside – a more formal structure. Equally, *Sink or Swim* is both pleasurable and perplexing, and its perplexing qualities seem to me to be essential to the pleasure(s) it provides. I do not mean to say that I do not 'get' the film. I think I do, but there are nevertheless passages which I find perplexing, and the precise reasons why the film gives pleasure, by moments and as a whole, remain to some extent unclear to me. These are the issues I want to explore in this chapter.

First, however, a good deal needs to be said about the film's formal structure. That structure is relatively easy to describe in outline – though, in my experience, very difficult for most viewers to perceive directly on a first viewing. This is, of course, true of many experimental films. Friedrich has admitted her interest in minimal and conceptual art and the kinship she feels with some of the so-called 'structural' North American filmmakers (like Hollis Frampton, Ernie Gehr), 'since I do like to play with the frame, the surface, the rhythm, with layering and repetition and texts and the other filmic elements' (MacDonald 1992: 308). However, as she also points out, she 'grew up through the women's movement' (MacDonald 1992: 310). If, as avant-garde films go, *Sink or Swim* is relatively accessible to a fairly wide range of audiences, this is in part because whereas some structural films have been criticized as being empty of 'content', purely formal, Friedrich's films have contents familiar to most people. And, as Laura Mulvey remarked of women's avant-garde film in general, 'women cannot be satisfied with an aesthetic that restricts counter cinema to work on form alone. Feminism is bound to its politics' (Mulvey 1989: 124).

The main sequences of the film are introduced by title cards with – except for the final one – one word, white on black, beginning with a capital letter: 'Zygote', 'Y chromosome', 'X chromosome', 'Witness', 'Virgin', 'Utopia', and so on, ending with 'Competition', 'Bigamy', and 'Athena/Atalanta/Aphrodite' (this 'final' sequence being the only one using more than one word in its title, and picking up very explicitly on earlier discussions of the three names). Put in print like this, it is relatively easy to see that the structure works on the basis of the alphabet, backwards, but this is much more difficult to 'see' while watching the film, when the spectator is working to make sense of all kinds of other information, visual and verbal. All but one of the sequences come without their own diegetic sound but are accompanied by a voice-over.

There are twenty-six sequences or segments – Friedrich herself calls them 'stories' – twenty-seven if we include the coda or epilogue (and the segment 'Memory' is divided into two parts). Each segment has a voice-over accompaniment, with the exceptions of 'Y chromosome' and 'X chromosome', which are silent, 'Kinship', which is accompanied by Kathleen Ferrier's rendition of one of Schubert's lieder, 'Gretchen at the Spinning Wheel' (sung in German), and 'Ghosts', which uses the sync sound of the typing of a letter addressed – though it cannot be sent, except via the film – to 'Dear Dad' (and, exceptionally, shown in negative). Thus, although there is clearly a 'system' at work here, it is a system with enough variations, or distractions, to make it less visible than it would otherwise be. Another important reason why the film's structure is hard to see is that the visual material shown is not all of the same type, and the relationship of the voice-over to the images is, again, very variable, even when the 'normal' pattern of image plus voice-over is maintained.

Although the segments do not adopt an absolutely consistent pattern, typically they begin with a title which does not relate at all clearly to the segment's opening image (though the first, 'Zygote', deceptively offers what might be considered predictable – found footage – images of human eggs, sperm, fertilisation, etc.). The title and initial images are always silent for some seconds, so sound offers no cue, and we are repeatedly faced with a challenge to make some connection. In 'Realism', for example, the title is followed by a silent long-shot image of a young girl riding a bicycle around an apartment rooftop area. When the voice-over comes in, it turns out to be about learning to swim. By this time we have also seen images of a Chinese-looking man and a young girl (presumably his daughter) standing eating together on another apartment rooftop and turning away – the girl following the actions of the man – when they see the camera looking at them. Eventually, we *do* get images of children learning to swim (though we return to the other images as well), but not before having been made to think about other dimensions of the subject matter. Elsewhere, the challenge to make meaningful connections is sustained over a longer period, as we shall see. Thus, only very rarely is there any sense in which the images may be 'illustrating' the story being told in the voice-over.

Friedrich's *The Ties That Bind* (1984) largely concerns the life story of the filmmaker's mother, Lore Friedrich, particularly the period of growing up in Nazi Germany and surviving the Second World War in Germany, but then also in the US in the 1950s, after Lore Friedrich had married a member of the US occupying military and later returned to the US with him and started a family. We hear a great deal in the film of Lore Friedrich's voice-over as she tells her story and we see much footage of her life in the US at the time the film was being made, and to that extent a description of the film as being 'about the filmmaker's mother' would be reasonably accurate. However, such a description also belies much of the complexity and challenge of the film, which uses a very wide range of visual materials and strategies (including found footage, home movies, 8 mm travel footage) and, crucially, reveals itself to be as much about the filmmaker's life and situation as it is about her mother's. This strongly autobiographical dimension is also clearly present in *Sink or Swim*, which could be said at one important level to be about the filmmaker's father – certainly, we learn quite a lot about him – but is also primarily about the filmmaker's relationship with her father and the effects of that relationship on her. Superficially, at least, Friedrich both concedes this and seeks to mask or generalise it (or mask it by generalising):

> The stories are read in voice-over by a 13-year-old girl, Jessica Lynn ... In the case of images that portray young girls interacting with their friends or fathers, an effort was made to include girls of different races, in order to show that the experiences described in the film are shared by many girls/children, regardless of race or class. All of the stories are based on the filmmaker's experience but were written in the third person, so that the distance provided by a less subjective voice would allow the viewer greater access to the material. The intent was not to make a film simply about an individual, but to present a series of events which are common to many children. (Friedrich 1991: 116)

But Friedrich has also put a different gloss on this: Fred Camper reports her conceding that 'it was only when she began to write about herself in the third person that it became possible to tell her stories at all' (Camper 1991).

As these comments imply, alongside or overlaying the very formal alphabet-in-reverse structure is a more or less autobiographical *narrative* structure: the film constructs – or allows the spectator to construct – the (albeit rather episodic) life story of the 'girl' from, effectively, conception ('Zygote', 'Y chromosome', 'X chromosome') to the filmmaker's adult present.

A late sequence ('Bigamy') – late in the film, obviously, as well as late in the filmmaker's life – has the girl, now a woman, visited by her father and the eleven-year-old daughter of his third marriage. Since the adult woman's story is being narrated by a thirteen-year-old girl, this has some intriguing effects, reinforcing what Camper calls 'the interpenetration of the past and the present' (Camper 1991) as well as the centrality to the film of the female age of puberty, approximately ten to thirteen years of age. As we can hear (even if we do not know from Friedrich's comment about the film), the voice-over is spoken by a thirteen-year-old girl; many of the children we see in the film are roughly of this age; the father's sister, whom we see in home-movie footage (presumably from the 1930s or early 1940s, presumably shortly before her death) appears to be of this age; and in the coda or epilogue that stands outside the other structures of the film the film ends with home-movie footage (presumably from the 1960s) of the filmmaker herself at this age, but now with an adult voice-over by the filmmaker herself in the form of the ABC Song.

The film's structure is also marked by recurrent thematic elements in the images or the voice-over, or both, and these build in resonance over the film as a whole. As might be expected from the film's title, one of the major recurrent themes involves sinking, swimming and water, which serve as a grand metaphor for the process of being brought up by and separating from the parent. At times, this is very explicit, as in 'Realism', where the voice-over tells of the girl learning to swim by being thrown in the deep end of the swimming pool by her father, and we see images of young girls swimming and thrashing around in a pool; or in 'Memory (Part One)', in which we hear the story of the father's sister drowning in a swimming accident as a young girl, accompanied by cheery home-movie images of what we take to be the girl and her brother (the filmmaker's father); or in 'Nature', which tells the story of the father nearly risking death by swimming in a quarry infested with water moccasins. The final alphabetical segment – 'Athena/Atalanta/Aphrodite' – returns directly to this theme, very movingly, with the story of the girl's return, as a woman, to the orange-coloured lake mentioned in 'Realism' and her breaking free from the desire and need to emulate the father and forge her own identity separate from his. At other times, the references to swimming and water are less obvious but nonetheless resonant – not least at the start with the swimming sperm. Early in the film ('Virgin'), 'the water running in the gutter was the Nile river' (in which floats a Becks beer bottle, much in evidence later); in 'Loss' we hear the story of the estranged father brutally ducking the heads of his misbehaving daughters in the bath; in 'Bigamy' we see a woman we will have come to assume is the filmmaker in various everyday situations, including in the bath, and ducking under the bathwater. Similarly, there is a network of references to goddesses which both begin the film – 'Zygote' shows the biological fertilisation of the egg, but is accompanied by voice-over narration about Athena springing fully formed from the forehead of Zeus – and come together at the end, not only, as we have seen, in the final alphabetical sequence, but also in 'Competition', in which the girl tells the story of scouring her academic linguist/anthropologist father's publications and reading from cover to cover a book by her father about the 'age-old schism between the two kinds of love', as embodied in Aphrodite, goddess of sexual love, and Demeter, goddess of maternal love.

Sink or Swim would be considerably less pleasurable than it is were it not also witty and humorous. 'Flesh', for example, recalls the young adolescent girl's Mexican vacation trip with her father: passing time with 'an Adonis of the beach', she forgets a lunch date with her father; though warned about repeating the error and in fear of her father, 'the next day she was late for both lunch and dinner'. In 'Homework' we learn from the voice-over that the father had forbidden the family a television set, but once he had left they immediately acquired one, and the girl spent many hours watching her favourite shows. These shows (heavily sponsored by the tobacco giants), from which we see silent, ghostly clips (filmed from the television screen, with rolling bars across the screen), turn out to be the 'happy family' shows of the 1950s and 1960s, such as *Father Knows Best, Make Room for Daddy* and *The Donna Reed Show*, with benign, understanding fathers or father figures like Robert Young and Danny Thomas. The contrast with what we have learned about Friedrich's own family is both funny and devastating. Indeed, some of the most biting – and bitter – sequences are also the funniest, as if the ability or power to laugh at them is a condition for being able to tell – and live with and live through – otherwise traumatic stories (though stories/sequences can also be traumatic and not funny). In 'Discovery' the voice-over tells of the girl's disappointment when her father, a university academic anthropologist specialising in linguistics and kinship systems – which Friedrich recognizes as the source of the film's alphabet structure – worked late, which meant she would not see him and be able to tell him about her day: 'Many years later she went to the library and looked him up in the card catalogue. She wondered what he had been writing while deciding to get a divorce.' She finds two articles about kinship: 'In the hopes of learning something about his approach to family life, she carried the book to a nearby table. For an hour she tried to read through the first one, but couldn't understand a word he'd written.' While the narration plays with these bitterly funny musings, Friedrich gives us, deadpan, on the image track 'The American Kinship System ca. 1950–1959', an animated family tree centred on the husband, giving us, first, Wife (1950–66) and three children (including Freidrich herself); then another line comes from the husband, 'Wife' becomes 'Wife # 1', and we get

Wife # 2 (1968–75); then a final line leads to Wife # 3 (1977–) and a further two children.

Most of the motifs and associations which criss-cross the film are relatively accessible, even if they do not always offer themselves up easily on a first encounter, but this may begin to suggest that *Sink or Swim* makes manifest its meaning(s) in more conventional and accessible ways than I think is the case. For a start, the relationships between the titles of the segments or stories – as is perhaps already implied – is more often than not at best oblique. Further, the relationships between the image track and the voice-over within the segments is as often equally oblique. For example, the sequence titled 'Journalism' (a word play) concerns the girl's diary, given to her on her tenth birthday, and focuses on her shame when her parents told the children they were getting a divorce and her inability to confess this to anyone except her diary; fearful that the act of writing it down would make it come true, she wrote it in pencil, only to find, next time she looked, that it had been erased ('Her mother was the only possible suspect'). For the duration of this sequence, the image track shows us a school playground, with children of many races (but many of them Japanese- or Korean-looking) aged about ten to twelve years, in school uniform, overseen by nuns, on what appears to be playtime at a private school. Girls are skipping, groups of children stand around, and at one point a girl chases a boy round and through the other children. This is in line with Friedrich wanting to include a wide range of races in the film, but each instance of 'generalising' brings with it its own particularity, as here. It is of course the film's apparent opting for generality via the non-personal particular that makes the surfacing of the personal so powerful. It is not that these images *don't go* with the voice-over narration, which does say at one point that the diary was mostly filled with 'stories about doing punishment assignments, fighting with boys and playing with friends', but nor do they *go* with them in any immediately obvious way.

As with any act of reading, there are many things in the film that only make sense, or are only fully or multi-dimensionally meaningful, in retrospect, when they can be locked into a system or network of references. But there are also segments with which one can only struggle to make sense. One of the more perplexing segments in *Sink or Swim* is 'Kinship'. The images – possibly home-movie type images – juxtapose what seems to be footage of a trip to a desert location with shots from a moving plane and a moving car, shots of the desert, and quite long-distance shots of a woman walking or climbing on her own in the desert with very grainy interior shots of two naked women in a sauna/shower, washing and embracing (Figure 10.1). These shots may be related to the previous desert shots, and one of the women may be the woman we saw climbing the rocks, but nothing here confirms such connections. None of these images have any sync or other diegetic sound,

10.1 *Sink or Swim* (Su Friedrich, 1990)

but this is the segment which is accompanied throughout by the recording of Schubert's 'Gretchen'. What can we make of this sequence as it unfolds? Very little, I think, or very little that we can do much with. One might read: two women on a desert vacation, even though only one is actually seen in the desert. Maybe, if this is a home movie, then the other woman is filming the scene. But this is not a very secure reading and it seems virtually impossible to see any obvious relationship to the Schubert song, which adds to the doubt about the reading. At the same time there is very little, if anything, that might be linked with previous segments of the film. The spectator must be more inclined to say, well, I don't get the significance of this, but I will wait and see. It would be very unusual for a sequence in a narrative film, even one in which ambiguity was paramount, to resist meaningfulness to this degree.

So, the spectator waits. Later sequences do, in fact, show images of a woman who is probably the same woman we saw in the desert sequence, and probably the filmmaker, the 'girl' grown up, and the later segment 'Ghosts' builds very specifically on 'Kinship'. It is a single close-up shot, in negative, of a letter being typed, addressed to 'Dear Dad'. The letter tells the father how, after he left, Mom used to come home after work and sit alone and play the Schubert Lieder, and that 'Gretchen' 'was the one that made Mom cry the most ... It's the one about a woman who yearns for her absent lover and feels she cannot live without him'. However, this explicit reference back to the earlier segment in which the song was played does not then open out into any obvious meaning for the earlier sequence. Could it be that the film wants to suggest that the choices open to the mother, reliant (as we learn in *The Ties That Bind*) on her secretarial skills, in the male-dominated and largely heterosexual 1950s and 1960s, somehow embodied in Gretchen's melancholic and lonely entrapment, are far different, given the intervening social changes around gender and the family, from the choices available to the daughter in the 1980s and 1990s – suggestions which seem to be reinforced later in the film? Maybe. I don't know, and I don't think we are supposed to 'know'. While the earlier segment is certainly not 'unreadable', nor is it conventionally 'meaningful'. It seems to want to resist interpretation and insist upon a suggestive perplexity, a mystery that cannot be plumbed.

This seems to me to be equally the case with the sequence 'Insanity', where the elements in play are not returned to in any obvious way in later sequences. The voice-over narration here tells of the intense emotional state of the family after the father has left, and in particular the chilling story of the mother, after a visit by the father, holding the two children on a high apartment window ledge, threatening and screaming at the father far below in the street. While we hear this story, the camera roves, hand-held, over a rather eerily empty hospital ward – incubators, trolleys, a wheelchair, with a slow zoom into a bed, a drip pouch, a television monitor – then, making some link with the voice-over, a movement towards a high window and a tilt down to the street (Figure 10.2). As with 'Kinship', there does not seem to be any easy way to relate sound and most of the images here, though both are perfectly comprehensible in their own separate rights. Camper suggests that the 'story about her mother's suicide threat is accompanied by footage of a hospital room – the place where unsuccessful suicides usually wind up' (Camper 1991). This seems to me, at the very least, plausible, given the title of the sequence (even if I am not quite convinced by 'mother's suicide

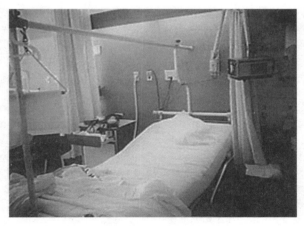

10.2 *Sink or Swim* (Su Friedrich, 1990)

attempt' as a description of the story itself, and though there is much else as well as the bed), but it does little to shift my own sense of not knowing, really, what relationship is being suggested here. If this is, indeed, suggestive of mental illness, then why exactly, and when, and whose insanity is being suggested? Is it the mother's, the father's, the children's, the whole family's, the institution of the patriarchal family's? This seems to me a good example of an explanation or interpretation which is certainly plausible but which fails to satisfy one's actual experience of the sound/image mix. And, of course, we should always remain open to the possibility that what we may worry over as a matter of interpretation may be more simply a failure on the part of the filmmaker, here, to find a juxtaposition with the multi-dimensionality or resonance which characterises other sequences/stories. Though I cannot *feel* that this is case here, making such a call seems to me more difficult with a film operating with these kinds of systems.

Different levels of perplexity and mystery also pervade other sequences in the film, though in very different, and less troubling, ways. 'Bigamy' tells the story, as indicated earlier, of the adult daughter being visited by the father and the eleven-year-old daughter of his third marriage. The images consist of a succession of shots of a grown woman – now, surely, taken to be the filmmaker herself – variously in the bath, in the park, smoking and drinking beer. Towards the end of the sequence we see this woman sit down at a desk, stub out a cigarette and begin to type; then we see the words being typed, and it transpires that they are the same words as those being spoken in the voice-over narration. The particular point at which voice-over and typed script coincide is also crucial: the voice-over has described the daughter of the third marriage being told by the father that the story she was telling did not inter-est him – just, as we have learned earlier, what had happened to the filmmaker at the same age: 'This was her childhood, being played out all over again by the young girl.' But the point at which voice-over and image finally converge exactly comes just a moment later: 'At that moment, she didn't know whether to feel pity or envy for the young girl who sat alone in the sunshine trying to invent a more interesting story.'

Even after many viewings, this remains a very moving moment, but the reasons for this are very difficult to articulate. Clearly, at one level, there is a convergence in the sense that the 'more interesting story' the girl is trying to invent for her father can be taken as the 'story' which the filmmaker is seen to be 'inventing' (and at least in part for the same father) at this very moment, both on the typed page and in the film we are watching. At another level, this sense of convergence is a 'coming out' moment on the part of the filmmaker. I do not mean 'coming out' in the sexual-preference sense – though this is a strong, but never simple or unambiguous, sub-text scattered across the film – but rather that the filmmaker 'comes out' from behind the mask of the voice-over 'girl' to reveal herself as both the film's author and its subject. Images of the filmmaker herself earlier in the film have generally not been easy to recognise as such. One effect of Friedrich's decisions about the voice-over is certainly to create a certain distance between the filmmaker and the girl's story. As the film develops, this distance is broken down: the personal, subjective element refuses to be 'third-personed', as it were, suppressed, and comes right to the fore. This is surely a calculated effect: the film has been constructed to have this tension and this sense of the subjective refusing to remain suppressed. This very much exemplifies Friedrich's comment in interview that 'it's often the case that the more a person pretends or insists they're not dealing with their own feelings, the more those feelings come out in peculiar ways in their work' (MacDonald 1992: 310). It is a moment of 'epiphany' in that whatever one has to say about the sequence and its place in the film, it does not seem to quite explain the deeply moving nature of the moment, or does not seem to explain it enough. It remains a moment which escapes any more precise interpretation.

This 'coming out' and convergence are built upon in the final sequences of the film. The 'Athena/Atalanta/Aphrodite' sequence continues with the young girl's voice-over, but continues to tell of the girl now being a woman. Bringing together the swimming and sinking metaphor – along with images of a woman who may or may not be the filmmaker, with other women, and, significantly, a toddler, lounging on the beach and swimming at the orange-coloured New Hampshire lake referred to earlier – the woman finally lets her father, real or imagined, swim away, ahead of her, the woman no longer feeling obliged to follow or compete with him, becoming her own woman, her own person. In the coda, the terms of the 'Bigamy' sequence are reversed and we see home movies of the filmmaker as gawky young adolescent in a swimming costume, on a beach, looking at the camera, footage which is overprinted in the same way that the filmmaker's adult voice singing the ABC Song is overdubbed, in the form of a round, until we are left with a single – frozen – image, and a single voice (Figure 10.3). Of course, having established in 'Athena/Atalanta/Aphrodite' the girl as a woman breaking free from the father, the coda/epilogue in some sense reverses this conclusion, and allows childhood and the past to reach again into the present. The woman, in voice, reverts to the child/girl in image (as well as in the song/game) and the line – 'Now you know my ABC/Tell me what you think of me' – seems as much directed at us, as spectators, as addressed to the father, whose judgement is still being sought, and whose shadow still shapes the woman's fate and identity. As Friedrich puts it, 'the conclusion of *Sink or Swim* was ... a way for me to acknowledge my absurd ambivalence' (MacDonald 1992: 314).

Avant-garde films tend to raise questions about pleasure – viewing pleasure, narrative pleasure – in more heightened ways than more conventional

10.3 *Sink or Swim* (Su Friedrich, 1990)

narrative films. I am constantly trying to persuade students that frustration of the 'normal' expectations and pleasures associated with cinema can itself be a source of pleasure (though there are plenty of more obviously narrative films – one only has to think of, say, *L'Année dernière à Marienbad* (Alain Resnais, 1961) or *Persona* (Ingmar Bergman, 1966) – which also raise such questions very explicitly). I suppose *Sink or Swim* should be regarded as a 'difficult' film. Certainly, like many avant-garde films, its perplexing qualities are essential and integral to the pleasure(s) it provides.

References

Camper, F. (1991) 'Daddy's Girl', *Chicago Reader*, 8 Feb. 1991, repr. at www.fredcamper.com./Film/Friedrich.html

Friedrich, S. (1991) 'Sink or Swim', *Cinematograph*, 4.

MacDonald, S. (1992) *A Critical Cinema 2: Interviews with Independent Filmmakers* (Berkeley, Los Angeles and London: Oxford University Press) (incorporates interview: 'Daddy Dearest: Su Friedrich Talks about Filmmaking, Family and Feminism', *The Independent*, v 13 n 10, December 1990).

Mulvey, L. (1989) 'Film, Feminism and the Avant Garde', in L. Mulvey, *Visual and Other Pleasures* (Basingstoke and London: Macmillan).

Russell, C. (1998) 'Culture as Fiction: The Ethnographic Impulse in the Films of Peggy Ahwesh, Su Friedrich, and Leslie Thornton', in Jon Lewis (ed.), *The New American Cinema* (Durham, NC and London: Duke University Press).

11

'Knowing one's place': frame-breaking, embarrassment and irony in *La Cérémonie* (Claude Chabrol, 1995)

Deborah Thomas

I would like to explore the nature of our emotional involvement in narrative films – the kinds of feelings that well up in us as we watch – or, at least, to look at one small aspect of this. Most writers who try to make sense of the capacity of the movies to pull us in and involve us intensely in their narrative worlds do so by assuming that we identify in some way with one or more of the characters on-screen. Such identifications have been described and theorised in a variety of ways, but these debates are not what I am interested in here. For the purposes of my discussion, I would like to put aside considerations of identification, not least because I am never quite sure whether I am identifying with a character or not – what would count as knowing this? – nor what sorts of evidence could adequately reinforce such claims. Just as important for our emotional involvement in a given film as our relationship with any of its characters is our awareness both of the film's tone (that is, the emotional and moral colouring of the experience that the film offers us) and of the point of view with which it provides us, through which we experience its narrative world and events. Because of the importance given to tone and point of view in my account, the textual specifics of the film I have chosen to examine have proved absolutely crucial. Simply reporting how we feel is not enough in order to address questions about *why* we feel that way, *where* our responses come from and what they are responses *to* (though, of course, the initial introspective reporting of one's response is a necessary first step).

Such questions about the ways a film may work upon us are impossible to address without paying close attention to the film in all its details, including those of which the film's characters are completely and necessarily unaware, thus producing a split between the characters' positionings and our own more 'knowing' alignment with the film as a whole. Although this is a general point about our experience of narrative films across the board, I wish, further, to suggest that there are specific films amongst them which much more emphatically hold us at arm's length from their characters to the extent that it makes little sense to couch our relationship with any of them in terms of identification, however that may be defined, but where we remain caught up in these films and implicated in their unfolding events with an emotional intensity undiminished by the lack of such figures. My choice of Claude Chabrol's *La Cérémonie* (a film from 1995, based on Ruth Rendell's *Judgment in Stone*) is partly arbitrary: it happened to be shown on British television during the period when I was beginning to think about these issues and struck me as a good example of a film whose characters are either unsympathetic or inaccessible in terms of motives and inner life, yet where my emotional reaction was uncomfortably strong.

I will only have time to concentrate on one particular segment of the film and one specific emotion. I have chosen a moment of what I can only call 'negative' emotional involvement, by which I don't mean the opposite of emotional involvement – which would merely be emotional detachment – but rather that the emotion I felt was an unpleasant one. The reason for this choice is that there is a clear criterion for when such negative emotions are at work, at least in the context of a solitary viewing of a film on video, which, as it happens, was the condition of my initial experience of the film. Thus, although my methodology for discovering and exploring the kinds of emotions involved in watching films is based on introspection – an empirical study of an audience of one – nonetheless, my sense that strong emotions are in play is not merely a matter of subjective impressions of inner states unavailable to anyone else. Instead, there is a clearly observable piece of behaviour to back them up: quite simply, at a particular moment while watching *La Cérémonie* for the first time, I felt anxious enough to switch off the video for a moment or two in order to 'recover' myself, and this reaction convinced me to examine that particular moment to see if I could discover exactly what was going on.

As the film may not be as well known as it deserves to be, at least in England, I will give a quick summary of the plot, up to the section we'll be examining, before we proceed. Briefly, Madame Catherine Lelièvre (Jacqueline Bissett) hires Sophie (Sandrine Bonnaire) to be her maid, and once Sophie is installed in her new job, she is befriended by the local postmistress, Jeanne (Isabelle Huppert), despite the objections of Catherine's husband Georges (Jean-Pierre Cassel). Georges's daughter Melinda (Virginie Ledoyen) finds out Sophie's shameful secret – that she is illiterate – and Sophie threatens to reveal Melinda's pregnancy to her father and step-mother if Melinda tells them anything about Sophie. However, Melinda tells her family everything, and Sophie is fired for attempted blackmail. Sophie and Jeanne return to the house to collect Sophie's things and, in the scene I'll be analysing, they pick up Monsieur Lelièvre's guns to scare the family – Georges, Catherine, Melinda and Catherine's son Gilles (Valentin Merlet) – who are gathered together watching *Don Giovanni* on television, and end up by killing them all.

La Cérémonie is largely concerned with the way working-class and upper-middle-class characters lack a common language and continually misread one another, as well as the way politeness hides an accumulating sense of mutual distrust and aggression. The early scenes, for example, show the family discussing Sophie when she is not in the room (though she is near enough to be able to hear their conversation), and their comments throughout reveal the extent to which they take for granted that Sophie will show gratitude and a properly subservient attitude – that is, that she will know her place. Sophie is at a double disadvantage, however, since not merely is the monied world of the Lelièvre family strange and unreadable to her, but her illiteracy makes the world's surfaces in a more general sense opaque. Sophie's skill at her job – the efficiency with which she cleans and polishes – may, perhaps, be taken to reflect her determination to 'erase' from the world meanings which she is unable to grasp and which disadvantage her so completely (this notion of cleaning as 'erasure' will be made more blatant when Sophie cleans up after the murder). At the same time, she herself remains opaque to the Lelièvre family, her face like a mask as she performs her role. This relates intimately, of course, to *Don Giovanni*, the opera the family are watching in the murder scene, with its use of disguises and its thematic interest in class and gender exploitation. So a number of crucial themes and motifs come together in this scene which have already been present as ongoing concerns leading up to this point.

Despite the way in which my description of Sophie's and Jeanne's situation may make them sound like figures of sympathy, Sophie's strangeness and Jeanne's vulgar bravado evoke a sort of clinically detached curiosity rather than anything approaching liking or identification. Their behaviour becomes increasingly embarrassing to watch in the build-up to the murders. However, if embarrassment can be understood primarily as an emotional reaction to the transgression of social conventions, then it can be experienced in two ways. First, it can flood over us when *our* transgressions make *us* the centre of unwelcome attention (or, in cases where we are self-conscious merely by finding ourselves at the centre of attention for whatever reason, it can make us anxious that we will not be able to carry off our expected social role but will botch it in some way: so the imagined prospect of transgression may be embarrassing as well as its actuality). Second, it can be felt when we are forced to witness the transgressions or social gaffes of others, or, once again, anticipate the prospect of their occurring before our eyes (even if, as in Chabrol's film, those characters whose behaviour is painful to watch are unembarrassable themselves). Thus, in the latter case, embarrassment is the result of our position as witnesses, and therefore well suited to the experience of watching films – more prevalent, perhaps, than has been recognised – while very different from the mirroring of characters' emotions which identification as a model of film spectatorship would seem to require. So some emotions seem attuned to the experience of watching films, while others – for example, jealousy – seem quite foreign to it, though frequently experienced by characters within films. In both these cases – where we are embarrassed by characters who are themselves unembarrassed, or where characters are jealous but we feel no such jealousy ourselves – there is a disjunction between the characters' emotional reactions and our own. Thus, what is telling in the Chabrol example is that we are consistently made to feel distanced from both the killers and their victims, yet remain intensely – and emotionally – involved in the film.

I would like to situate my discussion in the context provided by American sociologist Erving Goffman, in his book *Frame Analysis* (1974). He speaks of frameworks of rules and conventions which we make use of for understanding what he calls strips of activity. However, strips of natural or social activity can be 'keyed' in various ways: that is, they can be reframed in terms of a set of conventions which cause participants or onlookers to take them as something else (for example, what we assume to be children fighting may turn out to be only a game). Such frameworks may be layered (or 'laminated') one upon the other, producing increasingly complex frame structures. Thus, in Chabrol's scene of the family watching television, the various activities Don Giovanni gets up to (such as serenading Donna Elvira's maid) are keyed as an opera, which is keyed, in turn, as a television programme. The television programme is itself part of a larger frame – the family spending a cultural evening at home – which itself becomes part of the further frame of Sophie and Jeanne watching the family unobserved, and the whole thing is keyed for us as only a film, after all, so that the outermost rim of the frame structure is us watching Sophie and Jeanne who are themselves watching the family watching a television production of Mozart's opera in which (at the centre of the structure) Don Giovanni is serenading the maid. There are further complications to this laminated structure in the fact that Melinda is tape-recording the opera, as well as reading the libretto, while she watches.

In addition, frame issues are raised in other ways. Certain activities are taken to be outside the frame of the opera-watching episode by the family: for example, having coffee is put off until the interval, and Georges Lelièvre's viewing is interrupted by his having to investigate the noises made by Sophie and Jeanne elsewhere in the house. Secondly, the tape recorder which begins by recording only the opera, as underlined by Melinda hushing her family when their voices are in danger of being picked up by the machine, ends up with exquisite irony by recording the murder as well. Finally, although Jeanne and Sophie begin by keying the gun episode as play ('Let's scare them'),

Sophie suddenly turns it into murder when she shoots Georges in the kitchen. I think we see this coming before Jeanne and Sophie do themselves, since Chabrol signals it to us through the film's rhetoric, that is, at the outer rim of the structure to which the characters are necessarily blind. What all these examples around frames and the crossing of their boundaries have in common is a set of implicit rules and strictures as to what sorts of activities and roles are deemed appropriate to what sorts of contexts.

Thus, spatial transgressions are also important. The fatal gunplay in the kitchen is preceded by Jeanne and Sophie's transgressive intrusion into the master bedroom upstairs, where they break photo frames, spill hot chocolate on the bed, tear Catherine's clothes and fling them on the floor (mirrored by the flinging of a cape to the ground in the opera on television downstairs), and so on, all of which must be seen in relation to the family's cordoning Sophie off into her own space within the home. But Georges too intrudes into the kitchen, which has earlier been described as Sophie's domain. Feeding into this thematic as well are the various instances of eavesdropping in the film (Jeanne opening the family's post, Sophie listening in on Melinda's phone call to her boyfriend when Melinda's pregnancy is revealed, and the general atmosphere of gossipy speculation and moral judgement). There are also alliances within the Lelièvre family which exclude other family members: Melinda and her father, on one hand, and Gilles and his mother, on the other, as is made clear in two matching earlier scenes.

Madame Lelièvre's role in the scene we will be examining is crucial. In some ways she remains the most opaque character in the film for us, with Jeanne hinting that Madame Lelièvre has been hidden away in the country because of a disreputable past in Paris and that she may be continuing to be unfaithful now, the film implying that, were she to wander onto a more public 'stage', rather than keeping to her 'proper' place, she would bring scandal in her wake. We have no way of knowing whether Jeanne's gossip is true, just as we never quite know whether Jeanne and Sophie are each guilty of murder in the past (of Jeanne's daughter and Sophie's father respectively), though there are certainly indications that Catherine has difficulty coping. For example, she gets very anxious at the thought of losing Sophie, and she smokes heavily, her groceries containing numerous bottles of liquor as well. Her comment to her son Gilles that 'One can never really relax', in the scene when he advises her not to tell Georges that Jeanne has come to the house to visit Sophie, is also indicative of a nervous disposition, or at least an ongoing feeling of unease. In the scene leading up to the murder, she seems at odds with the rest of the family, and is the only one to be anxious and to suspect that something is wrong. Thus, Melinda assumes the gunshots in the kitchen are the sound of Jeanne's old car, and that earlier sounds of glass breaking were a stereo effect in the opera.

It is now time to examine all these issues more closely in terms of the build-up to the murders and the murders themselves, and, in particular, to note the way the murders relate to dramas within the family. In the moments before the televised opera begins, our growing sense of a family divided by blood relationships, already suggested in earlier scenes of Melinda alone with Georges and of Gilles alone with Catherine, is reinforced as Melinda sits on her father's lap. His comment that he hopes her boyfriend won't phone her in the middle of the second act may imply a wish that her boyfriend not interrupt his relationship with his daughter at all, though the second act will be interrupted much more forcefully by the murders. In line with this, Georges had earlier asked his daughter whether he should clean the guns so that they can go hunting together, and in this sense, Sophie's and Jeanne's gunplay is a direct appropriation of this activity of 'going hunting' with guns and, thus, a hijacking of the father's relationship with his daughter as well, just as much as the prospect of her boyfriend's telephone call during the opera – and his relationship with Melinda more generally – can be seen as an appropriation of the intimacy between Melinda and her father. This intimacy is reinforced as Melinda goes and sits in the middle of the settee, making it difficult for Georges and Catherine to sit side by side, and her father settles in beside her, with Catherine on her other side and Gilles fitting in at the end next to his mother, his mother's arm around his shoulder. So the scene of family unity is actually a scene of blood alliances within and at odds with the larger makeshift family.

The first chord of the opera is accompanied by our view of the television screen, but by the second chord, we have cut to a shot of a car (with Jeanne and Sophie inside) approaching from a distance, the headlights bright in the surrounding darkness. The effect is of the family's fate closing in on them – just as Don Giovanni's will close in on *him* – while they remain complacently unaware. Back inside a little later, a camera movement from the television to the window indicates to us that Jeanne and Sophie have arrived, though the family remain oblivious, producing a kind of complicity between us and the knowing camera which has an independence from both the family and the two girls outside. The continual cross-cutting between the spaces occupied by each – and the privileged knowledge we have of what both groups of characters are getting up to – reinforces our detachment from them all (though cross-cutting, in a context where we were more insistently involved with the characters, might have generated a heightened anxiety on their behalf instead). As Sophie prepares hot chocolate in the kitchen, Jeanne comes up behind her with a gun aimed at her in mock attack, then puts it down on the counter as they go upstairs. The camera stays on the gun, then cuts to the family, where Georges abruptly joins in with the opera for a few notes, his self-satisfaction and pretentiousness weakening our resistance to whatever danger the emphatic shot of the gun may have foretold.

11.1 *La Cérémonie* (Claude Chabrol, 1995)

At this point, there is a cut to a position upstairs looking down onto the tray with the hot chocolate which Jeanne is carrying, both girls moving into view as they climb the stairs. So although we are well placed to see what Jeanne and Sophie are doing, we are nevertheless positioned at one remove, allied once more with a camera that can predict their arrival and get there first. As they enter the master bedroom, their first irreparably transgressive acts take place, instigated by Jeanne, as she smashes framed photographs and proceeds to pour the hot chocolate on the bed and scatter Catherine's clothes on the floor (Figure 11.1). For the film's viewers – for me, certainly – any anxieties about whether the family will get killed are swamped by more pressing anxieties about whether the two girls will get caught and how embarrassing that would be. That their being caught is indistinguishable from their being *seen* is more emphatically underlined as they blatantly look down upon the family from a little balcony leading off the master bedroom. After a closer shot of Jeanne and Sophie, the film cuts a couple of times between them and the family down below them, and then to a close-up of the telephone line being cut, suggesting a greater seriousness of purpose than the girls' pretence of play would seem to acknowledge (Figure 11.2). Thus, when Jeanne asks, 'What next?' and Sophie replies, 'I don't know', Jeanne's response as she picks up one of the guns – 'Let's scare them' – again stops short of keying the gunplay as anything more than mere charade, even as Sophie is showing Jeanne how to load the gun (Figure 11.3).

That this moment is a crucial turning point is made clear as we cut back to the opera, where the intermission is indicated as the curtains close on the television screen. Melinda turns off the sound as Georges asks Catherine what she thinks. Catherine moves from comments on the opera to voicing her anxieties about noises she has heard beyond the world of openly fabricated

11.2 *La Cérémonie* (Claude Chabrol, 1995)

11.3 *La Cérémonie* (Claude Chabrol, 1995)

performance on the television screen (for example, the sound of glass breaking, which Melinda insists belongs to the operatic frame). Catherine is convinced that Jeanne is in the house, and, as Act II is about to begin on-screen,
Georges gives in to Catherine's anxieties and agrees to investigate. My own
mounting anxieties throughout this section of the film – from Jeanne picking
up the gun through to Georges going to investigate – are what led me to stop
the video at precisely this point. However, whereas Catherine's anxieties are
about what the girls may be doing – or what they may be on the brink of
doing – my own were very specifically focused on not wanting to see Georges
or the rest of the family catch them out. Indeed, the killings themselves come
as a welcome relief from this particular unease. With the sudden removal of

disapproving witnesses, the behaviour of Jeanne and Sophie is abruptly drained of all such affective power: it is no longer embarrassing to watch.

The lack of emotional display by either Jeanne or Sophie continues to keep us detached from either one throughout the murder of Georges in the kitchen, and the unsympathetic portrayal of Georges keeps us distanced from him as well. Such details as Georges's open collar and loosened tie are particularly effective in delineating what comes across as a sort of lordly ownership of his domain, with Georges insisting that Sophie and Jeanne observe the proprieties at the same time as he asserts his own right to flaunt them by presenting himself to them in mild disarray. I have already suggested that, if anything, we experience a degree of relief when Georges is no longer alive to make possible a scenario of embarrassment as he confronts the transgressive behaviour of the two young women. However, this is not the whole story. Jeanne's throwaway comment to Sophie following Georges's death – 'One down' – has the odd effect of making me smile, even as it signals the inevitability of the murders to come. Why, exactly, is this amusing? I can only make sense of this as a moment of complicity between Chabrol and us, something along the following lines: 'Let's see how far we can take this, after all we all know it's only a film.' It is a playful moment inserted in the midst of a scene where it really ought not to exist, a playfulness which acknowledges, perhaps, that the prospect of further murders which awaits us is also more exhilarating than it ought to be. And yet, as it is 'only' a film, our rising anticipation can be sanctioned and experienced as no more than cinematic fun. If Sophie and Jeanne turn gunplay into murder, then Chabrol seems to be giving us permission to relish the murders by turning them back into play.

Comparable to this moment of mischievous complicity between the viewer and Chabrol is an earlier scene, mentioned briefly above, when Catherine and her son Gilles are watching a film on television together, after she had responded to her husband's comment that he may be home late by telling him of their plans. 'With a tray ... without me,' he responds with mock mournfulness, and she replies teasingly, 'Without you. Good film, though!' The film turns out to be Chabrol's own work, *Les Noces rouges* (*Red Wedding*, 1973), about an unfaithful wife who helps her lover to murder her husband, a sly expression, perhaps, of Catherine's resentment at being put second to her husband's work. At one point, the lover (played by Michel Piccoli) turns to the camera with a conspiratorial smile at the wife in the film-within-the-film, but his direct address to the camera has the effect of implying a collusion with Catherine as well.

The way that the film-within-the-film provides a suggestive commentary on Catherine's situation and motives is echoed by the similar way the televised Mozart opera relates to the larger frame, and it equally privileges Catherine, though not exclusively. Thus, from the aftermath of Georges's murder, we cut back to the rest of the family watching the opera's second act, as Don Giovanni begins his serenade, and his words – 'Deh, vieni alla finestra ...' ('Oh, come to the window ...') are accompanied by an uneasy Catherine moving to the window of the sitting room as if in response to Don Giovanni's seductive invitation. Oddly, this has the effect of putting Catherine in the position of the operatic maid whom Don Giovanni is serenading, and, by implication, suggests a potential alliance between Catherine and her own maid Sophie, who in terms of the plot at that moment is, of course, her deadly adversary. The fact that Catherine sends her son Gilles after her husband to see what is happening elsewhere in the house, despite her strong suspicions that something is seriously amiss – in effect, sending Gilles to his death as she has already sent Georges to his – reinforces the sense of a potential alliance amongst the film's women, a shared set of interests, in opposition to the males. Further, it is surely not random that Melinda cites as her favourite bit of the opera the aria 'Ah! taci, ingiusto core' where Donna Elvira sings that Don Giovanni is 'un empio, è un traditore, è colpa aver pietà' ('a scoundrel, a deceiver, it is wrong to pity him'), just after her father has been killed in the kitchen.

However, although Melinda is extremely critical of her father at a couple of points in the film (referring to him as a fascist), and Catherine seems to be sending him to his doom with at least semi-conscious glimmerings of awareness of the fate which that entails, any alliance based on gender between Catherine and Melinda or between Catherine and Sophie is blocked by stronger loyalties based on blood and class. Indeed, the association of Melinda with Donna Elvira's words, and of Catherine with the situation of Donna Elvira's maid, suggests that class as well as blood may divide the step-daughter and step-mother, with the implication, perhaps, that Catherine has married above her station and is an interloper rather than a bona fide member of the upper middle classes. Nevertheless, the evocative shot of Jeanne and Sophie with raised guns aimed at Catherine and Melinda, who are standing face to face with them as if each pair of women is looking into a mirror, produces an overall image of blind self-destruction – of acting in opposition to their mutual affiliations through gender – despite the contrary alliances based on class, or at least on present position – which set the two pairs apart. This is in marked contrast to the various women in the televised opera who are damaged by Don Giovanni's seductive exploitation and form a more conscious and deliberate partnership to destroy him.

In the end, in any case, Chabrol's characters are *all* destroyed. The family are brutally murdered, as we have seen. However, Jeanne too is killed when she attempts to drive away, as her car stalls and is hit, with more than a little irony, by a car driven by the prim and disapproving abbé who had rebuked Jeanne and Sophie earlier in the film after receiving complaints about their insolence in the course of their charitable work for Catholic Relief. That the abbé is accompanied in the car by the equally disapproving female assistant we saw in the earlier scene may be innocent (he may merely be giving her a lift home after work, after all, even though it is already well into the evening), yet it is a detail which, at the very least, trails hints of possible improprieties of his own. However, we are given little time to speculate, for a far greater irony lies in wait: the police retrieve Melinda's tape recorder from the wreckage as Sophie watches and listens helpless from the shadows while the murder is replayed and the jaws of her trap snap shut.

The situation is so aesthetically delectable – and so intricately framed and laminated, like the earlier murder scene itself – that it is difficult to suppress a smile, as, once again, we embrace our utter complicity with Chabrol and the film, rather than with any of the characters who have been killed or caught before our eyes. The fact that the end credits have already begun to roll gives the moment an extra punch, presenting events which are so momentous for the characters as a sly parting shot from Chabrol to his audience, a sort of cinematic wink. This rekeying of the scene as 'only a film' is not merely an abrupt transition from narrative world to end credits. Rather, the end-credit sequence emphasises and continues to remind us of the narrative's most devastating events, whose consequences continue to unfold behind them just after Jeanne's body is removed, the memory of her death fresh in our minds, as the murder of the family is replayed on the tape recorder and Sophie looks on with something like bewilderment as her fate is sealed. Yet surely what we feel is Chabrol's irony rather than Sophie's blank helplessness and incomprehension of the workings of a world she is unable to read, nor any sense of profound emotional loss at Jeanne's death or the family's recent destruction.

However, despite the various instances throughout the film where we align ourselves with Chabrol and with the film's ironic placement of its characters within a class-bound frame, our embarrassment when the family's middle-class values are transgressed is clear evidence that we are caught within the very same frame ourselves. That is, our embarrassment – *my* embarrassment – when the frame of middle-class decorum is broken by Jeanne's and Sophie's behaviour in wreaking havoc in the master bedroom and playing with guns in the kitchen implicates us irrevocably in the family's middle-class values against which the film directs so much of its critique. The precariousness of our situation rests upon the fact that we are made complicit with the film's critical attitude towards the smug self-satisfaction of its middle-class characters and yet are simultaneously implicated in their values of decorum and cultivated good taste. Presumably, for viewers who are unembarrassed, the film's project as I have discerned it will falter and cease to work in the way I have described. So Chabrol's address is to an audience who share the values

of propriety and 'knowing one's place' which are endemic to bourgeois life –
at least if the strategies I have identified can be generalised beyond my own
experience of the film – and this sort of spectator appears, in fact as well as in
theory, to be the audience his films have mainly reached, at least in Britain.
(The screening of the film on BBC2 is evidence that the broadcasters made
some such assumption about the film's likely audience as well, though this
may have been mainly to do with its being a foreign-language film with
subtitles, rather than one that plays on middle-class anxieties in its viewers.)
In any case, just as Baudelaire famously addressed his putative reader as
'Hypocrite lecteur, mon semblable, mon frère' ('hypocritical reader, my likeness, my brother'), so too might we be admonished for our hypocrisy in
sharing values with characters from whom we strive to maintain an ironic
and complacent distance.

In this context, the family's destruction comes as a welcome relief not just
from our embarrassment that Jeanne and Sophie may be caught out, as
suggested earlier, but from the ideological tension of experiencing ironic
distance and acute embarrassment at the same time. Chabrol's use of
Les Noces rouges as a film-within-the-film looks much more calculated now.
Towards the end of that film, the illicit couple played by Michel Piccoli and
Stéphane Audran, who have murdered her husband so that they can be
together, are asked why they hadn't simply run off together instead, and they
reply that it had never occurred to them. Just as the killing of the Lelièvre
family solves the problem of our own position as a sort of 'hypocrite voyeur',
so too in Les Noces rouges does murder become the preferred solution –
indeed, the only one that presents itself – to an ideological conundrum the
couple cannot think themselves out of by other means, with furtive killing
more bearable than public disgrace.

Note

The translation I have used of lines of dialogue from the film is taken from the
English subtitles to the British television broadcast on 28 February 1999 on BBC2.
The translation into English of lines from Don Giovanni (sung in the original Italian
in the film) comes from the multi-lingual libretto accompanying the Decca recording
of a performance of the opera at the Royal Festival Hall, with Sir Georg Solti con-
ducting the London Philharmonic Orchestra and with Bryn Terfel as Don Giovanni.

Reference

Goffman, E. (1974) Frame Analysis (Harmondsworth: Penguin).

12

'Television aesthetics' and close analysis: style, mood and engagement in *Perfect Strangers* (Stephen Poliakoff, 2001)

Sarah Cardwell

'Television aesthetics' and close analysis

While the close textual analysis of film is undergoing something of a renascence (as this volume testifies), the same enterprise remains almost non-existent in television studies. Two principal reasons for this present themselves. First, the development of television studies out of sociology and cultural studies has led to a focus on television's import in political, ideological and socio-cultural terms, rather than in artistic or cultural terms. Second, television is still regarded as artistically impoverished in comparison with other arts. Little attention has been paid to what one may call the aesthetics of television: the analysis of thematic, formal and stylistic qualities; the exploration of 'questions which arise from a thinker's interest in beauty and in art' (Vivas and Krieger 1953: 5); and the consequent evaluation of an individual programme's achievements in these terms.

To some degree, the avoidance of such matters is understandable. I would not wish to make claims for the artistic or intellectual integrity and accomplishments of most televisual output. However, the customary focus on representation, ideology and socio-cultural context has had deleterious consequences for television studies, two of which concern me here. The lack of close analysis in the field has permitted work that is often derivative, unadventurous and under- or unsubstantiated to dominate. Scholars have strayed from an understanding that the most responsive and persuasive theorising arises from careful observations of the particularities of television texts. One of the objectives of this chapter is to demonstrate (in a necessarily limited fashion) how the methodology of close textual analysis can enhance television studies, by focusing specifically on aesthetic matters. The second consequence of the neglect of close analysis in television studies is that much of the genuinely exciting work that can be found tucked away in the television schedules has remained overlooked and undervalued. The second objective of this chapter, then, is to offer a critical appraisal of a small sample of the work of one of the most distinctive writers/directors in television today: Stephen Poliakoff.

In essence, I hope that this chapter will offer a modest starting point for a greater awareness of what might constitute a study of television aesthetics. Here, I draw upon a generalised understanding of the key foci of philosophical aesthetics: the criticism and evaluation of art, and the raising and tackling of questions that arise from our engagement with works of art. Thus, moving from a close analysis and critique of thematic, formal and stylistic qualities present in a particular televisual sequence, I aim to explore some of the questions that arise from the peculiarities of a single work. I wish to capture something of the individuality and distinctiveness of the programme, evaluate its achievements and also address the more 'theoretical' questions that the programme raises.[1] Through an exploration of a sequence from *Perfect Strangers*, I hope to be able to offer an engaged critical reflection upon central questions that arise in this case; these concern mood and engagement, and their intimate connections with style and form.[2]

The medium of television is the one which has most successfully cultivated Poliakoff's talent as a writer and director, and it is within television that he has developed distinctive and intriguing thematic preoccupations, formal techniques and traits of style and mood. He tends to work within a kind of inflected naturalism, which is inclined towards stylisation. Alongside naturalistic and realistic sequences, he constructs expressive montages using various media, which frequently traverse spatial and temporal boundaries; notably, these exhibit a formal responsiveness (between theme and style), forging links between images and moments, and emphasising their interconnectedness. The internal coherence of the montages echoes the broader structure and tone of Poliakoff's work, which is full of repeated motifs, patterns, obsessions and gradually elaborated themes.[3] Further, his idiosyncratic style creates an equally distinctive mood – or rather, a series of shifting moods.

The chosen sequence

I wish to focus on a sequence that occurs towards the end of Poliakoff's *Perfect Strangers*. This is a very complex, seven-and-a-half-minute sequence, containing 142 individual shots. It is difficult to capture such complexity within a chapter of this length, and I will not be able to offer a complete analysis of the entire sequence, but I hope that by focusing on a few representative moments from it, I will manage to convey a sense of some of the ways in which it works.

One of the abiding themes of Poliakoff's television work is family, and another is the relationship between past and present. In this sequence the two concerns are interwoven. The solutions to various puzzles of the plot are revealed, and their interconnectedness is elaborated. The sequence primarily involves Daniel (Matthew MacFayden), his father Raymond (Michael Gambon), and Stephen (Anton Lesser), a family friend and archivist. The narrative is centred on three still images: a black-and-white photograph of Daniel, as a young boy, dressed in fancy dress as a prince, and standing on a rather grand staircase (Figure 12.1); a large painted portrait of a young boy, dressed similarly (Figure 12.2); and a black-and-white photograph of Raymond's father (Jay Simon), who remains anonymous, garbed in a three-piece suit and a jaunty feather-topped hat, performing an arabesque in a

12.1 *Perfect Strangers* (Stephen Poliakoff, 2001)

12.2 *Perfect Strangers* (Stephen Poliakoff, 2001)

12.3 *Perfect Strangers* (Stephen Poliakoff, 2001)

sunny garden (Figure 12.3). The photographs are clues to a family history, and have remained unexplained and unconnected throughout the serial, despite Daniel's attempts to decipher them and grasp their significance.

In this sequence, Raymond and Stephen reveal to Daniel the truth behind the images, this being related to us through dialogue, voice-overs, flashbacks and montages. The sequence opens with Raymond and Stephen showing Daniel the portrait of the Little Prince that hangs in Henrietta's study.[4] Daniel recognises the costume in the portrait: it is the one he wore as a young boy, in the photograph. The connection is reinforced through a short montage that cuts between adult Daniel, observing the portrait, and 'young Daniel', dressed in the costume. Daniel is confused by this connection, unaware of why he was dressed after the portrait. Raymond and Stephen promise to reveal all, and the three men are shown walking purposefully towards the lawn upon which Raymond's father danced; it is here that Raymond says the answer will be revealed.

The three men assemble on the lawn, and Raymond discloses that his father had a long-lasting, illicit affair with Henrietta (Sarah Guyler/Iris Russell), his brother's wife. The picture of Raymond's father dancing captured his performance for Henrietta, as she stood almost completely hidden, in the bushes at the edge of the lawn. Raymond, as a child, had watched his father's dance without being aware of the secret audience, and thus without grasping its true significance. As Raymond divulges this, the events are replayed for us, in 'fuzzy' Super-8 colour images, intercut with the present: we see his father dance, and we follow Daniel's gaze as he looks into the bushes where Henrietta had stood – there, we see her, in 'flashback'. Raymond relates how Henrietta and his father would frequently meet in her study, and would make love underneath the Little Prince portrait. We see a beautifully composed image of this: the pair of them perfectly framed underneath the painting, kissing passionately; the two young lovers are handsome, the décor is impressive, the colours are warm: the image is both romantic and erotic.

After this image, we return to the three men on the lawn. Raymond clarifies: the portrait and the photograph, connected through the similarity of the costume in each one, are intimately related. Raymond describes how the photograph of Daniel was taken; we see this event in a montage that cuts between adult Daniel, and flashbacks of Raymond's father and Henrietta with young Daniel (the latter is seen in both colour and black and white, posing for the photograph). The scene is played out for us: we see Henrietta welcoming Daniel to a children's fancy dress party that she has organised, and we observe her smile of recognition as she realises that Daniel has been costumed by his grandfather to look like the Little Prince portrait, as a visual reminder of their private passion – a tangible token of his enduring love. The two lovers send the other children upstairs to tea, and tell Daniel to stand still on the stairs so that they can photograph him. Daniel obeys, and the picture is taken. Finally, we hear adult Daniel, as his memories begin to resurface, speaking of how he remembers pulling from his neck the uncomfortable ruff he had been forced to wear, and kicking off one of the ornate shoes. We see this, and then we see Raymond's father picking up a weary young Daniel and carrying him from the party, minus his shoe and ruff. As they leave, we see a shot of Daniel's face, gazing back into the camera, at Henrietta, and then we see Henrietta from Daniel's (retreating) point of view, as she looks sadly after them.

This scene is followed by another flashback montage, but this time we return to Henrietta as a young woman, shown in a series of shots posing for photographs and staring directly into the camera. We are then returned to the present, and to Daniel, for whom the pieces finally fit together. He does not speak, however; the final words of the sequence are uttered by Raymond: 'It's great. I love it. The two pictures – *our* two pictures – they're for the same reason, Daniel: my father's secret life.'

Moving moments: style, mood and emotion

In much television drama, melodramatic strategies are employed, which tend to prioritise emotional movement and climax. As Steve Neale has argued, citing Daniel Gerould, 'melodrama involves the subordination of all other elements "to one overriding aesthetic goal: the calling forth of "pure", "vivid" emotions"' (1990: 66). However, this sequence rejects the melodramatic mode, subverting its conventional dramatic strategies. Here, stylistic and formal features are not subordinated to emotion, even though in terms of narrative development this is a climax, a moment of revelation, of significant emotional importance to the central characters. Here, as in much of Poliakoff's work, rather than a determined movement towards a moment of intense emotion, there is a continual 'pulling back' from a clearly defined emotional release.

Further, aspects of style, theme and performance appear to be foregrounded as important in themselves, as potential sources of pleasure, not just as a means to an end. Perhaps I ought to clarify that I am making two implicit claims here: first, that much television drama can be broadly categorised as 'melodrama' (as defined above), and second, that *Perfect Strangers* refuses to fully embrace that familiar and widespread generic identity. Instead, *Perfect Strangers* forges connections with other 'genres' such as art cinema and the much less visible 'art television' at least as frequently as it draws upon melodramatic strategies. A full exploration of the programme's peculiar generic identity might shed light upon our evaluation of it, for it is possible that in its rejection of familiar melodramatic conventions, *Perfect Strangers* stakes its claim as 'quality' television – as an impressive artwork. (Unfortunately, there is not space here to pursue (or substantiate) this tentative but intriguing line of investigation more fully.)

Through its abjuration of melodramatic structure and movements, this sequence creates a distinctive, yet indeterminate and continually fluctuating mood.[5] 'Mood' is commonly understood to arise from stylistic particularities; according to Greg M. Smith, certain formal qualities constitute 'mood cues' which tend to induce comparable mood states in the viewer. Smith emphasises that 'a mood is not entirely self-perpetuating ... It requires occasional moments of strong emotion [emotion markers] to maintain the mood' (G. M. Smith 1999: 116). Yet this sequence avoids the emotion markers that would ordinarily be considered vital to the maintenance of mood; it creates an emotional expectancy and fulfils our expectations of the narrative (the puzzle is solved), but this is dealt with in an understated way and does not constitute a clear movement towards emotional climax and catharsis. There is a sense of a mist clearing, of a peeling away of the obfuscating layers of history and intrigue, and of revelation, conveyed primarily through Raymond's and Daniel's expressions of satisfaction and wonder. Yet instead of rushing towards *emotional* revelation, the programme seems to enact restraint, balancing movement, pacing and articulation.

The structuring of images and sounds (including music and dialogue) is such that they work together to achieve this 'holding off', this sustaining of mood. In broad terms, the music repeatedly rises and falls, rather than leading to a grand finale. And a comparable denial of climax is evident in the way in which the central revelation – of the secret affair – is dealt with. It is drawn out gradually, through fragmented images leading to longer series of shots, and to the presentation of a passionate moment shared by the semi-naked couple under the oil painting, but then we are led *past* that moment, on to the same couple in old age and in separation. The sequence refuses to linger on its most romantic and beautiful image, a picture of love consummated; it moves beyond the moment, undermining its potential as a classic, significant climax; it prefers a less explicit, non-sexual denouement that maintains the emphasis, inherent in the sequence's form, on the flow of time.

Images and montage

When Daniel looks into the bushes at the side of the lawn, he and we search the bushes as presented now in colour, now in a black-and-white photograph, seeking the person (Henrietta) who hid amongst them as his grandfather danced. Point-of-view shots consistent with Daniel's 'actual' view are intercut with point-of-view shots from the same space but looking 'into' the old photograph, so that Daniel and we seem able to look not just across space but also through time. Images of past and present are placed consecutively in order to construct a curious, sustained cross-temporal shot/reverse shot sequence. In mixing shots that are spatially consistent but temporally inconsistent, it is implied that emotional and thoughtful connections can be made across temporal boundaries. It is implicitly affirmed that places and people offer continuities between past and present, so that the past may persist within the present, through our cognition. The overwhelming emphasis is on the role of humankind – rather than places, objects or relics – in forging connections between past and present. The moving camera within both black-and-white and colour shots as Daniel searches for meaning within the bushes works to link the two, and to emphasise the active role that he and we must undertake: a literal refocusing, a determined search for meaning. Further, it is a human connection that is sought in the bushes: the revelation is of Henrietta's face. We discover not just a 'fact' but another human being.

While the formal technique of intermedia, 'cross-temporal' montage is vital in constructing a sense of potential connections through space and time – one of the preoccupations of the narrative – it is also pleasing in itself. Within this sequence, there are still images (paintings, photographs and motionless film images) and moving images (on 35 mm film, video and Super-8). The different media used bring with them other variations in grain, texture, density of colour, and spectra of colour (from black and white to full colour). The eclectic nature of the montage opens up various possibilities for engagement and interpretation (as we shall see), but the fragments are intimately related and narrative trajectories, character subjectivities and music all act as unifying or cohesive forces. A degree of openness thus co-exists with formal unity. The montage is carefully orchestrated: themes are developed and explored, movements are constructed, codas are reached. The

images and music work together to create a 'tertium quid': 'the comple-
mentarity inherent in this relation produces a level of meaning and emotive
significance that is qualitatively different from the meanings of the visual and
music tracks themselves' (J. Smith 1999: 157).

Music, dialogue and sound

Noël Carroll presents the common observation that music lacks emotional
specificity: 'typically, non-vocal music is expressive of emotional qualities
but ones that are inexplicit, ambiguous, and broad' (Carroll 1988: 220). This
sequence capitalises on music's lack of specificity, and on its capacity to be
expressive of emotion in a way that enables it to approximate a non-verbal,
and otherwise inexpressible, state.[6] Further, the sequence exploits the fact
that television (like film) is capable of combining the expressive qualities of
images, language and music simultaneously. Here, the configuration of the
three varies between concord and dissonance.

Concord

Adrian Johnston's music has become a familiar feature of Poliakoff's television work, and is integral to this sequence. It permeates it, yet it works not
in a conventionally reactive and supplementary way, highlighting moments
of intense emotion, but in a more nuanced manner, forging links with other
elements. Both Poliakoff's and Johnston's work can be broadly described as
characterised by repetition, wistfulness and thoughtfulness. The nature of the
music – its rippling, subtly changing emphases and shifts through its reiteration of themes and motifs – echoes the narrative concerns of the sequence –
the gradual uncovering of clues, the repeating of memories, the 'going back
over things'. The music links fragmented images together, continuing as it
does across the sequence, and thus operating to fulfil one of Jerrold Levinson's
fourteen functions of film music: 'the imparting of certain formal properties,
such as coherence, cogency, continuity, closure, to the film or parts thereof'
(1996: 258).

Yet the music also alters with the changing mood of the narrative. The
central repeated theme moves gradually and step-by-step up and down the
scale, and is picked up by various instruments according to the mood of
the moment. First, as the portrait of the boy in the 'Little Prince' costume is
revealed to Daniel, woodwind and string instruments playing low down the
scale underscore the moment, creating a suspenseful, questioning, expectant
mood. The discovery of the portrait signals that the mystery is about to be
unravelled and the pieces are to be fitted together, and the characters are
experiencing a sense of heightened involvement with the mystery and an
awareness of its imminent resolution. Then, the theme is picked up by jauntier

strings, with an increased sense of pace and movement; this echoes the purposeful strides of the characters as they walk towards the next 'clue' (the lawn where Raymond's father danced), and their quickening interest in the story being unravelled. At the moment at which the illicit affair is disclosed, and Henrietta's face is revealed through the leaves of the bushes, the music peaks, not through a crescendo, but on a sustained high note, followed by a moment of silence. This is an almost climactic moment: a question is posed as the camera lingers on her face (who is the woman and what is her importance?) and we are suspended, anticipating an answer. The use of fermata rather than crescendo marks the moment as important without shaping it into a climax in an obviously dramatic way. Moreover, the moment passes; slow strings and piano then take over and develop the theme, the piano bringing a fingered precision, marking time more precisely than the strings did, and echoing the urgent and constrained nature of the lovers' romance and the fact that it was ill-fated, always about to run out of time.

After the revelation of Henrietta, the music becomes temporarily sombre: the piano's interlude is succeeded by a melancholy and mournful oboe, backed with strings, which develops the central theme, as the inauspicious nature of Daniel's grandfather's romance is relayed. As the sequence moves to its end, the music gathers momentum towards a pleasing and broadly harmonious combination of piano, oboe and strings together, suggesting the closure that this solved mystery will bring to both characters and viewers. However, there is a break – a few seconds of silence – which marks a movement towards greater subjectivity, as the remainder of the sequence focuses on Henrietta's feelings and on the young Daniel's place within the story (as the Little Prince). This final section shows how Henrietta had to come to terms with the futility of her secret love for Raymond's father, and how Daniel was 'used' by his now-aged grandfather, formed into a visual echo of the portrait in order to symbolise his love for Henrietta.

Dissonance

In attempting to express the different experiences and emotions of these two characters, the final part of the sequence displays a dissonance between their respective subjectivities that complicates its mood. The music and images enter a strange relationship, and our sympathies are pulled in two directions. In many films and television programmes, emotional foci are clearly established, so that the emotional vibrancy of the musical score is directed towards something. But here, the use of montage and the presentation of two subjectivities within the same sequence work to multiply potential foci, preventing obvious particularisation, and music's fundamental indeterminacy is exploited.

The emotional tenor of this final section of the sequence guides our sympathies to lie initially with the two thwarted lovers: Henrietta and Raymond's father. The music echoes the progress of their romance, its ultimate demise and their always unresolved feelings for one another, and the shots of Henrietta throughout this section enhance our engagement with her. From the shot of Henrietta as an old woman, watching Raymond's father as he leaves her party, the section moves to the montage of shots of Henrietta as a young woman. The first of these is of her having her photograph taken as she lies on a chaise longue (we hear the shutter click and the image is briefly still) – but just after the photograph is taken, she turns and looks thoughtfully and sadly into the distance, suggesting something of her repressed feelings. The following montage is of her posing, motionless, for more photographs, but these are formal portraits and she stares directly and in a detached manner into the lens. Juxtaposed after the previous image, and linked together with poignant, almost plangent, music, this montage highlights the hidden nature of her true feelings, indeed of her 'liveliness', and sets up a tension between the polished, perfect woman in the photographs and the unhappy yet 'real' woman behind them. In this sense, the music is expressive of the feelings of Henrietta. This seems a perfect example of affective congruence: the 'music ... influence[s] the interpretation of visual information by moving the affective meaning of the visual event closer to the specific affective character of the music' (J. Smith 1999: 161).

Jeff Smith has explored how filmmakers may choose between 'playing the mood of the scene [or playing] the mood of the character' (J. Smith 1999: 156). One of the finest accomplishments of Poliakoff's work here is that he manages to do both at once, setting up a dissonance within the otherwise harmonious section. This section does not sustain a straightforward mood; nor is it univocal. The congruence between music and images is not wholeheartedly expressive of Henrietta's subjectivity, for there is a focus not just on Henrietta but also on Daniel. Notably, Daniel, in flashback as a young boy, frequently looks directly into the camera just as Henrietta does. Like Henrietta, his face is almost expressionless, and is legible only with reference to other elements.

Daniel as an adult discovers that he, as the Little Prince, is the key to the mystery, but this involves a discovery that he is little more than a clue, like the photographs, the portrait, the ruff, the shoe and the staircase. Within the story being told, he is little more than an object that was used by someone else. He was given meaning by his grandfather by being dressed up as a Little Prince. Indeed, Daniel understands himself as both a significant individual and a potential 'thing' – objectified by others for their own ends: on seeing the portrait, he says, 'There it is. That's the Little Prince. There I am'. Whilst one function of this line is to stress the pertinent connection, its expressive use of near-repetition ('There it is ... There I am') draws our attention to the change in pronoun from 'it' to 'I'. Daniel is both an object and a person within this mystery, and this is emphasised by his father's words: 'He must have hired the costume. No doubt it was a form of signal: a sign of his continuing love for her, a message. *You were a visual gift* (emphasis mine).

This objectification of Daniel is not presented unproblematically, and Daniel's expression as he stares into the camera, head tilted downwards, with pouting lips and a direct gaze, can be read as reproachful and resentful: he wishes to resist being used by those around him. The voice-over of the adult Daniel educes this reading: he states that he disliked the costume he was forced to wear, and emphasises his frustration with looking different from the other children. His direct gaze at Henrietta and his grandfather is again ambiguous, but within its context one might surmise that it is not so much uncomprehending, as comprehending that something is being kept from him – he realises that he is being made to do something and that the reason for it is not being explained.

The presentation of Henrietta's and Daniel's contrary perceptions of the Little Prince story within the same section creates two counter-currents, complicating the question of with whom we might be aligned, and for whom we might feel sympathy. The music plays a part in this. Although the theme has been linked with Henrietta (as described above), it is also connected with Daniel's point of view. First, the music, while expressive of Henrietta's internal experiences, is also necessarily presented as an accompaniment to her 'story' as it is told to Daniel and to us – it consequently reflects Daniel's changing understanding of her story. Even more clearly, the music is shown to be expressively linked with Daniel's thoughts and perceptions, as the final shot of this sequence makes manifest. The camera lingers on Daniel's face as he makes sense of the narrative with which he has just been presented; a small but perceptible eye movement indicates that he has 'refocused': he no longer stares into the mid-distance but now directs his gaze towards his father. As this eye movement occurs, the music comes to an end, implying Daniel's progression from inward reflection and thought to a clearer connection with the external, present world. The link between the music and Daniel's (rather than Henrietta's) subjectivity is thus affirmed.

In this way, the music is connected with both characters, and thus refuses its potential function of expressing one particular character's feelings. The tone of the music is such that it can be regarded as expressive of Henrietta's feelings of loss and irresolution and simultaneously, yet almost contradictorily, Daniel's feelings of disturbance and resentment. The mood is thus sustained by the existence of two counter-currents, and the music sustains both rather than prioritising one over the other. The non-object-directed nature of music is successfully exploited here to reinforce the scene's ambivalence. The score neither simplistically enhances nor bluntly establishes the mood of the sequence, and it does not work to establish a 'preparatory' mood that is then developed towards an emotional climax and release.

Music is not the only element of the soundtrack that is vital to this sequence. The tonal qualities of the spoken word cannot be overlooked. Appropriately for a programme that is concerned with the importance of human beings as storytellers and players, dialogue features strongly in the sequence. Raymond and Stephen relate their findings to Daniel, and Daniel's questioning draws out further details of the narrative. All three characters are educated, eloquent, highly articulate and expressive; their language is frequently stylised, even poetic, rather than everyday. The use of such language opens up possibilities for greater expressiveness and meaningfulness, and the verbal development and reiteration of themes. Most notably, the dialogue utilises near-repetition to great expressive effect.

The pleasures of repetition

One of the most singular aspects of Poliakoff's dialogue is in its emphasis on near repetition or, more precisely, rearticulation. Mirroring Poliakoff's own concern with expressiveness, many of his central characters appear relentlessly to strive for some kind of ideal articulation – a perfect intelligibility and vividness – although this is, understandably, rarely achieved. Rearticulation is a primary means by which the characters convey their thoughts and feelings to others, and think through their own dilemmas. So when one of the central characters, Charles (Toby Stephens), distraught, calls his sister, Rebecca (Claire Skinner), from his workplace bathroom, he describes himself as 'crying on the phone, weeping in the lavatory'. The unnecessary reiteration of what is visibly apparent emphasises both his distress and his desire to communicate his situation, to state it, to put it into words, and to discover for himself why he is feeling as he is. In this way, one may observe a character undergoing a process of self-reflection and gradual self-realisation – although again this is a process that will rarely attain completion.

The use of repetition in dialogue as a means for characters to come to know themselves and their situations is seen again in the sequence explored here, when Daniel and Raymond attempt to elaborate and affirm their awareness of their own roles within the story of Henrietta and Raymond's father:

RAYMOND: Of course I realised – Stephen helped me realise – and what I remembered for the first time, is what was really going on in the picture.

DANIEL: You mean someone else was there, in the photograph?

RAYMOND: Exactly. Somebody else was there; there was someone else in the picture.

And when the reason for his Little Prince costume suddenly dawns upon Daniel, Raymond's search for synonyms emphasises the importance of attempting to capture accurately in language the truth, the meaningfulness, of a moment or a situation: 'He must have hired the costume. No doubt it was a form of signal, a sign of his continuing love for her, a message. You were a visual gift.'

There are several consequences of this stylistic trait in Poliakoff's dialogue besides the part it plays in character development. The repetitive reshaping of ideas into different words has the effect of stalling the narrative, slowing the pace more generally, and allowing the 'patterning' motif present in the music and the montage of images to be extended into the dialogue. This tallies with the programme's preoccupation with the processes of returning to, reconsidering and re-evaluating relics of and clues to the past, and of renegotiating one's relationship with that past. It simultaneously expresses that all such processes are ongoing, never-ending, a necessary part of human existence. It is also a source of satisfaction, fulfilment, resolution and even pleasure – for the characters, and potentially for the viewer. Going back to something, going back *over* something, as all three characters in this sequence are bound to do, is an experience which heightens our awareness of that something's potential significance – its meaningfulness. In this sequence, the three central images are found to be valuable not just (not even) because of their own inherent qualities, but because of their role in a wider context – one which can only be grasped, vitally, through human agency and a resolute commitment to understanding.

It becomes clear, then, that the use of repetition and near-repetition in *Perfect Strangers*, present in music, in images and in dialogue, is the primary way in which themes and ideas are developed (and left open). Repetition is a formal quality that permeates the work, delivering a sense of coherence and unity. Music and dialogue, intricate and expressive in themselves, become part of a coherent whole through the way in which they are intimately connected with other elements of narrative, theme and style. Yet through its constant revisiting and rearticulation, the programme also retains a sense of 'open-endedness', of the perpetual possibilities for developments, amendments and revisions, while the use of montage, mixed media and ambiguous subjectivities resist homogenisation and simple uniformity. Even the three central images of the sequence (the photograph of Daniel as the Little Prince, the portrait and the photograph of Raymond's father dancing) are themselves less clearly delineated and more mutable than one might expect; in this sequence these images are fragmented and multiplied. An alternative shot of Daniel on the staircase, peering through the banisters, is included alongside the 'original' photograph with which we are familiar, and new photographs are introduced into the sequence, with no explanation as to their origin. For example, we see a photograph of Raymond as a child, watching his father dance, yet this image has not been previously displayed, nor is it referred to by any of the characters. It is almost as if the concrete existence of these alternative and multiple images in the diegetic world is questionable; the montage sequence thus moves outside the bounds of the narrative and into an alternative space, in which the fragmented images suggest something of the breadth and variety of human stories and experiences.

The programme affords the viewer varied pleasures. As a formal quality, repetition can give rise to pleasurable experiences, as Bruce Kawin has persuasively shown (Kawin 1972). In *Perfect Strangers* repetition opens up a wealth of affective and interpretative pleasures. One effect of Poliakoff's 'wordiness' on the viewer is that one has time to engage with and reflect upon the ideas, thoughts, feelings and themes being articulated, both emotionally and intellectually. Further, the coherence, the internal beauty of the sequence, works to sustain a thoughtful, wistful mood that encourages reflective responses from the willing viewer.[7]

Whilst many popular television serials can be regarded as having 'transparent narratives', Poliakoff's narratives require unravelling. They make demands upon the viewer; they elicit concentration and thought as well as emotion; they require the interested viewer to engage in interpretation and evaluation. Carroll writes, 'interpretative play ... remains a characteristic from of interaction with artworks [and] if we encounter an object designed to support interpretative play ... then we have a reason to believe it is an artwork' (Carroll 2001: 15). If this is the case, the fact that *Perfect Strangers* permits, even demands, interpretation and subsequent evaluation means that one may regard it as an artwork. Again, I find myself needing to draw out the two parts of the claim I am making here. Explicitly, I am merely making an assertion about how one may categorise *Perfect Strangers*, in a similar way to that in which I earlier attempted to delineate its generic categorisation (that is, to explicate its links with and distinctions from melodrama, and art film and television). Yet I am aware that I am additionally, and implicitly, making a rather different kind of claim – an evaluative one (a critical judgement); for inherent within words such as 'artwork' is an implication of value, a suggestion that the programme ought to be more highly regarded than others. Although this is not the place to draw out the complexities of this matter, it is nevertheless important to acknowledge it, and to recognise that such claims must inevitably lead us back to the question of the appropriateness of developing our awareness of 'television aesthetics'.

Reflections: television, close analysis and aesthetics

When I first watched *Perfect Strangers*, the sequence explored here struck me as particularly accomplished. I felt unable to take it all in on a first viewing; it demanded closer attention. In particular, I was struck by the curious mood of the sequence and, relatedly, by the ambiguous feelings it aroused in me: I was wholeheartedly drawn into the moment, yet I was unable to describe precisely what I felt about it and about the story and characters presented. Being interested in recent theoretical work on film style and mood, I wanted to see how valuable my favourite 'theories' would be in helping me to understand the sequence and its effects upon me. I discovered that this recent work on filmic moods does not unproblematically offer the explanatory power it has done on other occasions, and requires further development. Simultaneously I found that Poliakoff had achieved something extraordinary in this sequence in terms of mood, through his manipulation of stylistic and formal elements.

Thus the close analysis of this particular sequence allowed me to address certain critical questions that arose in my mind because of my engagement with the sequence itself, and because of my related interest in theories about style and mood. Why is this important? It is important because there is still a widely held perception that the close analysis of films means negating or avoiding 'theoretical questions'; this is even more true in television studies, where close analysis is rarely seen as a useful contribution to the field at all. Yet in focusing on a sequence which engaged, intrigued and pleased me from my first viewing of it, I was led 'outwards' to consider how I ought to revisit and revise my understanding of larger theoretical issues. In short, I was led to those 'questions which arise from a thinker's interest in beauty and in art' that are particular to the field of aesthetics. If television scholars were to undertake such journeys more often, we would be led to a greater critical appreciation of individual programmes and programme-makers (writers and directors), and a more mature understanding of television forms and genres, structures and styles. We would also feel more able to offer evaluations and critical judgements. Such work can only enhance the field of television studies and its object: the art of television.

Notes

1 It is important to emphasise that the theoretical questions I will address are 'raised by' the text. That is, the sequence demands that we explore its affectiveness and its power, and in undertaking this exploration we are led to certain theoretical issues and not others. This is to be distinguished from the more usual approach that begins by making assumptions about which theories might be 'applied' to the text in question.
2 *Perfect Strangers* (Talkback Productions, UK), broadcast on BBC2, May 2001.
3 In this sense, the way in which Poliakoff organises his montage sequences owes more to Kuleshov's notion of 'linkage' than to Eisenstein's notion of 'conflict'. (See Stam 2000: 37–47).
4 The appellation 'Little Prince' is used by the characters in *Perfect Strangers*.

5 I use the term 'mood' rather than the alternative term 'tone' for a number of
   reasons. First, because 'mood' seems somehow more ambiguous, and less easily
   determined and described (which reflects the nature of this sequence), whereas
   'tone' has associations with attitude and voice that I do not particularly want to
   suggest. Also, the word 'mood' can be related to the viewer's emotional state as
   well as to something present within the text. For a fuller discussion of the term
   'mood' and its difference from emotion, with particular reference to nostalgia,
   see Cardwell (2002: 144–7).
6 Poliakoff employs music and repetition, both of which, it is claimed, afford us
   'non-verbal' modes of expression and comprehension (see Kivy (1993, 1997) on
   music, and Kawin (1972) on repetition).
7 I use the phrase 'the willing viewer'. This is to say that I am not assuming 'this is
   how one does respond' but 'this is how one *can* respond'. The sequence permits
   one to engage with it in certain ways, if one is a 'willing viewer': an interested and
   enthusiastic viewer who wishes to thoughtfully engage with and interpret the text.

References

Cardwell, S. (2002) *Adaptation Revisited: Television and the Classic Novel* (Manchester:
   Manchester University Press).
Carroll, N. (2001) *Beyond Aesthetics: Philosophical Essays* (Cambridge: Cambridge
   University Press).
Carroll, N. (1988) *Mystifying Movies: Fads and Fallacies in Contemporary Film Theory*
   (New York: Columbia University Press).
Kawin, B. (1972) *Telling It Again and Again: Repetition in Literature and Film* (Boulder:
   University Press of Colorado).
Kivy, P. (1993) *The Fine Art of Repetition: Essays in the Philosophy of Music* (Cambridge:
   Cambridge University Press).
Kivy, P. (1997) 'Music in the Movies: A Philosophical Enquiry', in R. Allen and
   M. Smith (eds) *Film Theory and Philosophy* (Oxford: Clarendon Press), pp. 308–
   28.
Levinson, J. (1996) 'Film Music and Narrative Agency', in D. Bordwell and N. Carroll
   (eds) *Post-Theory: Reconstructing Film Studies* (Madison, WI: University of
   Wisconsin Press).
Neale, S. (1990) 'Questions of genre', *Screen*, 31, 1, 45–66.
Smith, G. M. (1999) 'Local Emotions, Global Moods, and Film Structure', in
   C. Plantinga and G. M. Smith (eds), *Passionate Views: Film, Cognition and Emotion*
   (Baltimore and London: Johns Hopkins University Press), pp. 103–26.
Smith, J. (1999) 'Movie Music and Moving Music: Emotion, Cognition, and the Film
   Score', in C. Plantinga and G. M. Smith (eds), *Passionate Views: Film, Cognition and
   Emotion* (Baltimore and London: Johns Hopkins University Press), pp. 146–67.
Stam, R. (2000) *Film Theory: An Introduction* (Oxford: Blackwell).
Vivas, E. and M. Krieger (1953) *The Problems of Aesthetics: A Book of Readings* (New
   York: Rinehart).

13

How cinematography creates meaning in *Happy Together* (Wong Kar-Wai, 1997)

Cathy Greenhalgh

> I think cinematography is very close to my physiological or psychosomatic state
> of mind, which is ... you think on your feet, you move around a lot, you resolve
> conceptual problems or emotions visually. (Doyle 1998c)

This chapter situates a sequence analysis within the production context
surrounding cinematographer Christopher Doyle's work on the film *Happy
Together: A Story of Reunion*, his fifth collaboration with Hong Kong
director Wong Kar-Wai and production, costume designer and editor William
Chang. It draws on interviews conducted with Doyle (Doyle 1998c; Doyle
et al. 2002), and on his published diaries. Cinematographic elements
are extrapolated from three consecutive sequences which exemplify the
filmmakers' approach, as evidence of particular ways in which cinematography affects meaning in this film.

Cinematography is rarely discussed at length in film criticism, and the
practices of image making, embedded in the complexity of production,
are even less frequently considered. Feature-film cinematography has many
inherited shooting conventions, but also exploits ways of seeing discovered
in the making. This is an attempt to indicate through an examination of one
cinematographer's work how an exploration of these processes can enrich
our understanding of films.

Cinematography is usually judged simply by its service to the narrative.
Yet film viewers often recall specific images and pivotal moments in the
storytelling as experienced through their bodily and sensory perception, when
they may not remember whole plots. Vivian Sobchack argues that film
theory generally ignores this 'somatic intelligibility' and attempts 'to locate
the sensuous *on* the screen as the semantic property of cinematic objects
and the semiotic effects of cinematic representation, or *off* the screen in the
spectator's fantasmatic psychic formations, cognitive processes, and basic
sensory reflexes' (Sobchack 2004: 4, 15).

Cinematographers, on the other hand, tend to assume that viewers engage with characters and stories emotionally through experiencing the 'feeling' of images. For Doyle, finding the rhythmic flow is a way of engendering a presence on screen which might have this effect. He claims: 'You don't know why an image works or not ... the only thing that really works and communicates is the energy of the shot' (Doyle 1998b: 49).

Some cinematographers come up with choreographic or musical metaphors when asked how they visualise a film and what they do on set. Though appropriated from other disciplines, these analogies more accurately evoke the physical and mental process of regulating an activity which simultaneously integrates framing, camera movement and lighting with the developing narrative than the standard descriptive nomenclature of film language. To see what the effect of the cinematography may be, identifying the space-time frame of a film or a sequence may be more useful in that it directs our attention to the fluid aspects of shooting (as well as sound design and editing). It can offer a way of grasping what film criticism often struggles with or ignores – the physical and emotional experience of movie-going.

The professional relationship between Wong Kar-Wai, Chris Doyle and William Chang, and the working practices they have developed, provide a particularly rich context for thinking about these issues. In Kar-Wai's films mise-en-scène is not coordinated by traditional rules. Space cannot be viewed simply as physical space to be organised for the camera. Objects and actors are not placed within a preconceived staging but the elements of mise-en-scène are improvised and mobilised in fluid relationship with each other. Temporality is treated as kinaesthetic and mutable experience, using registers of movement, lighting tone and texture to express characters' feelings and events. In his diary about *Happy Together*, Doyle describes how they imagine space and one of their 'trademark' shots:

> It's the concepts of space = context and repetition = identity. ... These familiar themes occur in almost every Wong film to date. Closeness vs. 'impossibility of love' and dynamism vs. 'the need to hold on'. (Doyle 1998a: 106)

> There's no word in English. In Chinese we say 'kong jing'. They're not your conventional 'establishing shots' because they're about atmosphere and metaphor, not space. ... The only thing they establish is a mood or totally subjective point of view. They are clues to an 'ambient' world we want to suggest but not explain. (Doyle 1998a: 24)

Critics have identified Kar-Wai's films as revolutionary, but many of their features stem from a background making films in Hong Kong. David Bordwell notes, in his discussion of the broader traditions of Hong Kong filmmaking, that 'as a script is not the core of production, but a director's idea, action is constructed reel-by-reel, not by three act structure' (Bordwell

2000: 122). Many of the practices and stylistic tropes he identifies in this context – 'speed changes and "collision editing" for action sequences', for example – equally characterise the particular films directed by Wong Kar-Wai (2000: 35).

These methods derive from the non-unionised context in Hong Kong, which also provides collaboration opportunities rare in the West. Australian-born cinematographer Doyle, who has lived in Hong Kong for many years, also exhibits photo collages and writes about the films he shoots. William Chang is a well-known production designer, costume designer and editor. Kar-Wai worked as a graphic designer and wrote feature scripts. They, and lead actors Tony Leung and Leslie Cheung, had previously worked together on Hong Kong action movies, commercials and pop promos.

During handover fever in 1996, Kar-Wai, Chang and Doyle deliberately exiled themselves, leaving Hong Kong with a small crew and some of the industry's most famous actors, bound for Argentina, to make the film which turned out as *Happy Together*. The intended six-week shoot ended up as five months. The feelings of both actors and crew about exile and their home city were an influence on the improvised nature of the filming process. [1] Though the film was influenced by tango music and the novels of Manuel Puig, they found they made 'another love letter to Hong Kong' (Kar-Wai in Charity 1998: 74).

Happy Together is a romantic, wistful, almost farcical tale of two Hong Kong gay lovers, Ho Po-wing (Leslie Cheung) and Lai Yiu-fai (Tony Leung), on a long 'holiday' escape. The only love-making in the film happens at the beginning: a black-and-white sequence of the two men having sex in a seedy hotel room. Lai's voice-over tells us they've come to Argentina to 'start over', but between intimacies, sulking and rows they are trapped in cycles of isolation, togetherness and longing for each other. Lai saves money to return home and works in a tango bar, a kitchen and an abattoir, whilst Ho loses himself cruising the streets as a prostitute. Inspired by the optimistic young Chang (Chang Chen), Lai takes a bus to the majestic Iguazu falls, eventually returning to Hong Kong alone.

'Nostalgia can be found in all Chinese and Hong Kong cinema', but Kar-Wai is obsessed with themes of 'home, homelessness and belonging ... diaspora, exile, travel, and migration' (Chow 2001: 231). Home in *Happy Together* is Lai's one-room apartment, where a few objects, such as the warm, stripy, brightly coloured blankets and the lampshade, with its flickering Iguazu waterfalls 'cartoon' effect, take on enormous symbolic significance, standing for the potential of the relationship. But home is a precarious space, coloured in both art direction and lighting with a rather sickly warm golden green and red tone. The lovers eat, wash, tidy, caress and argue in the tiny apartment.

The streets and the empty docks are places where the lovers have walked together as travellers, or which they have sloped through without each other, remeeting by accident. Intimate incidents of the film often occur in border spaces: the doorway of the tango bar, when Lai gives and lights Ho's cigarette; the men's lavatory when Ho teaches Lai tango. The spaces are metaphors for extremes of the relationship: cosseted and delicate to polluted and desolate.

The narrative is revealed through gesture, space and the repetition of the theme of loss and belonging, rather than specific linear plot points. 'The prosaic rationales of acts and arcs' are abandoned in favour of something 'more fragmented ... more akin to flicking through a photo album ... character and emotion seep through landscape and image' (Charity 1998: 74).

In the following three sequences, which last around four minutes in total, we witness the final break-up of the lovers and find an anguished Lai facing his isolation and loneliness. Lai has decided to look after the beaten-up and injured Ho, who has turned up at his apartment, and they start over again. The film is now flooded with saturated colour. Once in domestic bliss, Ho feels trapped and disappears out at night. Lai knows Ho is out cruising, and moons over the waterfall lamp with its picture of the Iguazu falls, the romantic place they never reach together. Lai tries to hold on, hiding Ho's passport. The atmosphere which has built up is one of mutual suspicion, followed by accusation, violence and eventually melancholy.

The improvisatory method of shooting in the restricted space of the apartment, and the shifting texture of shots and editing, give the sequences a strong, even visceral effect, which it is difficult to capture in analysis. But in the shot descriptions and commentary that follows, several tendencies will be identified. These include:

- the use of wide-angle lens, shooting from high and low angles;
- differential focus and film speed changes;
- assymetrical framing with blocked bodies and close-up profiles;
- hand-held camera entering into varying relationships with the actors and the space;
- abrupt jump cutting of long takes;
- choreographic repetition;
- lighting discontinuity, saturated colour and extreme tonal contrast;
- prominent pattern detail, colour and movement in art direction and costume.

[*Code*: BCU = big close-up. CU = close-up. EC = exposure change. FSC = film speed change. HH = hand-held camera. JS = jump cut. LC = 180 line cross over the cut. LS = long shot. M = medium. OV = over-shoulder shot. R = reverse. W = wide angle. 2S = two-shot.]

Sequences

1   HH-WLS. Dusk for night interior. High-angle empty decayed yellow corridor outside apartment. Lai climbs up corner of stairs carrying tray with plates of food up from the kitchen for himself and Ho.

2   HH-WCU. Abrupt cut. Wardrobe mirror view. We have seen Ho in mirror before. He seems to be dressing up to go out. Waist-level view: Ho tucks garish yellow and brown geometric patterned shirt into jeans and buttons flies.

3   HH-WCU. Ho's face looks down. Camera tracks (steps) back slightly wider as out-of-focus silhouetted Lai enters the door behind left and Ho looks up, eyes very near us, mildly scowling, deliberately ignoring/back to Lai. His slicked black hair is sharply backlit, a yellowish green soft light to the right side. The apartment has mixed artificial blue light which looks like day and artificial yellowish light which accentuates the characters' in-between netherworld. In the small apartment there is just a dining table and two chairs, an iron bed and a couch, small tables and lamps, a shower curtain and washbasin. We have seen this view many times – the small waterfall lamp is to the back by the washbasin, a miniature portable television near the wardrobe and portable tape recorder stacked on top. Probably cut from a take of 2.

4   HH-WMS-2SR. Orange squared patterns of the apartment wallpaper and top centre-frame hot-green ruched lampshade above the hot overexposed whited-out tablecloth. Ho, back to us, is obscured by Lai, back to us, who sets tray down on table. Middle of frame is empty, displaced. Lai sits right, leans over to set out chopsticks for Ho, and raises own chopsticks to eat rice. Ho, belabouring turning around, puts on striped cardigan and passes, blurred, to extreme right of frame behind Lai. Ho – 'Where's my passport?' Lai mocking half-heartedly – 'I don't know'.

5   HH-WMCU. Camera tracks in (steps in) to high angle behind Lai's overlit head, as Ho's furry cardigan wipes frame right to left. Lai is both vulnerable and defiant, back turned to camera.

6   HH-WCU. Angle slightly looking up left of frame. Profile Ho looks down accusing, tight lipped.

7   HH-WBCU-JC. Profile Ho left of frame. In middle of dialogue. Ho – 'Then why can't I find it?' His face is picked out by sharp near focus and top lighting.

The whole film so far has been shot in wide-angle lenses, but here they express just how far apart the lovers have become, giving the tiny apartment a spread-out but still paradoxically claustrophobic feel. The psychological tussle between them is exacerbated by blocked views and asymmetric framing. We notice small defining objects and textures of the room.

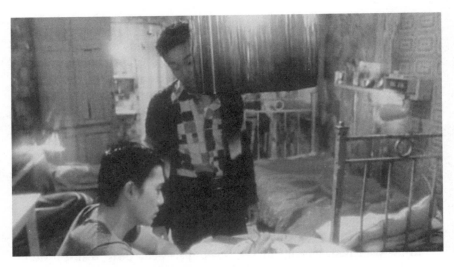

13.1 *Happy Together* (Wong Kar-Wai, 1997)

8 HH-WOV2S-JC. Ho's loud furry cardigan left to Lai sitting right. Lai's head and T-shirted shoulders small in frame. Lai – 'No idea'. Ho is reflected in the mirror behind Lai.

9 HH-WCU. Sharply near-focused back of Lai's head almost as 5, Ho left (head oddly decapitated.) Camera jibs up (carried up) to Ho, almost losing Lai's head off bottom of frame. Green lampshade above slides up frame right.

10 HH-WM2S-almost LC. (Figure 13.1) Eye-level Ho, angle down on Lai, seated bottom left. Ho partially blocked by prominent green lampshade centre top frame, the shower curtains beyond. Ho – 'I want my passport back!'

11 HH-WM2S-LC. Lai right of frame seated, Ho beyond (decapitated), 'window' framed by orange curtains either side. Dialogue over cut. It may be that this shot was through a mirror as it has the feel of slight patina effect over the image, which is further distancing.

The pattern established, of Lai as carer and Ho as receiver, breaks down as Ho now has his strength back. The characters'/performers' action begins to speed up. Frames within frames, profiles of Ho and back views of Lai visually split the pair further. The hand-held camera lunges in and out or in circular motions which are jump cut in the editing, crossing the 180-degree line. Differential focus favours Ho. The organisation of bodies in the space seems to follow a choreography with repeating gestures and movements of performers and camera.

12 HH-WMOV2S, Ho to high angle on Lai turning to look up, burnt out under light, displaced very small at bottom right of frame. Lai – 'What do you want it for?'

13 HH-WBCU almost as 7. Sharply near-focused profile Ho looks down, grimacing.

14 HH-WBCU-LC. Very abrupt short cut. Near-focused slightly high angle on Ho. Looks down left and leans in shouting, face then shadowed. Ho – 'It's none of your business!'

15 HH-WMS-LC. Suddenly eye-level Lai, (powerful) centre-frame, part of Ho's body to right, toying with chopsticks and rice in bowl, slowly, deliberately smirking. Lai looks up right, smiling to Ho almost off-screen. Lai – 'I'm not giving it back to you'.

Though the green lampshade and waterfall lamp are in the scene, we cannot really tell if it is night or day. The lighting is mixed day/tungsten. The tonal contrast is extreme, with hot spots of exposure pinpointing Lai or outlining Ho in profile. Exposure 'accident' is left uncorrected. Textural detail of costume, parts of bodies and faces, are attended to by the camera as it hovers hand-held between the performers. (We are familiar with this from previous scenes where Lai caresses Ho when he sleeps, or Ho rifles through Lai's possessions looking for his passport, and in the camera's obsession with small images of possible intimacy and 'home' such as the steaming rice held between Lai's chopsticks.)

16 HH-WBCU-LC to WLS. Starts as 14. Very tense Ho looks down at Lai below left, turns and strides back in frame and out of door left. Leaving lingering view of both beds with stripy yellow/red blankets and small shower area and wild flowery yellow ochre/brown wallpaper beyond. The camera holds steady as the white/blue shower curtain sways in breeze from slammed door at end of room. The small waterfall lamp in the background looks almost discarded, unimportant on small side table beyond the two empty beds.

17 HH-WLS. Reverse-view low angle, empty bed to left, Lai alone, small, at table right, blown-out lampshade above. 'Perfect', composed, straight verticals frame Lai as if in a static painting (pictorial).

18 HH-WMS-WCU. As 15 but tracks (steps and lunges) in. Hot glaring light above, accentuates rice (home food), chopsticks, eating alone. Lai slowly raises rice on chopsticks and opens mouth. The film speed does not change as previously in the film, but the actor slows down the action choreographically altering the flow, food barely reaching his mouth.

One minute fifteen seconds to here from start.

19 WS. Dusk exterior. The ultramarine silhouetted shapes of the docks and lights at La Boca. The bridge where the lovers have walked together

before. Ho is out there somewhere. The opposite of home, a vignette of bleak, lonely, urban industrial scene. Emptiness ambience.

20 HH-WBCU. Night interior, the apartment. Blue leaf pattern white plastic curtain texture. Scuffled noise as Ho enters off-screen. Camera almost swish pans left blurring to Lai (view waist up) waiting, stepping to lean back lolling against wall pretending indignation. This could be early the next morning, or days later ... Now wearing the open-necked, red-and-navy check warm shirt that Ho wore a few scenes back, his face shadowed, blue, looks off left. Lai – 'What are you looking for?'

21 HH-WLS-WBCU. Reverse Ho chucking blankets across the apartment. The frame starts with the blur of a thrown blanket hurled in Lai's direction. Ho yanks the mattress off the bed to left. Ho – 'You know very well'. Ho strides across the apartment pulling out papers, glaring at Lai, then turns back to him with hands on hips. Fast track (stepping) back as Ho turns, rushes and lunges into close-up, sharp near focus, backlit, looking to Lai off-screen right. Ho – 'Give it back!' The whole shot is like a reverse movement but the same view as 16 when he left before. Ho wears a much less loud (than Lai) mid-blue T-shirt. When the two are both in shot our attention is honed to Lai because he is like a red beacon in the frame. Ho's clothing drew attention to him in the first sequence.

22 HH-WMOV2S. Ho to Lai centre-frame. Lai is silent.

23 HH-WMS-LC reverse. Ho to right of frame, looks left. Almost as if in a mirror, displaced. Ho silent, extremely tense, fuming.

24 HH-WBCU. Reverse just lower than eye-level Lai as in 20 but closer up, cocky, looks left at Ho off-screen left. Lai – 'How many times must I tell you ... I'm not giving it back', smiles triumphantly.

25 HH-WMOV2S-JC to WMCU2S from further back than 22. Ho out of focus foreground left, Lai mid-left, partially blocked by Ho. Decayed tiles, mirror and décor to right. Displaced awkward frame. Lai turns away right and Ho lunges back in frame to swing a punch at him. Their backs to us, the camera tracks in fast (steps in) following line of punch action to both of them fighting and shouting. Camera shifts (steps) right, blurring the fight behind blue/white patterned shower curtain.

The blue cold of the docks contrasts with the warm, if uncomfortably oversaturated colours of the apartment. The wide-angle space displayed is at its most extreme, exacerbating the faster action of the performers. The bodies become more chopped, blurred, swiped past by the camera as the film jump cuts, repeating the encircling pattern of the first sequence at double the speed. Focus accelerates before the characters, or conversely decelerates, rather than simply going with the action.

26   HH-WCU2S. Ho and Lai tussle behind the curtain, its dark-blue leaf patterns graphically loud against the action. This may be a very short cut from the continuous take of 25, but bodies are further back in the blur.

27   HH-WBCU2S. Ho left grapples with Lai. Blurred fighting. Lai – 'Yeah, hit me!'

28   HH-WBCU2S-LC reverse. The camera moving right. The two continue fighting. Lai – 'Ah! Ah! Hit me!' Ho pulls Lai to right of screen. Camera pans left to favour Ho right in near-silhouette profile. Ho tries to headbutt Lai, pushing him off-screen left. Ho – 'Fucker!'

29   HH-WLS. Camera pans fast right, the intimate green lampshade slides across the top of frame, the empty bed frame appearing below. The same view towards door as 16 and 21. Ho in long shot scoops up jacket and strides towards the lit doorway.

The textural detail in art direction, costume, lighting and differentially focused close-ups enhances the sudden violent action.

30   HH-WMS. View past wall edge blocking right as Ho leaves frame left in silhouette.

31   HH-WCU. Outside in apartment corridor, Ho's shoulder leaves left of frame. The doorway out of focus beyond. Garish green wallpaper outside the apartment is striped with rough lines of light – almost like an animal or jungle print effect.

The reappearance of the curtain and the lamp is prominent and noticeable: they are almost like running gags, humorous or ironic elements which seem to comment on the interior battle and outer netherworld of our characters. Repetition occurs in the performances, clothes swapping, swapping of points-of-view, positional echoes of past shots in the film.

32   HH-WBCU. Very near-focus silhouetted profile Lai now alone. Echoes framing of earlier profile of Ho in 7. The apartment is so small, Lai and Ho keep appearing in each other's positions. Astor Piazzolla's melancholic tango jazz music begins.

Two minutes to here from start.

33   HH-WCU-WLS-WCU. FSC and EC. Day exterior, cloudy dull weather. Dark-blue inky water fills the frame. Slight slow motion. Underexposed and blue filter accentuate. (Possibly pushed in development to increase graininess.) Piazzolla's music gets louder and continues as camera pans up to wider view of the oily water, bridges and architecture of docks at La Boca. The effect is of graphic industrial shapes, ultramarine blue monochrome, viewed at almost water level from a tug/barge moving

13.2 *Happy Together* (Wong Kar-Wai, 1997)

back, gently revealing its wake in the picture, with reflections of the sky breaking up in the water. The camera moves right/tilts down to reveal Lai lying stomach down to bottom left on the barge edge, musing sadly towards the inky water, head in hand. The blue filter has bleached any warm colour from his skin, and he appears almost ill. Lai's jacket is ribbed white (corduroy?). The camera jibs (kneels down) to eye level lying by Lai, the dock's horizon near the top of frame. The exposure changes, bleaching out the jacket and lightening his face, much larger in frame. Lai looks at the camera, his eyes blinking in slight slow motion; the effect has caused the exposure change, which has been deliberately left to happenstance, uncorrected. Lai slides his head in his leaning arms. The camera hovers to the left and jibs up (stands up from kneeling) above his body, then tilts up to the water, pulling exposure again to increase the inkiness of the water against the horizon and docks.[2] The music continues.

34   HH-WCU-WMS-JC. (Figure 13.2) A similar frame to before, functioning as a jump cut. Lai lies with his head in his hands, then holds forehead looking right. This time the camera hovers and pans right. Though the actor moves at the same speed, slowly, this in normal motion and the water wake and camera moves a bit faster. The camera tracks back (kneels/leans back), keeping Lai to left as dock cranes and bridge appear in brooding graphic shapes above. Depth of field accentuates the bridge. Music continues. It has repeating melancholic jazz tango long notes, like the water movement.

The deep-blue colour is very strong and the changes in light and film speed quite noticeable, as if drawing our attention to them. This is one of few wide scenes of a daylight landscape, and prefigures the film's Iguazu falls end sequence with the same blue filtering. Lai almost appears to look out at the audience in the moment of overexposure. The hand-held camera moves back and forth in a choreographic rhythm with the music.

35   HH-WMS. A similar frame to 33 and 34 with Lai lying left of frame. The camera hovers and pans left. Focus pulls to near, with steaming blurring docks going out of focus behind. The camera jibs down (kneels down) to Lai's level. His eyes blink in slight slow motion, as if trying to go to sleep/forget. The music dies and picture fades to black.

Total time to here three minutes fifty-five seconds.

In these three sequences a narrative cycle with which we are already familiar is repeated: pattern of tension, followed by violent action, followed by long reflection. The two lovers, lonely and far from home, try to be happy together, but cannot escape a push/pull of attraction and repulsion. These cycles are played out in spaces like Lai's small apartment and the oil-polluted urban wasteland of the docks. The pattern of back-and-forth action in the performances, shooting and cutting creates tension which reaches a climactic explosion, gives way to calm and eventually gathers energy again. Fast cuts and loud dialogue give way to music and contemplative melancholy.

The first two sequences take place in the apartment, in which Ho lives on sufferance, recovering from his injuries, behaving like a recalcitrant teenager in front of an aggravated, barely controlled Lai. The tension has built to breaking point in the first sequence from shots 1–18. In the second, 19–32, violence breaks out between the pair and Ho leaves. In the third sequence, 33–5, we witness Lai's melancholic reverie at the docks, to the accompaniment of Piazzolla's haunting music. The first sequence (eighteen shots) lasts seventy-five seconds, the second sequence (thirteen shots) forty-five seconds, the third sequence (three shots) one hundred and twenty-five seconds. Medium, fast, very slow – there is a particular rhythm which we have experienced as identifying the speed and tone of how Ho and Lai relate to one another. It is part of the time–space organisation which is consistent throughout the film.

Happy Together uses the tango as a visual motif which extends beyond the scene in which the men dance together, forming a metaphor for their relationship. The whole film can be seen as having the form of a 'milonga', an early tango form which while sensual and melancholic has a sub-text of aggression. This extends to the way the characters circle and stalk around each other, with backward, forward and almost duplicated movements which entwine us deeper in the emotional tangle, through the delicacy of pace changes, stretching or suddenly speeding up the momentum (as if the performers were connected by elastic).

The tango is a slow dance using a syncopated rhythm. It displaces accents in the music, strong becoming weak and vice versa. Jeremy Tambling's description of the dance in his account of the film could be about the film's camerawork: 'It requires a couple who move at a slow walking pace. Its distinctive feature is "cutting" or suspending, a break in the motion manipulated by the male or dominant lead skipping a note; obliging his partner to lift and twine her leg round his; he leans her backward from waist up, his hips now against hers in "perfect fit"' (Tambling 2003: 43).

The tango choreography rhythms can be felt in the sequence shots 4, 5, 6, 7 and 8 as Ho hovers and circles while Lai sits in the chair. The camera lunges in and out, the editing jump cuts, and the focus is very close up so that we remain psychologically close to Ho, though not sharing his optical point of view. We see Lai in shots 5, 8, 9 and 10 in medium shot only, with Ho always partially blocked by the green lampshade, decapitated, or with half his body in frame. Ho and Lai are never together in a balanced compositional frame. We can apparently be right in the headspace of one character, then suddenly flung out, and then flung into the headspace of the other – like tango partners, flung out, grabbed in, flung out and swirled around. The effect is repeated again then in the second sequence in shots 25, 26, 27, 28 and 29, much faster as they fight.

A combination of shooting and editing methods is used. A disturbing effect is created by constant chopping and blocking of our view of one actor by another or by objects; by differential focus on wide-angle lenses; and by Doyle's small lunges in the hand held-camerawork: in and out, and in a circular stalking motion anticipating or following Ho. (Doyle describes actors as 'dancing partners [who] control the rhythms', and camerawork as 'anticipation and response' (Doyle 1998c; 1998a: 73).) It is exacerbated by Chang's jump cutting in or out from medium shot to close-up, to extreme close-up, and by constantly crossing the 180-degree line. What might conventionally be seen as poor continuity editing because characters appear to have jumped into each other's positions, here creates the tango dance relationship.

Ho moves with animal stealth before his sudden violent outburst in the first sequence. In the second sequence in shot 21 he swings in wild curves across the apartment, sweeping objects off tables, lifting up the mattress from the bed, ransacking Lai's home while trying to find his passport. He is given power by the amount of space he has to stride around in the wide-angle lens view. Lai then assumes the powerful position with the camera holding him in centre-frame in shot 22. This position acts as a pivot for Ho, whom we sense just off frame left (following normal screen logic and Lai's eyeline to left of frame), but then in shot 23 he enters from the right of frame. This is another jump cut (the actor having walked behind the camera), and increases the encircling of Lai, as we are very near to Ho's point of view. Lai is about to become victim, but also 'holds' the space.

To quote Doyle: 'Space = context and repetition = identity' (1998a: 106). Since the pair are addicted to love and argument they cannot stay away from each other. They play 'musical chairs' in the apartment, wearing each other's clothes and catching each other's gestures. The camera even repeats the view from the wardrobe mirror (as in shot 2), or the waterfall lamp, or the doorway when the characters are not home in the empty apartment, so we begin to long for them to be in this view we have already inhabited earlier in the film. While Ho appears to have the more reckless lifestyle, it is Lai who often seems aggressive in the face of Ho's passivity. But the characters are in love and co-dependent on each other's dramas. It is in the power games of the apartment, where they swap or repeat each other's physical positions, that these antics are grounded for the audience through a poetics of repetition. In the art direction, Chang also integrates this idea of repetition or reversing power roles through visual cues such as Ho wearing a loud striking jumper in the first sequence, followed by Lai wearing an equally gaudy shirt, which we have seen Ho wearing before, in the second.

Long lenses are sometimes used in the film, but wide angles are mostly employed. One important consequence of using extreme wide-angle lenses is that the camera operator (in this case also Doyle), is physically very close to the actors. Physical proximity was intensified in the flat location which was so minuscule that sometimes a video assist was used and Kar-Wai watched the performers on a monitor cabled through to the next room. Wide-angle lenses are commonly used in action filming to accentuate violent movement and physical distance between characters. In the apartment the wide angles reveal the whole space at once, with Lai or Ho surrounded by the personal objects and clutter of their lives always in frame, though at times differentially focused. The split focus between foreground and background can be achieved with considerable velocity as during shots 3, 16, 21 and 29.

These shots reveal the widest spatial gap between the lovers in these sequences. Lai enters behind Ho in shot 3; in 16 he leaves; in 21 he strides up to the foreground in sharp focus to confront Lai; in 29 he leaves, the view held for several moments, before the cut and time jump to Lai's profile in 30. To take the tango motif again, Ho is locked metaphorically in a competitive gripping tango embrace from which he is desperate to escape. When he decides to leave, unable to get his passport and beat Lai's control, he leaves, 'catapulted' also by Lai repelling him. Both are then consumed with regret as they have lost connection with the 'figure of eight' entwining embrace. When the two actually dance the tango earlier in the film, it is much more intimate, caressing, happy together.

Things that are conventionally avoided whilst using wide angles – such as accidental blocking of one character from another, decapitating heads and body parts, and sudden empty middles of frame – are creatively employed here to emphasise closeness and distance, as in shot 4. Jump cutting and blurring focus with wide angles is jarring and draws attention to the space, as does sudden framing out, as in shot 11, which gives the feeling of a view just off set (beyond the 'fourth wall' – i.e. where the film crew are or beyond what the viewer has conceived so far as the geography of the apartment) – as if momentarily we are transported outside the characters' own little world. Wide-angle shots can also enable us to experience space in ways that intensify our response to the situation of the characters: shots which begin or end empty, or emphasise loneliness by keeping one character differentially focused far apart from the other in the depth of field. When empty, they often feel like a character's point of view – for instance in shot 16 we see Ho, then realise we are inhabiting Lai's POV of him by a sense of foreground presence nearside of the camera after Ho has exited the frame.

Small body movements of the camera operator relative to the actor can open up physical/psychological spaces: suggestions of action, spaces for thought, a 'breathing' space for the audience – as in shot 3, when Ho dresses up in front of the off-screen mirror (camera point of view) and shot 25 at the hovering moment just before the fight. Symbolic objects such as the green lampshade above the table can be moved past and integrated with the action more easily than in a cutaway, as in shot 29. A character's indecisiveness can be tracked, responding to the actors' gestures very precisely because of the operator's proximity. This is especially potent when the camera can be feather light and 'hover' in a close-up reaction, like shot 10 of Ho glaring with accusing tension at Lai.

Focus may be roughly pre-planned with an assistant at hand, but Doyle's response is to use this as another register as the sequence develops. 'Focus is not a technical detail. It is a feeling, an intuition, a perception, a direction, a drama. The most irritating of film compromises is "racking" (adjusting focus) back and forth between characters in a conversational two-shot' (Doyle 1998b: 84). Focus can be used as a way of delaying or propelling time, by accelerating pulling focus before the actors move, or the converse. Keeping the focus on Lai in the second sequence before the fight starts exacerbates and stretches out the tension for Ho. However, like elastic, when he pings back in, lunging with fists towards Lai, it is with more force and shock. The focus holds us back in the past slightly, as if gathering breath in the calm before a storm, as we can feel violence is imminent. Lai's holding on isn't going to work. The flexibility afforded today by remote-control focusing and aperture means these technical effects are profoundly affecting storytelling. For this film Doyle wanted to keep the accidents in, even seek out mistakes.

His presence, our presence in this drama is intensified by the slight hesitancy or else adrenaline rush caused in the image when the camera operator tries to follow an actor by hand.

Doyle also refers to cinematography as 'jamming' and understands the MTV generation to be part of the audience for the films (Doyle 1998c). There is much influence from the music video world in *Happy Together*. Kar-Wai often plays music on the set, whilst actors perform. This happens in pop promo production, where playback is used to help performers to move choreographically. Doyle believes that 'Rhythm is the essence of a script' (Doyle 1998b: 99). He perceives a 'movement-narrative' within a project, through which he can both intuit a shooting process and find metaphors which will work for lighting camerawork in practice. Chang also states: 'I edit the same way I design. I go by emotion and a sense of rhythm. ... Moments in life are like that ... memory is essentially ephemeral and so are relationships. It is in this context that one should look at all my "techniques", be they jump-cuts, freeze-frames, opticals, slow motions, or inter-cutting between black and white and colour' (Chang 2001).

In *Happy Together* as well as previous films, Kar-Wai works with the actors moving at different speeds in combination with film speed changes (stop-frame animation and shots at 8 or 12 frames per second (fast) ramping to normal 25 frames to 75 frames per second and back). This requires experiment and precision timing between camera operator and actor. Chang then adds or deletes frames in the editing. The effect is of different time elements unfolding in the same physical space. With respect to *Happy Together* Doyle comments:

> I've always associated our 'blurred action' sequences with the adrenaline 'rush' that fear or a violent act excites. This time round it's more 'druggy'. We change speed at 'decisive', 'epiphanal' or 'revelatory' moments. The actor moves slowly while all else goes on in 'real time'. The idea is to suspend time, to emphasise or prolong the 'relevance' of what is going on. (1998a: 104)

In the first and second sequence the film speed is normal, though the pace of the actors and the editing increases dramatically. But when we reach Lai's melancholy in the third sequence, we see him blinking in slight slow motion. Shot 33 starts on the swirling, turbulent, dark-blue oily water, the wake of the barge on which we will see Lai lying alone, head in hands. We are not consciously aware of slowed-down motion, just that something temporal has gone out of tune. As the hand-held camera pans and tilts to Lai, Doyle pulls the exposure, overexposing Lai. The weather is dull, but the effect is of too much light in his eyes, literally and emotionally raw – too much exposure. Lai is metaphysically as well as actually overexposed in shot 33 in his stretched moment of realisation.

With in-camera movement we become aware that something changes in the camera eye, but it seems optical and cerebral rather than visceral and physical as actual camera movement does. This could be achieved digitally, but would not have the presence effected by Doyle's sleight of hand, improvising with the actors' performance. As the tonal range gets lighter, more bleached out, the slow motion returns to normal. The actor also moves more slowly. This contra-flow effect doubles our sense of temporality being confused. The colouring in these shots is a rich ultramarine blue, which quite often surrounds Lai. It is the same colour filtering used at the Iguazu falls. It seems to be something to do with Lai's destination, which at this point is a bottomless depth, beautiful but very cold.

Filtering is important in the film, both on the camera and on the lights. The early part is shot in bleached green/yellow monochrome tones, or black and white, as we witness a round of arguments and drama. The frame floods with rich saturated colour when Lai and Ho start over again. Strong yellow, red, green and blue filters are used variously in the apartment throughout the film. Blue seems to symbolise Lai, and yellow and red Ho, or being 'happy together', but sometimes these are improvised with natural light in certain locations. In the apartment Doyle creates mixed colouring, so that we never really know whether it is night or day.

Lighting and colour are intimately linked to film stock. In Doyle's view, 'Colour is subjective, an accumulation of perceptions and experiences by which we interpret the world' (1998b: 14). He believes film stocks have personalities, tempers and tendencies. *Happy Together* was shot on Fuji film, because he sought a particular colour feel:

> Film stock doesn't see like anyone you or I know; it only appropriates a cultural mean. Fujichrome is a late Edo Period woodblock heroine skirting a brilliantly blue-green wave, delicate but hard-edged, with skin as sacred and white as Mount Fuji backlit by the moon. Kodak is Whistler's old sitter, well-placed, straight, and no-nonsense, as abrupt as black and white in colour, as functional as a newly built shaker chair. (Doyle 1998b: 15)

The décor and lighting filter colours in the apartment are enhanced by this stock, which some believe has more 'poppy' colours and degree of split between colours in flesh tones and between warm and cold tones. The film stock is also pushed in the development process in *Happy Together*, which increases the grainy, gritty texture of the images throughout the film. This is especially apparent in blurred out-of-focus parts of the frame and in dark areas.

Doyle and Chang are 'obsessed with textures' (Doyle *et al.* 2002). Texture is another register at play in both the art direction and lighting. The camera often lingers over the actors' bodies and the texture of flesh and clothing (as in shots 2 and 8). Leung and Cheung are famous actors; this fetishism is also found in music videos where 'shots are used to confer authority on the performer and assert their sexual charisma, by highlighting the erogenous zones' (Vernalis 2001: 28). In *Happy Together* there is apparent pleasure in this mobile micro-geography and surfeit of surface texture, where the particular rhythm, presence and identity of the characters can be found.

The lighting in *Happy Together* is left very contrasty in most situations by adding some lighting but leaving small practicals (in the set lights) to burn out with overexposure, as in shots 3, 9, 16, and 29. This gives the effect of hotness and hot spots in the frame, again something normally avoided and calmed down. Generally when creating naturalism, lighting follows the natural light of the sun, moon or man-made sources in their logical lighting effects. These rules are adapted from realism in painting going back to Dutch and Flemish art. Non-logical light sources and discontinuity are useful when trying to create a netherworld feel, as in this film. The makeshift quality and absurdity of the waterfall lamp and the green lamp over the table seem to amplify the lovers' desperate games and temporary liaison. Extreme shadow and extreme overexposure are another register in service to emotional effect. The burned-out, overexposed table lamp which spotlights Lai as he is encircled by Ho in the first sequence (shot 9) and the discarded waterfall lamp in shot 29 (small in frame when Ho leaves but lingered on long enough to notice where this iconic object has now gone) are expressive of what is happening in the relationship. Lai is overexposed in comparison to Ho, in the spotlight, while Ho appears around the darker edges of frame. Doyle uses exposure as another register or scale with which to mark emotional flow from scene to scene. Continuity rules are observed, but stretched to the limit.

I suggested above that the visceral, almost physical effects of the cinematography in this film are difficult to analyse (or even capture on the page) but I hope to have shown that breaking down the medium into its constituent elements of composition, camera movement and lighting can assist in analysis and discovery. Attempting to unpick some of the complexity of the cinematographic process is essential if simplifications about visual style are to be avoided and if an awareness of cinematography is to take its appropriate place in film criticism. In cinematography, composition and use of specific lenses can define power relationships between characters, focus attention on particular areas, define point of view, play with our sense of what we see and don't see. Movement creates interrelationships and can accentuate an actor's choreography, gesture, physiognomy and presence. Lighting contributes to creating emotional tension and releases through a huge variety of tonal, focal, colour and rhythmic values. In-camera movement of exposure, focus and film speed, together with combinations of

moving lights and dimmers, can also be used as expressive registers. These
elements provide the primary expressive possibilities of the cinematographer's medium.

Understanding these possibilities inevitably requires some technical knowledge of the nature of the decisions taken and the way the effects are achieved.
This is one advantage for students of courses that root analysis in practice.
But the pay-off is more than technical: taking critical account of cinematography and its specific practices can enrich interpretation.

Notes

1   The documentary accompanying the DVD of *Happy Together* reveals the cycles of
    exuberance, energy and camaraderie, lethargy and homesickness experienced by
    both crew and cast choosing to work in this way on a low budget for a long
    period in cramped locations.
2   This is the 'loneliness incarnate' image and metaphor Doyle discovered during
    the location recess: 'The first day of filming [is] not really a shoot ... just an
    affirmation we're here. We "pick up" the "ambience" shots in and around the
    stinking oil-slicked port called La Boca ... just playing it by ear, trying filters and
    film speeds, not looking for inspiration, just ideas. Then we luck out with a bus
    disgorging passengers, turning under the derelict bridge into a vast expanse of
    setting light. It's loneliness incarnate, at last I've got a visual theme to build on, a
    direction to explore the "character" of this space.' (1998a: 20–2)

References

Bordwell, D. (2000) *Planet Hong Kong: Popular Cinema and the Art of Entertainment*
    (Cambridge, MA and London: Harvard University Press).
Chang, W. (2001) 'Interview', in D. McGrath (ed.) *Screencraft: Editing and Post-
    Production* (Hove: Rotovision), pp. 156–63.
Charity, T. (1998) 'The Wong Answer: The Latest from Hong Kong's Visionary
    Master', *Time Out* (22–29 April), 74.
Chow, R. (2001) 'Nostalgia of the New Wave: Structure in Wong Kar-Wei's *Happy
    Together*', in M. Tinkcom and T. Villarejo (eds) *Keyframes: Popular Cinema and
    Cultural Studies* (London and New York: Routledge), pp. 228–41.
Doyle, C. (1998a) *Buenos Aires* (Tokyo: Prénom).
Doyle, C. (1998b) *A Cloud in Trousers* (Santa Monica, CA: Smart Art Press).
Doyle, C. (1998c) 'Taped Interview with Cathy Greenhalgh', by phone to Los Angeles
    (23 Aug.).
Doyle, C., E. Lachman, C. Greenhalgh, N. Deville and N. Kellgren (2002) 'Taped
    interview and conversation at *Camerimage* Festival, Lodz, Poland' (1 Dec.).
Greenhalgh, C. (2003) 'Shooting from the Heart: Cinematographers and Their
    Medium', in Imago (eds) *Making Pictures: A Century of European Cinematography*
    (New York: Abram; London: Aurum Press).

Sobchack, V. (2000) 'What My Fingers Knew: The Cinesthetic Subject or Vision in the Flesh', www.sensesofcinema.com/contents/00/5/fingers.html

Tambling, J. (2003) *Wong Kar-Wai's* Happy Together (Hong Kong: Hong Kong University Press).

Vernalis, C. (2001) 'The Kindest Cut: Functions and Meanings of Music Video Editing', *Screen*, 42, 1, 21–48.

14

Notes on teaching film style

Andrew Klevan

Can the *advanced* study of film style exist within the undergraduate curriculum? The study of film style is often merely preliminary: students acquire basic viewing skills and recognise features of film form as part of an introduction to film study. The student will then be in a position to pursue enquiries more worthwhile and will, given these foundational skills, successfully provide textual evidence. As a lecturer in film studies at the University of Kent I have developed a second-/third-year undergraduate course entitled Film Style, Interpretation and Evaluation which treats the study of film style as special, rather than preparatory. The course encourages the students to involve themselves in the intricacies of a film's style, while showing how that involvement refines interpretation and enables sensitive evaluation. This chapter is not intended as the gospel on teaching film but rather, in fashionable quality-assessment parlance, to draw attention to particular methods that produced exciting outcomes. Students on the course repeatedly emphasised that the advanced study of film style invigorated undergraduate teaching conventions (lectures, seminars, reading lists, essay titles) and offered them a distinct learning experience within the university.

The moment

Stanley Cavell's book *Pursuits of Happiness: The Hollywood Comedy of Remarriage* begins with a list of suggestive quotations. Two are of particular pertinence for teaching film style. Ludwig Wittgenstein writes (translated): 'I should like to say that what dawns here lasts only as long as I am occupied with an object in a particular way' (1981: 43). The use of the 'dawn' suggests coming to light (now I see the rabbit), coming into the light, an awakening, perhaps an awakening of feeling, only when we are occupied with an object. Occupied another way, or with another object, and something else will dawn.

Ralph Waldo Emerson writes: 'Since our office is with moments let us husband them' (1981: 43). If we take 'our office' to be our work, then moments are unavoidably our *business*. We should 'husband' moments, by managing them carefully and cultivating them as a husbandman would his seed. Wittgenstein and Emerson's sense of moments being essential to us, but still needing care (and attention), provides a preliminary justification for a cultivation of moments in life – and film.

Suspensions

Honing in on moments is a method of magnification. We can survey the interweaving contours of the drama and better discern the undulating lines without needing to straighten them out. Christopher Ricks takes a quotation from William Empson: 'Life involves maintaining oneself between contradictions which can't be solved by analysis' (Ricks 1998: 321–2). The use of 'contradictions' may too heavily emphasise mutually opposing, or inconsistent, elements, but 'maintaining oneself' draws attention to a state of suspension. Life suspends us between aspects – sometimes precariously, sometimes more securely – and there is rarely a situation that does not include various forms of overlap. V. F. Perkins writes that the good film tries to maintain the elements of style 'in productive tension and neither ... push them into symmetrical alignment ... nor ... let them fall into blank contradiction' (1972: 120). Perkins writes about 'stress without strain' in a film moment, and students can profitably embrace this stress. Students are encouraged, in Empson's terms, not to 'solve films by analysis', or to straighten them out with their analysis, but rather be responsive to the overlaps, keep in play the balance of meanings.

The seminar is not simply the place where these overlaps can be recognised and discussed but rather it offers a format where the overlaps can be successfully re-enacted. The seminar dramatises the process of appreciating the film. The amount and variety of the contributions, each interlocking and layering, mirrors the density of the moment on the screen in front of us. The seminar offers a forum for replicating the intricate weave of the film's strands. Perkins says that the good film is built up from the organisation of details that 'simultaneously complicate and clarify the movie's viewpoint' (1972: 119). Equally, the students' viewpoints need not fall into 'symmetrical alignment' or 'blank contradiction'. Each contribution in the seminar may 'simultaneously complicate and clarify' the overall viewpoint. Perkins says of a film's organisation (and it is equally true for the seminar), 'The separately discernible meanings become important less for their independent value than for their contributions, mutually deepening and defining' (1972: 119).

Interpretation

Concentrating on a moment may be the prerequisite for complex involvement – and dedicated interpretation – but it cannot ensure it. Many undergraduate essays look to be dissecting the form of a film, engaging in what
is often called 'close textual *analysis*', but good films will not allow themselves to be 'solved by analysis' (in Empson's terms), so for all their apparent
closeness, the interpretations remain far away. Crudely speaking, without
guidance students tend towards two approaches when interpreting style: in
one approach, meaning is obvious, and in the other, it is obscure. In the first
case, elements of style guide our responses to the film, straightforwardly,
and the interpretation becomes a deliberate step-by-step articulation of this
process. In the second case, elements of style work more 'unconsciously',
meaning is hidden, and the interpretation deciphers and translates. The former
takes meaning to be broadly explicit, and the latter takes it to be implicit.
Both find a favourite vehicle in *The Alien Cycle* (Ridley Scott 1979; James
Cameron 1986; David Fincher 1992; Jean-Pierre Jeunet 1997): there is the
essay on suspense that tells us about how elements of style trigger the spectator to feel this, that or the other, or we have the essay that reveals the vaginal
imagery of the Mothership. The insights of each essay have their place, but
they are too often derived from methods that are systematic rather than from
critical principles encouraging flexible and agile involvement.

There is an alternative. V. F. Perkins interprets a three-minute sequence
from *In a Lonely Place* (Nicholas Ray 1950):

> Suppose that you were planning the first few minutes of a film whose central
> issue is to be the uncertainty of emotion, a story of passion dogged by mistrust
> in which only the strength of feeling (not its nature) remains constant. You
> want to establish that neither hero nor heroine is sure whether the man's
> embrace is protective and loving or threatening, murderous.
>
> That was Ray's problem at the start of *In a Lonely Place* (1950). His answer
> was to give the same gesture to three different characters within the brief space
> of the scene that establishes the film's Hollywood setting: each of them ap-
> proaches another character from behind and grasps his shoulders with both
> hands. The first time, it is a perfunctory and patronizing greeting whose pretense
> of warmth is a bare cover for the assertion of superiority. Then, between the
> hero and an old friend, it conveys intimacy and genuine regard. Finally, when
> a large-mouthed producer uses the shoulders of the hero himself as a rostrum
> from which to publicize his latest triumph, it is seen as oppressive and openly
> slighting. (Perkins 1981: 1144)

Perkins says these moments are significant in themselves but 'their deeper
purpose is ... to dramatize the ambiguity of gesture itself' (1981: 1144). By
carefully patterning its gestures in this way, the film allows for the possibility

14.1 *In a Lonely Place* (Nicholas Ray, 1950)

that we may pay special attention to them although they may appear peripheral or incidental. The gestures are not clear prompts, signals or cues, nor is the quality of their meaning, as set out here by Perkins, well established by claiming them as flagrantly symbolic or 'allegorical'.

There is a famous scene late in the film where Dix and Laurel are in the kitchen together. Before Laurel's entry, Dix straightens a grapefruit knife, as if he were unaware that the utensil should be bent, and stabs down into the fruit. This is an extract from an essay in which a student has attempted to interpret the meaning of the characters' behaviour. He draws out the significance of the characters' positioning and movements, and crucially their significance *within* Laurel's kitchen:

> Dix is screen left, Laurel screen right, the distance between them filled by the tranquil, mundane domesticity of the kitchen. Dix then crosses this space to grasp Laurel by both shoulders and position her with some authority on a stool, then returning to his labours ... [Figure 14.1] Dix now represents to Laurel both love and fear, threat in comfort. His occupancy of the kitchen, surely the very heart of domesticity, underlines this as the threat that he now embodies has now forced itself into her everyday, domestic life; and he has in a very real sense taken command of it, therefore redefining it. This idea of redefinition is then articulated by his reconfiguring of the grapefruit knife, which itself becomes threatening, transformed from its mundane state. Following the dream sequence, the details of this scene combine to imply that Dix is a brutal force ... When Dix crosses the domestic space it is to control and dominate Laurel, fixing her in her place. When she crosses the space, it is to inform him of his mistake concerning the knife. Significantly, Dix does not attempt to bend the knife back into shape. He is instead puzzled as to what thought processes sought to bend it in the first

place. This is in keeping with his consistent failure to redress or even recognise the effect of his physical actions. Laurel sits down again re-establishing the distance between them ... [B]y redefining both love and domesticity as threatening, Dix also redefines marriage ... She begins to realise that a normal life together is impossible, as Dix, 'doesn't act like a normal person'. For Laurel this is something that can be loved but not lived with. (Paul Telfer, film studies essay, University of Kent, 1998/9)

This approach to interpretation is continuous with interpreting – and valuing – human behaviour in real environments. Encouraging this method avoids the possible rigidity of approaching style mechanically through a technical taxonomy (this week 'editing', next week 'the long take').

Which aspects of a human's behaviour, which of his or her postures, gestures, movements or expressions, are relevant to an assessment of them – in which places and at which moments? *In a Lonely Place* enacts and scrutinises these great questions. It is a possibility of film, because of its ontology, that human behaviour can be suitably and concretely integrated into the wider dramatic environment. This enhances continuity and creates the opportunity for the significance of postures and gestures to easily pass us by. Encouraging students to be alert to the difference between significance and prominence is a crucial aspect of teaching film style.

Perkins has elsewhere enlarged on this approach to interpretation:

I suggest that a prime task of interpretation is to articulate in the medium of prose some aspects of what artists have made perfectly or precisely clear in the medium of film. The meanings I ... discuss ... are nether stated nor in any sense implied. They are filmed. Whatever else that means ... it means that they are not hidden in or behind the movie, and that my interpretation is not an attempt to clarify what the picture has obscured. I have written about things I believe to be in the film for all to see, and to see the sense of. (1990: 4)

Perkins says that *In a Lonely Place* reconciles 'clarity with depth of suggestion' (1994: 231). The challenge for students writing about films – in the process dissolving the implicit/explicit dichotomy – is to convey both a moment's clarity *and* its suggestiveness. This student continues to outline, clearly, the scene's suggestiveness:

The shot of the kitchen shows Dix's physical domination of the room (he is both standing and in action) contrasting with Laurel's dozy, reclined position on the stool. It is, superficially, the very embodiment of easy going familiarity and domesticity. This is what leads Dix to assume that 'anyone looking at us could tell we're in love'; the idea being that the meaning of the scene is straight forward and obvious, whilst not being explicit. In fact, as Dix identifies when talking about the love scene he has written, it is the fact that this meaning is inferred and not announced that makes it seem genuine: 'That's because they're not always telling each other how much in love they are.' The genius of the scene is to qualify Dix's remark that they are acting out a scene that is much the same as the one he wrote, whilst also adding another level of inference of which he is not aware. Although the couple's love can be seen in the way that Dix suggests, it is tempered with an equally palpable but implicitly expressed threat. Just as anyone can see they are in love, one can also sense that something is wrong, that the apparent domestic tranquillity is undermined by a sense of danger. The scene can be seen as an exquisitely subtle exercise in subtlety. By articulating the failure of conventional love scenes, and demonstrating how it should be done, only to then undermine the notion through a further implied sense of menace, the shot of them in the kitchen realises graphically the tensions in the relationship and the problems faced by Laurel. (Telfer, essay, 1998/9)

Synthesis

Students are encouraged to be responsive to the gestures and postures of performers as they develop – to the performers' continually evolving rhythms and patterns of conduct – and, crucially, to their changing place within the shot, sequence and film as a whole. Studying the synthesis of style, attending to the complex and shifting relationship of the stylistic elements, ensures that interpretation, hence essay writing, can never become a matter of grossly summarising meaning. If the student is attentive to the developing relation- ship of elements and the adjustments of meaning which that necessarily involves, they are less prone to the tendencies of vague condensation. This attentiveness discourages, for example, one-note deciphering of a specific aspect ('this red rose *represents* x'), and assertion through summary ('the film is *about* x, y and z'). As Perkins writes in *Film as Film*: 'In order to compre- hend whole meanings, rather than those parts of meanings which are present in verbal synopsis or visual code, attention must be paid to the whole content of shot, sequence and film' (1972: 79).

The following is from another student essay; it concerns Lisa (Joan Fontaine) in the fairground carriage in *Letter from an Unknown Woman* (Max Ophuls, 1948), and the *handling* of a rose. The student accounts for the rose's syn- thesis with other aspects of the film:

The rose which Lisa toys with reflects upon her own being. For instance, it is a single white rose which is slowly opening; Lisa is like the rose in this respect for her evening with Stefan is one of a sexual awakening. The rose is also a beautiful and fragile creature, but an aura of inevitability surrounds it because of the knowledge that it will wither. This description of the rose can be transferred onto Lisa whose first words are, 'By the time you read this letter, I may be dead.'

Lisa's appearance also concurs with the whiteness of the flower. Her face is often lit giving it a luminous quality. She also wears dresses that have noticeable white in them, such as the white collars she wears as a girl, the white shirt which contrasts with her black skirt, coat and hat during their evenings together, and the white evening dress and coat she wears to the opera.

The fact that Lisa is holding a single white rose is also relevant because she is consistently portrayed as an isolated figure, detached from the world. Her isolation is evident during the supposed romantic evening with Stefan, for he often leaves her alone ... In the train scene, Lisa's isolation is reinforced by the camera placement and the frame composition. The first shot is a tableau with camera placed at a medium distance ... The static frame contrasts with much of the film's cinematography wherein the dominant technique involves moving the camera alongside the moving characters. The stillness of the frame in this shot emphasises the artificial and untypical stillness of Lisa ... The shot enables the spectator to see the physical, and perhaps emotional, distance between the two characters who are separated by the mountains of Switzerland and the canals of Venice. For example, Lisa initially had no view of Stefan, as the walls of his flat allowed her to only indirectly hear his music. His later views are impeded by several barriers, such as a social status which prevents her from visiting his public performances, or by the window panes of doors which she peers through. Thus when they are in the enclosed train compartment, Lisa's discomfort with the close physical proximity is noticeable in several ways. Amongst these is her gesture with the rose for it suggests fidgety unease. In addition, the rose provides an escape from the close-by Stefan by offering an alternative location for her sight to fall onto. [Figure 14.2] This evasive look is most evident when Stefan first gives her the rose. As they sit side-by-side in the horse drawn carriage, Lisa is almost completely absorbed in the flower, only once glancing up at Stefan briefly. This lack of eye contact is consistent throughout their evening together. One senses that Lisa is afraid to look too deeply into Stefan's eyes for they will expose the reality of him and the situation. Later she demonstrates

14.2 *Letter from an Unknown Woman* (Max Ophuls, 1948)

that she also dislikes being the receiver of his stare, fearing that the truth behind her protective mask, or veil, will be revealed.

Throughout the film she moves in circles, continually returning to the moments in her life which she shared with Stefan ... here her relative stillness is disrupted by the twisting of a rose. (Katherine Cruickshank, film studies essay, University of Kent, 1998/9)

The meanings that the student associates with the rose have been made through an evaluation of the other elements in the shot, the scene and across the film. The student has been responsive to the rose's relationship to colour; to the performers' movements and gestures; and to the placement of the camera.

The essay goes beyond simply 'using examples from the film'. The student is immersed in the intricacy of the synthesis, and endeavours to elaborate *involvement*. What can be achieved by students who set their own essay titles, and who are free to make any small detail the focal point of a whole discussion? They are released from the pressure of steering a route through pressing, and sometimes bullying, module 'topics'. The student now makes incidental aspects – of a film, of film scholarship – the focus of academic concern. These aspects become *critical*: the clasping of a shoulder, the cutting of a grapefruit or the turning of a rose.

Words

Before the seminar, the film is watched in full. In the seminar, also on a big screen, we view a sequence a number of times. Then we move through it, reviewing a few seconds repeatedly where necessary, and freezing the frame while we talk. This means a frame of the film is *always* suspended before the students. Looming, and pressing in this way, the spirit of the film is more likely to pervade our dialogue about it, and we are more likely to find words appropriate to an assessment of it. While in its presence we feel obliged to do it justice; if the film is absent, we will too easily betray it.

The search for the appropriate descriptions of what is projected before us is then the primary challenge of the seminar on film style. Although I have a broad sense of moments that may be eventually revealing, I only intermittently have a prepared articulation of these moments ready and waiting. Where possible, I want to be involved in the students' moment-by-moment endeavour to find appropriate words, and I want them to sense my involvement, so their pursuit will feel original. Students can show unease if they sense a teacher is artificially withholding his or her own perspectives and I consider it necessary to present my own assessments of the film as a crucial part of the ongoing conversation. My main concern, however, is to press students to become more exact and vivid in their expression, so that they may *distinguish* their interpretations. The challenge of studying film style is to search for suitable words to evoke a medium that is originally visual and aural. This is the *discipline* of film study (and my best justification to those who still look on the field with suspicion).

Distinctions

Considering appropriate words encourages articulate distinctions; observing distinctions encourages appropriate words. Students are stimulated to make fine distinctions about a good film, so that they may attempt to do justice to its delicate suspensions. In lectures, I *attempt* to provide examples of the density in that delicacy, and of the durable in the transient, possibly fleeting – momentary – aspects of a film.

The following example intends to show that a range of meaningful modulations exists in simply a few words spoken by a good performer. One critical challenge in writing about the final scene of *The Awful Truth* (Leo McCarey, 1937) would be to evoke the delicious suggestiveness of Irene Dunne's performance. Jerry (Cary Grant) and Lucy Warriner (Irene Dunne) find themselves in adjacent bedrooms in a house in Connecticut, divided by a faulty door, approximately one hour before midnight, at which time their divorce becomes official. The urgency of the deadline is set against their necessary tentativeness with each other: their agreement to avoid their divorce must be carefully managed so that they come together on the right terms. The scene, therefore, revolves around playing with their separateness as a way of negotiating their reunion. Lucy says of the faulty door, 'not so very practical but I guess it will serve its purpose'. What does she take to be the purpose of the door's practical failure: will the door work adequately enough to keep them separate or will it be faulty enough to keep bringing them together? Her words fall gently and quietly to almost a murmur, and this undemonstrative address gives room for the ambiguity to breathe. Indeed, Irene Dunne's voice is breathy, and slightly creaky, as if it were being gently stretched by the wind (her voice quivering in the draught, perhaps, which drifts through the bedrooms on this windy night). It makes her sound dreamily faraway – nearly lost yet lulling. A little later when Lucy says 'Good night', one simple and common pleasantry is made to sound complicated and uncommonly provocative. It is conclusive, curt – surely, you must curtail this exchange? It is sexually alluring, tantalising – surely, you are not prepared to curtail this exchange? It is a touch shaky, hesitant – surely, I should curtail this exchange? Lucy tries to encourage, but furtively, by means of cautious rejection.

Consider the relevance of one item of clothing. At the beginning of *The Woman in the Window* (Fritz Lang, 1944), Joan Bennett's performance of Alice skilfully evokes and plays against plot possibilities, and probabilities,

14.3 *The Woman in the Window* (Fritz Lang, 1944)

which are suggested by conventions, generic and otherwise. One critical challenge therefore is to establish the film's distinction within its generic family; and propose it as something other than conventional, so rescuing Alice, *femme fatale*, from the shadowy streets. The first section of the film exploits our presumption that the woman will be sinister, pursuing dangerous strategies through sexual provocation. Alice picks up Professor Wanley (Edward G. Robinson) from the street, and after they have had a drink together at a bar, she takes him back to her apartment. Her glistening outer garments removed, she is now shown wearing a chiffon top (Figure 14.3). Given the situation, the top might be interpreted (transparently) as a strategic, or eager, sexual invitation. Yet, given our developing understanding of Alice's hesitant personality, her wearing of the top seems less purposeful and committed. Rather than producing an erotic suspension of her flesh between concealment and revelation, it represents the way she is caught in ordinary situations between hiding and disclosing. It may allow her to trifle with amiable mischief. Probably, she is seduced by the idea of appearing more provocative than she feels, while she seeks to seduce someone who, generously recognising her *design*, will prolong the flirtatious possibilities. Many of the film's tensions are delicately gathered together in a simple item of clothing, and suitably this lightweight top wears its meaning lightly.

Reading

Stanley Cavell often writes enthusiastically about Ludwig Wittgenstein's desire to bring words back home, bring words back to the contexts in which we use them, and appreciate words as being in the stream and flow of life (for example, 1988: 192–3). The reading list for the course primarily contains film criticism which uses words that are in the stream and flow of the films. Information, points, topics, interventions are then secondary considerations, although in many cases these features will also be contained in the writing. I want students to experience film scholarship where the words are loaded with life and then attend to the moments in that reading as they would to the moments in the film. In the seminar on *In a Lonely Place* we looked at a sequence lasting approximately only two or three seconds near the beginning of the film where Laurel passes between Dix and Mildred in the courtyard, and at some accompanying sentences on it by V. F. Perkins:

> On her first appearance [Laurel's] ... indirectness is apparent as well as her pronounced investment in poise. She walks between Dix and Mildred in the courtyard of the apartments where both she and Dix are tenants with an 'Excuse me' that commands attention but also positions her to claim that she was only minding her own business and being polite. Here and later, she is skilfully dressed in costumes so well supplied with edges and angles as to construct the space for movements simultaneously elegant, erotically promising (she passes close enough for Dix to catch her perfume) and – hands pushed forward inside the pockets of her overcoat – held off from any risk of contact. The stiffness that possesses Dix at climaxes of anxiety is always more or less a feature of Laurel's bearing. She is ever so neat. Finding her way through without being touched is one of her prime objectives. (1994: 227) (Figure 14.4)

In the first sentence, 'apparent' alongside 'indirectness' suggests an incongruity, but conveys how Gloria Grahame is capable of manifesting her obliqueness (making her obliqueness manifest). Similarly, Laurel's 'poise' suggests

14.4 *In a Lonely Place* (Nicholas Ray, 1950)

her bearing has an ease which might seem ill at ease with an 'investment' which is 'pronounced'. In fact, the word 'poise' draws out the performer's multifaceted display of self-possession, as Grahame integrates aspects of elegant bearing with effort, deliberation and strategy (showing them as aspects of each other). Her 'poise' makes her appear, in both senses, *composed*. This also fuses with the other senses of 'poise', meaning to be in balance, suspended, ready or prepared – poised to do something. Hence Laurel's 'investment': deliberately suspending herself, albeit gracefully, as she passes here, and preparing, eventually, to catch Dix. The repetition of 'p' sounds across the sentence – 'On her first a*pp*earance, her indirectness is a*pp*arent as well as her *p*ronounced investment in *p*oise' – folds together the multiple aspects of her manner. It also has the effect of giving our pronunciation a rather correct, even haughty, air that matches Laurel's lordly passing.

The sentence which begins 'Here and later' lays out aspects of Laurel's bearing that she manifests simultaneously (she is 'elegant' and 'erotically promising' and 'held off from any risk of contact'). Choosing these three aspects, and placing them together, already establishes the layers of Laurel's display. Furthermore, however, the sentence includes two inserts: one held within parentheses and the other between dashes. The parentheses have the effect of separating and connecting the clauses: the clause within the parentheses 'passes close enough' to the main body of the sentence, in much the same way that Laurel, also making a connection while remaining separate, 'passes close enough to Dix'.

Within the parentheses, Perkins makes a claim about the presence of the perfume and about its desired effect ('close enough for Dix to catch'). We cannot, given the medium, smell the perfume and no physical actions evidently indicate a smell (Bogart is not seen, for example, taking a sniff), and yet it would be hard to refute that Laurel, given her behaviour and presentation, is not wearing perfume at this point. Perkins wants to claim that the perfume is inside the drama but recognises that it is outside its visible or aural aspects – it is present to the characters whilst not presented to the viewer – so the clause is inside and outside the main drama of the sentence. The parenthetic clause enables Perkins to point it up whilst recognising that he cannot point it out; the clause, like Laurel, is 'pronounced' and 'poised', and it allows the critic to suggest the obvious.

The other separated clause – 'hands pushed forward inside the pockets of her overcoat' – observes an aspect that is more prominent within the moment's design and therefore, by comparison, does not warrant parentheses (unlike the perfume, we can see it). Furthermore, if Laurel's hands are pushed forward in her overcoat to hold her off from any risk of contact, the clause is also 'pushed' into the sentence by the dashes, and 'held off' from absolute contact with the other clauses.

The sentence, 'She is ever so neat', when compared to the previous longer sentences, is 'ever so' clipped and terse and neat. 'Finding her way through' interprets a general feature of Laurel's behaviour throughout the film – her careful negotiations – while at the same time being specifically tied to this particular moment. Perkins could have used words like 'carefully negotiates', or 'manages', but the idiomatic 'finding her way through' evokes the actual movement at this moment. She does indeed pass between Dix and Mildred – 'finding her way through'. Similarly, using the word 'touched', with its different physical and emotional connotations, draws out how this passing moment is suggestive of a principal personality trait that the film, quite appropriately, might be reluctant to bring to the centre of our attention. The whole sentence – 'Finding her way through without being touched is one of her prime objectives' – crisply conveys the way a fleeting moment that could be considered tangential or merely preparatory physically dramatises a significant feature of Laurel's personality. It is a feature that will contribute to the eventual breakdown of her relationship with Dix.

When the students read writing which contains such fine-grained distinctions, more often than not they will be convinced that the film contains its own fine-grained distinctions. Having experienced criticism exhibiting this care and attention, the students will become less patient, unavoidably, with writing that evades a film's finesse. The pursuit of persuasive evaluation encourages students to execute detailed interpretations of style. The desire to share their involvement with the complexities of a good film is a stimulus for *creating* an appreciation of film style, rather than *producing* arid textual analysis or lifeless formalism.

The conceptual

The practice of criticism is sometimes presumed to be antithetical to conceptual thinking. However, those writers associated with exact criticism on film style – Perkins, William Rothman, George M. Wilson – are simultaneously executing sophisticated conceptual understandings. Stanley Cavell writes:

> [T]he question what becomes of objects when they are filmed and screened – like the question what becomes of particular people, and specific locales, and subjects and motifs when they are filmed by individual makers of film – has only one source of data for its answer, namely the appearance and significance of just those objects and people that are in fact to be found in the succession of films, or passages of films, that matter to us. (1988: 182–3)

(I take 'matter to us' to be as crucial in finding the answers as the encouragement to search in 'passages of film'.) We might ask what becomes of a shoulder grasp in *In a Lonely Place*, or a rose in *Letter from an Unknown Woman*, or a woman's top in *The Woman in the Window*. Always acknowledging these matters in their contexts, we might, for example, want to enlarge our discussion about Laurel to matters of costume or walking, and then, maybe, between a woman and her instruments of seduction, and then, more generally, to matters of female performance on film. We might even then consider how Laurel's passing in this film tells us about the possibilities for the medium of film. These enquiries should be flexible and generously reciprocal. Perkins's reference to Laurel's perfume subtly prompts our thoughts on the possibilities of the medium: the relationship between what film can show and what it may infer. His conceptual exploration is at one with his observation 'of things ... in the film for all to see' (1990: 4). If our 'office' is with moments then we should keep in mind why the film prompted the questions in the first place, and any conceptual thoughts should remain faithful to the tensions, weightings, balances and adjustments within the moments of the film. Students are encouraged to move deftly between the detail of the film and conceptual rumination, and then allow them to coalesce in their writing. Perkins's criticism folds together description, examination, explanation, suggestion, appreciation and conceptual rumination within individual sentences, clauses and even words. Here film style, interpretation and evaluation achieve exemplary synthesis.

References

Cavell, S. (1981) *Pursuits of Happiness: The Hollywood Comedy of Remarriage* (Cambridge MA and London: Harvard University Press).

Cavell, S. (1988) *Themes Out of School: Effects and Causes* (Chicago and London: University of Chicago Press).

Perkins, V. F. (1972) *Film as Film* (Harmondsworth: Penguin).

Perkins V. F. (1981) 'Moments of Choice', *The Movie*, 58, 1141–5. (Repr. in A. Lloyd (ed.) *Movies of the Fifties* (London: Orbis Publishing, 1982), pp. 209–13.)

Perkins, V. F. (1990) 'Must We Say What They Mean? Film Criticism and Interpretation', *Movie*, 34/35, 1–6.

Perkins, V. F. (1994) '*In a Lonely Place*', in I. Cameron (ed.) *The Movie Book of Film Noir* (London: Studio Vista).

Ricks, C. (1998) *Essays in Appreciation* (Oxford and New York: Oxford University Press).

15

Repetition and return: textual analysis and Douglas Sirk in the twenty-first century

Laura Mulvey

Repetition and return

A conference on style and meaning, the relation between cinematic language and its interpretation, was extremely timely in 2000. To my mind, it not only brought a welcome spotlight back onto an important form of criticism, but also drew attention to the way that the passing of time had affected the cinema itself, its technologies, its criticism and its position within academia. The conference offered me an opportunity to reflect on the relation between the time when textual analysis arrived in academia as a critical tool and its place at the beginning of the twenty-first century. For instance, my generation of British film academics only gradually moved into a more serious consideration of film theory out of a decade or more of cinephilia, concentrated, above all, on the Hollywood cinema of the last years of the studio system. Although a variety of theoretical and critical angles and approaches emerged during the 1970s, all learnt from, and built on, this cinema and were preoccupied by the question of how to mediate fascination with its films into more serious assessment and analysis. Textual analysis made a crucially important contribution to this process, providing a key means of critical access to a cinema made within industrial conditions for mass circulation. Textual analysis, as it prioritised mise-en-scène and the formal language of cinema, was an antidote to traditions of film criticism that invested importance in high-cultural, more literary-based, values. Whereas the traditional association between film criticism and art cinema could certainly use these criteria, they were of little or no relevance to evaluating Hollywood. There was, however, a built-in time lag. By the late 1960s or early 1970s, the studio system cinema that inspired the first wave of British film theory and criticism was, to all intents and purposes, over. Perhaps this historical asynchronicity is a necessary precondition for a form of popular, mass culture to be taken seriously by theoretical, academic criticism.

The 1960s and 1970s pioneering work on Hollywood took place within a tenuous, twilight, continuity with the great days of the studio system, which have, by now, become integrated into film history. There is a difference between how change is understood as it takes place and how it is understood once it has become ordered and relegated into a definitive past. Paradoxically, to become part of history also brings new cultural status, and Hollywood cinema of the studio system, especially its elite 'auteur' directors, can hardly any longer be seen within the original popular context from which they were 'rescued'. At the same time, cinema history in general, and perhaps Hollywood in particular, has gained a new lease of life from new technologies with DVD commentary and 'add ons'. New technologies have also brought new dimensions of possibility to textual analysis, not only for critical and for academic purposes, but also for the spread of film appreciation outside these limited circles. Once again, there is an echo across the decades, with a return to speculation about how the insights acquired through a specialised critical practice, such as textual analysis, might or might not have been available to original, popular, audiences. I hope to indicate later that there is quite a wide spread of possibility here, with some meanings no doubt decipherable at twenty-four frames per second. Others, however, have been difficult, even impossible, to perceive without slowing or stopping the speed of the film and have waited, like time capsules, to be discovered and discussed. One reason why I have chosen to return to Douglas Sirk's *Imitation of Life* (1959) is that I recently found interesting, previously overlooked, details in its opening sequence.

For personal reasons, I was particularly grateful to be invited to the Style and Meaning Conference. Both strands of this chapter bring returns to the past, to my own introduction to the practice of textual analysis and then to the recurring importance that Sirk has had for my thinking about cinema. To begin with: my first formal academic appointment, in 1979, was to the Department of Film and Drama, Bulmershe College (which organised the Style and Meaning Conference), now incorporated into the University of Reading. My appointment replaced Victor Perkins, who had recently moved to the University of Warwick. Although I had known Victor for quite some time and was in sympathy with the journal *Movie*, I had no first-hand experience of the actual practice of textual analysis that had become the linchpin of film teaching at Bulmershe. With Victor's legacy, and under day-to-day tutelage from Doug Pye (as we collaborated on courses in which textual analysis was a key critical tool), I began to see clearly, materially and in detail how meaning could be generated from the cinematic image itself. This critical commitment, and the excitement that went with it, could not have been sustained without the appropriate technology: Bulmershe had a 35 mm editing table, the Prevost, and a16 mm Steenbeck that made it possible to do close work with film in its original celluloid form. I had, by then, some experience of editing, through the films I had made with Peter Wollen, and had thus experienced 'the heady delights of the editing table', in Annette Michelson's evocative phrase (1976: 119). However, seeing great movies, in their 35 mm form particularly, frozen into a single frame, fragmented into a sequence or a fragment of a sequence, seeing another world open out behind the flow of narrative, was an indelible experience for which I am extremely grateful to the Bulmershe film culture. It was also a time when the British Film Institute and the education sector were 'in synch' and in sympathy; the BFI's distribution policy both responded to the critical and aesthetic priorities of early film departments and also initiated new possibilities by bringing prints of 'lost' films back into circulation. The early 1980s were a period of transition for cinema studies as the widening availability of VHS made the close study of film more accessible. Although there may be no substitute for textual analysis derived from the celluloid original, VHS has brought with it the advantage of repetition and return that was not so easy to secure in the pre-video days. Then, it might have been possible for a film studies department to own one or two, at most a few, prints. Now, individuals as well as institutions are able to build up collections of films that can be re-seen and reinterpreted along lines that might change with changes in interest and knowledge but also are open to the chance insights and unexpected encounters that come with endless repetition.

The question of repetition then returns to Douglas Sirk. When I was planning this chapter, I realised that I had written about his films at least once during every decade since (and including) the 1970s. This, latest, return was inspired by the National Film Theatre retrospective held in 1997–98, the BFI's reissue of *Written on the Wind* (1956) on a new 35 mm print and Criterion's publication of *Written on the Wind* and *All That Heaven Allows* (1955) on DVD in the US around the same time. In this context I looked back at the 'Sirk criticism' that had accumulated over the years. I was struck not only by the persistent attention to the relation between style and meaning that characterised this body of critical work but also by the variety of cinematic and political positions that had generated it. While histories and priorities changed, Sirk continued to be an extremely important point of reference for reflection on film language and how it is read.

The different critical perspectives on Sirk are telling and indicative of how his cinema has figured in the discussion of 'style and meaning'. In 1972 Thomas Elsaesser used Sirk, among other directors, in his pioneering article 'Tales of Sound and Fury: Notes on the Hollywood Melodrama'. He made the case for the melodrama as a genre in which meanings were to be found dispersed across its various, characteristic, signifying and stylistic elements. Although this anti-literary, mise-en-scène orientated, style was certainly to be found in other Hollywood genres, Elsaesser saw it heightened in melodrama due to generic content and constraints. Specifically cinematic values (lighting, camera movement, editing and framing, objects and so on) carry meaning when the intensity of emotion rendered characters' feelings or situation 'unspeakable'. Later in the 1970s, feminist film theory, already influenced by Freud, drew on and adapted the Freudian aspect of 'Tales of Sound and Fury'. Sirk's 'women's weepies' came to encapsulate a melodramatic aesthetic that was further charged and inflected by the cultural marginality of women and the constraining space of home and family – for instance, the problems of motherhood, family relations, older women and their sexuality. Both these, interconnected, discussions of melodrama emphasise the way that mise-en-scène 'fills in' meaning at the point where speech fails. Here, there is a sense of a social unconscious, touching those aspects of family and emotional life that are recognisable and, while not being completely inaccessible to consciousness, are subject to social convention or taboo and thus either uncomfortably difficult to articulate or rendered so within a particular drama. In this line of argument, roughly modelled on the psychoanalytic concept of the unconscious, in a melodramatic, cinematic, visual translation, meaning is displaced onto its surrounding mise-en-scène, invested in particular objects or inscribed onto the body through inarticulate gesture. Inevitably, this produces a style that demands to be deciphered and thus, in turn, produces rich material for the practice of textual analysis. While an alert and practised spectator of the melodrama may well read the cinematic language of displacement, consciously or subliminally, textual analysis enriches and illuminates these signifying elements. Furthermore, in the process of slowing down, freezing or repeating images, key moments and meanings then become visible that could not have been perceived, hidden under narrative flow and the movement of film at twenty-four frames per second. Not only does the style of melodrama demand a deciphering spectator, but textual analysis itself involves stretching out the cinematic image to allow space and time for associative thought, reflection on resonance and connotation, the identification of visual clues, the interpretation of cinematic form and style.

To interpret Sirk's use of mise-en-scène within terms of a displacement of emotion from character to cinematic language is certainly valid. But melodramatic mise-en-scène also acts as a means of narration, contributing a kind of cinematic commentary or description, inscribing into the scene significance that goes beyond the consciousness of characters. This is almost like an extra-diegetic mode of address, reaching out to the spectator who is prepared to find meaning through cinematic style. In this case, rather than a displaced expression of the unspeakable, meanings are encapsulated, materialised and mapped on to the image through the signifying potential of the cinema itself.

In certain staging, Sirk, in common, of course, with other directors, brings into play symmetry, rhyme and binary opposition, building into a segment its own integral pattern. This kind of 'segmentation' (to follow Metz and Bellour) signals the way in which fiction films are not necessarily smoothly structured to move inexorably forward, driven by a narrative dominated by cause and effect. To identify such segments is to acknowledge that privileged moments or tableaux have an aesthetic life of their own, detached from the whole. Once identified, such segments can only be analysed by means of repetition and return, by the extraction and juxtaposition of signifying elements, by analysing an opening visual premise in terms of its closing. I will return to this kind of sequence in my analysis of the opening of *Imitation of Life*. The paradox here is that, while it would be almost impossible to pick up these aesthetic reverberations consciously at twenty-four frames per second, once halted and analysed, the meanings invested in such a segment are not hard to identify. From this perspective, there is a built-in or 'pre-programmed' demand, within the film itself, to break down its more obvious narrative continuities, its forward movement, in the interest of discovering these, otherwise hidden, meanings.

On the other hand, Sirk's style is known for its use of significant objects or things, extracted from their ordinary place within the mise-en-scène, and invested with added value to the point at which the audience becomes aware and 'deciphers' the image. These objects are given an emblematic status through their framing, editing and melodramatic accompanying music. By means of these rhetorical devices the audience cannot but see the added value and, as these visual tropes draw attention to themselves, they often provoke laughter at the very moment in which they 'work' emotionally. This reaction marks the gap between the unselfconscious 'I see' and the self-consciousness of '*I see!*' The audience reacts as it might to gags or jokes, for which decoding is not only essential to the very process of understanding but also involves a similar moment of detachment, a moment, that is, of self-conscious deciphering. As Paul Willemen put it, in homage to Brecht in one of the earliest Sirk articles (1971), these moments of cinematic melodrama distance the audience into the process of reading. He further compares the working of these images to clichés in which pre-existing significance is recycled and recognised accordingly. For instance, in *Written on the Wind*, Kyle Hadley's fear of sterility and his desire to father a child are materialised into the image of a small boy, riding a drug-store rocking horse and brandishing a gun. With this one image various themes are condensed: Kyle's inability to escape from childhood into fatherhood, the child he might have fathered, his own infantile obsession with phallic objects. The overdetermined nature of the image, its citation of 'dollar book' Freud, and the rhetorical cinema within which it becomes an element of emblematic punctuation, all register with the audience, which then reacts with self-conscious laughter and the amusement of '*I see!*'

In an NFT seminar during the 1998 Sirk retrospective, José Arroyo gave a lucid account of another kind of self-conscious audience reading in his discussion of Sirk's place within a camp aesthetic. He pointed out that the very duality of the melodrama, its play on the relation between a surface appearance and an implied, hidden, vulnerability in which the theatricality of masquerade also acknowledges the pain it conceals, would inevitably appeal to a gay audience. The presence of Rock Hudson as Sirk's most significant star and Ross Hunter as his most consistent producer during his Universal period led to direct misreading into *double entendres* of lines and gestures within the films. According to Arroyo, a 1950s gay audience constructed a shared, underworld, camp sensibility around the Hudson/Sirk melodramas.

Textual analysis: pattern, iconography and gesture in the opening sequence of *Imitation of Life*

The opening of *Imitation of Life* is structured around two iconic images of femininity. The iconography and attributes of Lana Turner (as Lora Meredith) connote woman as eroticised spectacle. Those of Juanita Moore (as Annie Johnson), on the other hand, connote femininity as domestic and maternal, enclosed and enclosing. These connotations are built into the organisation and ordering of the mise-en-scène and the topography around a further, spatial, opposition between 'high' and 'low', 'above' and 'beneath'. The particular beauty of the sequence lies in the way the cinema translates the resonance of place into filmic space, turning the literal location into the pattern of space on the screen out of which another layer of meaning emerges.

The film opens in Coney Island and, after establishing shots of the beach, a complicated crane shot introduces Lana Turner. A tracking movement along the Coney Island boardwalk carries her into the scene but also isolates and emphasises her body and sexualised attributes, her legs and then her breasts, in a 'part for the whole' rhetorical figure. Pushing through a crowd of passers-by, she reaches the top of the steps that lead down to the beach. As she runs down, a man (John Gavin as Steve Archer) positioned at the bottom takes her photograph but, without seeing him, she crosses to the left of the screen and questions another man, who ignores her. Crossing back to the right of the screen, she bumps into the photographer and the crane shot ends with an abrupt cut. As he directs her towards the police, positioned in the middle of the steps, she crosses paths with Annie, a black woman who has found Susie. The camera then follows Annie under the boardwalk where she gives hotdogs to Susie and to her own daughter, Sarah Jane.

15.1 *Imitation of Life* (Douglas Sirk, 1959)

Lora's blonde, sexualised femininity has an immediately recognisable, iconic, quality that is enhanced by the upward look of the camera at the boardwalk, as though it were a stage (Figure 15.1). The background to this shot is theatrical rather than naturalistic. The stark, bright lighting and uniform blue backdrop flatten out any suggestion of perspective into a two-dimensional space. In contrast, Annie occupies an enclosed, as it were, interior, space underneath the boardwalk, which has depth and modulated lighting, so that the iconic qualities of each woman are echoed by their immediate settings (Figure 15.2). These attributes and resonance are not hard to identify. However, watching the film at twenty-four frames per second, not only is it difficult to find time to explore the scene's significance but the movie also carries straight on into its story, so that the rhymed pattern of its opening scene gets lost. Once halted, returned and repeated, the two images find a new relation to each other, each one gaining by contrast with the other, and the scene's integral structure acquires an aesthetic significance of its own. This sequence calls out for a return to its opening premise once its closing is inscribed into the scene. Furthermore, the attributes of place, ordered into cinematic space, not only enhance the contrasting iconography of the characters, but also introduce further meanings. Lora's space, the 'above' mapped out by the boardwalk, not only allows her to be seen as theatrical spectacle, but also, through the workings of antinomy, creates a space of 'above' in relation to Annie's space as 'below'. This spatial opposition carries with it further terms of high and low, so that connotations of class and social status merge with those of differing images of femininity. It is this ordering and

15.2 *Imitation of Life* (Douglas Sirk, 1959)

organisation of a 'poetics' of space that makes the sequence cinematically special. Its internal rhyming pattern, the beginning and the end, the 'above' space and the 'below' space, is linked by the stairs on which the two women's paths cross, when for a moment they are in the same frame. The spatial values of the scene give a visual rendition of race and class, and the domestic connotations associated with the enclosed space under the boardwalk also carry an association with confinement and containment.

The opening sequence points in two directions. In one, it gives an elegant, visual, pre-figuration of its own story and theme. Lora will become a big theatrical success, spectacularly rich and famous. Annie will be her maid. Sarah Jane will rebel against her mother's inescapable destiny, overdetermined as it is by race and class, and struggle to move up from the space of oppression and exploitation into the light of whiteness. Modelling herself on Lora, her means of social transition will be the iconography and attributes of femininity as erotic spectacle. But the film's opening premise also points in another direction. Mapped through the metaphoric significance of high and low, it reaches out beyond the diegetic world of the film into the society to which it refers. For instance, by this time the film was released in 1959, the Civil Rights movement had brought questions of race into the forefront of American consciousness. The pause for thought that comes with the practice of textual analysis not only brings with it the close reading of a scene in its primary, cinematic, terms. It is also a pause in which further associations and connections can arise that are, in the case of *Imitation of Life*, unusually rich and rewarding.

15.3 *Imitation of Life* (Douglas Sirk, 1959)

The signifying elements in the opening sequence are further dramatised by small details or gestures. The first takes place when Lora goes hastily down the steps of the boardwalk, distracted from her surroundings by her distraught search for Susie, and is photographed by Steve Archer. Just as he raises his camera, she pauses on the step, takes off her dark glasses, apparently to scan the beach, but actually to take up a pose for his photograph (Figure 15.3). Clearly unaware of the photographer and his camera, her pose seems to speak from her unconscious; that is, her behaviour as actress surfaces for a second through her behaviour as mother. This moment, and the meanings it brings in its wake, only really find visibility when the image itself is frozen and, once again, there is time to pause the flow of the story and to think through the implications of Lora's gesture. As Judith Butler (1990) points out, such a moment of exaggerated gesture is a characteristic not only of the performance of gender, but also of the melodramatic aesthetic itself, with its privileging of 'frozen moments'. However, Lora's frozen gesture is, in fact, a response to the presence of a camera, a still camera that, in turn, itself conjures up the 'frozen moment' of the photograph. Within the aesthetics of cinema, the presence of stillness, particularly the stillness of the photograph, necessarily brings with it a threat to the credibility of the moving image itself, the ghostly presence of the still strip of film on which the illusion of movement depends. Of course, to still a 'frozen moment' on celluloid, on an editing table, is to redouble the effect and to trigger immediately a reflection on the cinema's essential duality, its tension between movement and stillness. Although electronic and digital media cannot generate the satisfaction of such a literal doubling, the relative availability of the technology, and the ease with which a frame may be frozen, necessarily evoke the material nature of celluloid. In this sense, Lora's unconscious gesture reaches beyond her character into the hidden, secret nature of film itself and the stillness that has to remain repressed, as it were within its unconscious, for its own performance to keep its credibility. Ultimately, this line of reflection gives an extra edge to the film's title, suggesting the imitation that is the cinema and its mimetic relation to life.

The second detail relates to Annie. Apparently, she is the only black figure among a mass of white extras that make up the carefully choreographed crowd in which the child lost by one mother is found by the other. However, a close analysis of the scene reveals that black extras both foreshadow and accompany her first appearance. The extras are not only on the screen so fleetingly that it would be difficult, if not impossible, to register their presence at twenty-four frames a second but they are also placed at the edge of frame. As the spectator's eye is concentrated on the action of the main characters in the centre of the frame, it is only when the film is halted and the frame can be scanned that these significant details become visible. First of all, in the closing seconds of the first crane shot, a single figure creates a remarkable pivot point between Annie and Lora, perhaps subtly, questioning the accuracy of the antinomy between them. As Lora crosses back towards Steve, he is just raising his camera to photograph an elegant young black woman descending the steps on the far right edge of the frame. For a few seconds there seems to be a repetition of the scene a few moments earlier. But Lora's sudden collision with Steve knocks against his camera, disrupts the photograph and precipitates the cut. The next frame shows Lora and Steve together in a two shot. The choreographed movements of the camera, the stars and the extras are perfectly timed and synchronised throughout the whole of this complex crane shot, demanding not only considerable pre-planning but also very careful direction on set.

As Steve turns Lora round to face the police, now standing in the middle of the steps, a black woman extra, with her back to the camera, 'leads' its upward movement to where Annie is reporting that Susie has been found. At the same time, two black extras move through the top left-hand corner of the frame (Figure 15.4). This detail is, once again, impossible to detect at twenty-four frames per second. But this moment has the impact of a gesture, not one that is acted out through a character, but one that seems to materialise out of the texture of the film itself, mysterious but present and relevant. Lana Turner's performance of Lora Meredith makes the most of melodramatic gesture and the stillness that it brings with it. Juanita Moore, on the other hand, gives a certain swiftness to Annie's movements – until, that is, she is literally slowed down by the illness in the middle of the film that is closed by

15.4 *Imitation of Life* (Douglas Sirk, 1959)

her death. While Lora is blind to her surroundings, Annie is able to read the world around her and the social conditions determined by racial oppression. Melodramatic gesture is alien to Annie and it seems appropriate that the film itself should make a gesture on her behalf. Inscribed on to the screen but only subliminally visible, the fleeting presence of the extras relates to Annie's invisibility as the worker on whom Lora's visibility depends. But they also have a further significance for the theme of race that is so central to the film. Halting the image, concentrating on the sudden appearance of the black figures on the screen, they take on added power and weightiness, standing in for and conjuring up the mass of 'coloured people' rendered invisible by racism and oppression, marginalised within culture and representation. From this perspective, they foreshadow the apartheid invisibility that surrounds Annie's social life, which is unknown to Lora because: 'Miss Lora, you never asked'. This is the world that becomes visible, filling and overwhelming the screen during the film's final spectacle, Annie's funeral. Here black people line the streets and walk as mourners in the funeral procession and black culture appears with the church service and Mahalia Jackson's singing. The fleeting image of the extras in the opening moments of the film refers to a social unconscious, the 'unspeakable' nature of race that haunts the film, acted out by Sarah Jane's rejection of her mother. But their presence also makes a gesture towards the unconscious of the story itself and Annie's place within it.

Textual analysis has always generated a tension between the coherent narrative 'whole' and its forward drive, on the one hand, and, on the other, the desire to slow down the movement of film so that narrative, if not quite fades away, at least falls into the background. With a completely altered sense of time, it seems possible to capture the cinema in the process of its own coming into being. A segment extracted from the flow of narrative points to the way that there is always a pull towards tableaux in cinema. Now that films on DVD come with chapters, the linearity associated with film projection begins to break down further. It is easier to perceive the lack of smoothness that has always been an aspect of film narrative, its resistance to the forward movement to which it has always been tied by the movement of celluloid through projector. The discovery of a particular sequence or segment that responds to textual analysis necessarily leads to questions of film form in terms of both material and language. To halt, to return and to repeat these images is to see cinematic meaning coming literally into being as an ordinary object becomes detached from its surroundings, taking on added cinematic value. But halting the image, extracting it from its narrative surroundings, also allows it to contribute something to the story's narration.

For instance, when Annie and Sarah Jane first arrive to stay with Lora and Susie, Sarah Jane rejects the black doll she has been given and wants Susie's white one. The sequence ends with Sarah Jane's protest at their new quarters – 'Why do we always have to live at the back?' – and she drops the black doll on the floor behind her. The camera moves down, leaving the human figures, following the doll into a close-up, further underlined by accompanying melodramatic music. With this simple movement, the doll is taken out of its role as a contributory player in the scene between the two little girls and transformed into 'object image'. As the camera holds the shot, it allows a few extra seconds for the spectator to interpret the meaning invested in it: the significance of blackness that then mutates into an even more poignant signifier of Sarah Jane's feelings. It stands for her desire to leave blackness behind her, for her association of colour with class and 'the back', and also for the way she associates both with her mother's colour. The discarded doll pre-figures the way that Sarah Jane will choose to abandon her mother in order to escape into the world of privileged whiteness. Finally, the close-up of the 'object image' sums up the sequence and acts as its full stop, as a point of punctuation.

This is clearly an example of the way that Sirk uses clichés to create readable images with emotional impact that will address the audience directly. While the object's overstated poignancy may be obvious, even banal, in its demand for emotional response, the semantic process is always fascinating. Inevitably, there is a difference between the emotional impact that an image might have on an audience and how the process might be analysed academically through textual analysis. But both depend on an initial inscription of recognisable connotations, meanings that already have a cultural currency, and their reinscription into the language of cinema and onto the screen. In the Coney Island sequence, Sirk exploits existing connotations, resonance and reverberation while giving them a form and pattern that only the cinema can offer. A simple rhetorical flourish, such as the foregrounding of the little black doll, is also a reminder of the cinema's chameleonlike qualities. Not only can it shift from image to image, from shape to shape, but it can also shift meaning from one moment to the next, using framing, camera movement, lighting, music to invest 'added value' into a simple object. The doll shifts from a metonymic relation to Sarah Jane to a more general, amorphous, metaphoric relation to the abandonment that her mother will undergo and her inability to escape her fate. While this sliding of significance takes only a few seconds on the screen, it can be endlessly elongated and further enhanced by textual analysis. Halted and repeated, for instance, on video, the process through which an object's referential status is overtaken by rhetorical 'value added' becomes visible. As it is repeated, the image insists and persists so that the repetition and return enabled by the machine are echoed in the image's own repetition of meaning. This process is not only useful for an academic or critical practice, it has its own visual pleasures and rewards that do not replace, but complement, those of watching a film in its correct circumstances.

In Sirk's films, his highly stylised, rhetorical tropes lead back into the film's story and then further out into the social conditions to which the melodrama refers. These moments of semiotic 'value added' render visible the despair or desire that traps Sirkian characters within what he, Sirk, would call their destiny, the social and psychic constraints that act upon them, from which they may or may not escape. The close-up of the doll, with its melodramatic accompanying music, ends with a fade to black. The next scene fades in to show Annie in the kitchen, the next morning, already having assumed the role of maid. The foreboding and pre-figuring invested in the previous shot have been realised and naturalised within the story. While Sirk will always emphasise the fact that the cinema does not reflect life, he also sees it as a reflection on life, inescapably caught up with it. As a point of mediation between the two, Sirk uses places, rituals and dramatic moments that are embedded in everyday life but also heighten its hidden tensions. Here, reality, drama enacted within reality, and the highly evocative semiotic transformations inherent in the cinema merge together.

Ending

For me, *Imitation of Life* is a landmark film. Within the history of the Hollywood studio system it represents a high point in the successful restructuring that Universal Studios had undergone during the crises of the mid-1950s. As audiences dropped from eighty million in 1950 to twenty million in 1958,

Universal streamlined its production, cutting its investment in film by 50 per cent. While production focused on genre movies that could be made comparatively easily and economically (horror, Westerns and the weepies for which Ross Hunter was responsible), the studio also generalised the use of Technicolor. But Universal also supped with the devil. Increasingly, it leased its studios out for television production (Hitchcock's relation with Universal is a telling sign of changing times) and it had been taken over by the entertainment conglomerate MCA (Revue Productions). While larger, more glamorous and prestigious studios struggled, these initiatives ensured the studio's survival. However, this kind of diversification inevitably signalled the end of an era. Hollywood movies would no longer be the single and most important form of commercial entertainment that the world had ever seen. *Imitation of Life* was one of Universal's top box-office grossers ever, and Sirk's career, which had only really flourished during his Universal period, seemed finally to be secure. But he decided it was time to leave Hollywood. He retired and moved to Lugano, Switzerland, where he and his wife would live until his death in January 1987. Looking back at his decision to leave, he described how felt that the old Hollywood studio system was coming to an end and that the future would lie with small, independent productions and European new waves (Halliday 1972). Although his predictions might not ultimately have been fulfilled, and his views closely parallel the line of thought that brought Hitchcock to make *Psycho* in 1960, his retirement is emblematic. During the 1960s the old great 'auteur' directors such as Alfred Hitchcock, Howard Hawks and John Ford would make a few last swan songs, while the new great 'auteurs' (Samuel Fuller and Nicholas Ray, for instance) would see their careers falter and fail.

While there is no real reason why textual analysis should be tied specifically to the Hollywood cinema of the studio-system period, it is undeniable that the critical practice of close reading has greatly enhanced understanding of 'auteur' cinema. But there is a political dimension to this relationship. The strictly regulated, highly censored and standardised Hollywood that had been, ultimately, imposed by the mid-1930s was beginning to show cracks of unsustainability by the mid-1950s. Sirk's *Written on the Wind* (1956) had already signalled Hollywood's new need to be adult in the face of daring European imports and in the interests of distance from television's family values (Klinger 1989). And the political climate itself was changing. In a rather similar way to its earlier, 1934 John Stahl version, Sirk's *Imitation of Life* belonged to a period of political thaw. Donald Bogle points out that the film 'hit a chord in black Americans, acknowledging on the screen, as it did, that a race problem existed in America' (2001: 57). However, the depiction of the 'race problem' in *Imitation of Life* still belongs firmly to a pre-1960s, pre-Malcolm X, pre-Black Power era. From this perspective, it clearly belongs to that style of filmmaking in which a social 'unconscious' is both acknow-ledged and displaced and in which the melodrama flourished. It is, perhaps, for this kind of reason that Todd Haynes's *Far from Heaven* (2002) can only mimic Sirkian cinema stylistically, as it is necessarily more literal and explicit about taboo issues than would have been possible in Hollywood even by the late 1950s.

To my mind, the new ways of consuming old movies on electronic and digital technologies should bring about a 'reinvention' of textual analysis and a new wave of cinephilia. Now, anyone can view a favourite movie by selecting special scenes, stopping the film on a privileged moment or gesture, returning to and repeating images that suddenly seem to acquire new signi-ficance and beauty and demand further thought and interpretation. I have described this elsewhere as a 'democratisation' of textual analysis and this process of viewing as 'pensive' spectatorship which brings with it a special pleasure in watching the cinema's meanings materialising on the screen (Mulvey 2003). However, as I pointed out at the beginning of this chapter, the cinema is deeply affected by the passing of time itself. Although textual analysis was born after the decline of Hollywood's studio-system cinema, its practice has been primarily one of aesthetic interpretation. Now, to look at films such as those made by Douglas Sirk is to have the impression of look-ing into history. Even studio sets and stars take on the status of document, and close readings inevitably lead to questions of context as well as text. But reflection on film now leads not only to its surrounding history. If the moment when Douglas Sirk left Hollywood in 1959 is, for me, emblematic of the end of an era, seeing his films now, after the death not only of his stars but of the extras surrounding them on the set, is to see time itself caught and fossilised into the illusion of movement. Now, as Lana Turner runs down the steps on the Coney Island set, conjuring up the meanings inscribed into Sirk's film and her performance, she also shifts between the ghostly and the living. Her presence brings with it the cinema's unique ability to return to and repeat the past, which becomes both more real and more mysterious as the film's fragment is itself subject to endless repetition and return.

References

Butler, J. (1990) 'Lana's Imitation: Melodramatic Repetition and the Gender Per-formative', *Genders*, 9, 1–18.
Bogle, D. (2001) *Toms, Coons, Mulattos, Mammies and Bucks: A History of Blacks in American Film* (New York: Continuum).
Elsaesser, T. (1972) 'Tales of Sound and Fury: Observations on the Family Melo-drama', *Monogram*, 4, 2–15, repr. in C. Gledhill (ed.) *Home is Where the Heart Is* (London: British Film Institute, 1987).

Halliday, J. (1972) *Sirk on Sirk* (London: BFI/Martin Secker & Warburg).

Klinger, B. (1989) 'Much Ado About Excess: Genre, Mise-en-scène and the Woman in *Written on the Wind*', *Wide Angle*, 11, 4, 4–22.

Michelson, A. (1976) 'Reading Eisenstein Reading *Capital*', Part 1, *October*, 2.

Mulvey, L. (2003) 'The Pensive Spectator Revisited: Time and its Passing in the Still and Moving Image', in David Green (ed.) *Where is the Photograph?* (Brighton: Photoforum).

Willemen, P. (1971) 'Distanciation and Douglas Sirk', *Screen*, 12, 2, 63–7.

Index

Page numbers in italics include one or more relevant illustrations. Names with initials only for first names indicate bibliographical references. Full names indicate the names of actors, directors, etc.